LOOKING AT LANGLEY PARK

MEMORIES OF A VILLAGE

View of Langley Park from Esh Hill Top – 2006

COMPILED BY JOHN C. FOSTER

John C. Foster

Langley Park is a small ex-colliery village. It is situated in the Browney Valley about 5 miles North West of Durham City in the North East of England. Its main claim to fame is that it is the childhood home of former Newcastle United and England Football Manager Sir Bobby Robson. Although the colliery closed in 1975, Langley Park has actually grown in size with the development of a number of new housing estates increasing the population of the village. This is despite the fact that most people now have to travel elsewhere for employment.

JOHN C. FOSTER

John C. Foster was born in Langley Park in August 1937 the only child of John C. Foster (known as Jack) and Lillian Marshall (nee Flowers). Young John attended Langley Park Infants School and the Langley Park County School. Leaving school at the age of 15 he was employed as an office boy with Lanchester Rural District Council for two years and then joined The Durham County Council Surveyor's Department. In March 1956 he was conscripted into the Royal Army Pay Corps for two years National Service, most of his service being in the Aldershot area. In 1958 he returned to the Durham County Council and remained with that organisation until he retired.

Developing a keen interest in theatre he became at first a regular theatregoer and in 1958 joined the Durham Amateur Dramatic Society and took up acting. Most of his appearances were with this Club but he was also a member of the Langley Park Players and appeared in other productions for Elsie Craig Shaw. At Durham he was a producer for the Society whose plays were staged in St. Margaret's Hall and later at the Assembly Rooms. During his time with D.D.S. he adapted 'A Christmas Carol' and 'Dracula' for the stage.

He became an avid collector of theatrical memorabilia particularly programmes and handbills and is a member of The Ephemera Society of Great Britain.

Left:Ex Police Sergeant Thomas Foster and his wife Sarah the grand parents of the compiler of these memories. Mr. and Mrs. Foster had a large family. Their sons Jack and Norman and daughter Dora were long time residents of Langley Park. Another son Thomas was killed during the First World War. Sergeant Foster died in 1931 and his wife in 1944.

Ken Hoggart
who provided
original photos

LOOKING AT LANGLEY PARK

MEMORIES OF A VILLAGE

COMPILED BY JOHN C. FOSTER

TO THE PEOPLE OF LANGLEY PARK WHO WERE BORN, EDUCATED, WORKED AND CONTRIBUTED TO THE DAILY LIFE OF A VIBRANT COLLIERY VILLAGE.

What follows is not a history of Langley Park but a random collection of memories mainly covering the period 1930s – 1960s with some recollections of earlier and later years. The reader is invited to recall his or her own memories of days gone by and share them with relatives and friends.

No part of this publication may be reproduced, stored in a mechanical retrieval system, or transmitted, in any form or by any means, electronic, mechanical, photocopying, recording or otherwise, without prior permission of the publisher

ACKNOWLEDGEMENTS

The author acknowledges the assistance given by the under-mentioned without whose help these memories would not have been produced.

I.T. Co-ordinator: Mr. D. C. Rider

I.T.@The Tute, Langley Park
The staff of the Reference Section, Clayport Library, Durham City
The Durham County Advertiser Series
The Durham County Record Office
and the people of Langley Park who have added their own memories included in the following pages.

Original Photography by Ken Hoggart

ISBN 10:	ISBN 13:	Title Information
0-9554626-0-6	978-0-9554626-0-3	Looking at Langley Park

Published by John C. Foster, 15, Pine Street, Langley Park, Durham DH7 9SL

© JOHN C. FOSTER 2006

CATEGORIES

Introduction: Living in Langley Park
1. 1939 – 1945 War
2. Comforts Fund
3. The Unknown Soldier
4. The Home Guard
5. Evacuees
6. Air Raid Wardens
7. Special Constables
8. The War Is Over
9. A Woman With A Past
10. Civil Defence
11. A Chinese Incident
12. Army Cadet Corps
13. National Service
14. British Legion: Women
15. British Legion: Men
16. School
17. Transport
18. Doctors
19. Nursing Association
20. Dr. Robert Rutherford
21. St. Johns Ambulance Brigade
22. Isolation Hospital
23. Friends Of The Hospital
24. Entertainment
25. Recreation Ground
26. The Colliery Band
27. Public Houses
    a) Langley Park Hotel/Ball Alley
    b) The Workmen's Club
    c) The Rams Head
    d) The Board Inn
    e) The Station Hotel
    f) Langley Park Social Club
    g) The Union Jack Club
28. Langley Park Players
29. Methodist Drama
30. Primitive Methodist Chapel
31. Trinity Methodist Chapel
32. Baptists Chapel
33. All Saints Church
34. Mothers Union
35. Girl Guides
36. Roman Catholic Church
37. Funerals
38. The Lynmouth Disaster
39. Murder of A Kitchen Maid
40. Coronations/Golden Jubilee
41. The Fire Brigade
42. The Women's Institute
43. Literary Institute and Library
44. Women's Co-operative Guild
45. The Aged Peoples Treat
46. The Over 60s Club
47. Shopping List Intro/Adverts
48. The Post Office
49. The Co-op
50. Newsagents/N. Anderson
51. J.W. Cousins
52. T.R. Watson/E. Eccleston
53. Thomas A. Coates
54. Around The Shops
55. Football Langley Park Villa
56. " Langley Park C.W.
57. " Langley Park St. Josephs
58. " Langley Park Hotspurs
59. " Langley Park Juniors
60. " Langley Park Methodists
61. Sport: Allen Ferguson
62. Sport: Schoolboys
63. Sport: William T. Surtees
64. R.Robson/O. Lee/D.G. Harron
65. Cricket
66. Amateur Boxing
67. Johnny Cuthbert
68. Chess
69. Bowling
70. Angling
71. Sport Miscellaneous
72. Gardens Guild/Association
73. Village Policeman/Sledging
74. Women's Labour Party
75. Rebecca Rutherford
76. Joseph R. Robertshaw
77. Snippets
78. Robbie Irons
79. Joan Wadge
80. Jack Ardley

81 LANGLEY PARK PEOPLE; C. F. Burdon, Jane Buchan, Matthew King, Richard A. Swinbank, Martha Heppell, John Peel, W. E. Cooper, Harold Ardley, Ann Wood, Eleanor Mulcaster, Richard Shorten, William Dunn Hall, Dawson G. Harron, Westgarth Adamson, William Foster, Robert Howe, A. W. Elliott, J. S. Elliott, Ned Miller, A. Model Man, Mr. and Mrs. John Agar, Molly Agar, Norman Richardson, Ella McNay, John Dodgson, David John Ough, Henry Suttersfield, Dan Gregory, David Richardson.

INTRODUCTION

LIVING IN LANGLEY PARK

With the establishment of the Colliery the village of Langley Park grew in size. The ten streets that existed around the year 1895 soon became more in number. Woodland in the area behind Front Street was cleared and new rows of terraced houses were built, all the new streets being given the names of trees. Referred to as 'Newtown' the houses were referred to as 'two up and two down'. The accommodation consisted of two bedrooms upstairs and downstairs there was a kitchen that was the living room and a back kitchen where meals were prepared and washing and ironing took place. Central heating was unheard of and there was no hot water laid on. In the kitchen (living room) there was a large black leaded range in one of the walls that had a coal fire. To the right there was an oven and on the other side a boiler for heating water. Above the range there was a mantelpiece and underneath a line was stretched and used for drying towels or small items of washing. No electric irons. Irons were heated on the fire; while one was being used another would be 'heating up'. Washing day, usually a Monday (washing on a Sunday would never be considered!) and that would take all day. There was a set-pot in the corner of the 'back kitchen' under which a fire was lit and it was here that clothes were boiled. In earlier time a 'poss-tub' would be employed for doing the washing. Later along came a 'washer' but the work was done by means of a hand-operated lever. When washed and boiled the clothes were put through a mangle, a process that was repeated some three times. No wonder washing took nearly all day and if the weather was inclement the clothes had to be dried on lines placed around the living room.

Friday was baking day when the housewife made the bread, cakes, pastries etc. that would be required for the next few days.

There was no bathroom or shower. The bath was a tin tub placed in front of the fire and water came from the fireside boiler. The bath was usually kept on a nail on an outside wall at the rear of the house. Toilets were outside. In some of the earlier houses the toilet was across the road and sometimes facilities had to be shared with neighbours. Initially earth closets but later water closets were installed. In early houses there was no electricity just oil lamps. Later electricity was laid on downstairs and in some houses the upstairs was not converted until the late 1930s. Under these conditions large families were often raised.

Stone floors were a feature of much downstairs accommodation. Comfort being added by oilcloth laid on the floor and rugs placed over a large centre carpet. This was periodically lifted and beaten with tennis racquet type carpet beaters. Rug making in the home ('clippy mats'-old clothing cut into short strips which produced a rough short ragged surface or 'proggy' mats – old clothing cut into long strips producing a tight ball type surface) was a normal feature of home life a task that occupied most members of the family during leisure time.

There were ladies in the village that could be called upon to attend births, which very often took place in the home and ladies who would come to the aid of families in the case of deaths. Discreetly stored away in their homes would be trestles and boards etc. for use when required.

Before the Second World War new council houses appeared on land above All Saints Church and the cricket field most of which had gardens.

During the years of the Second World War village life continued as normally as it was possible despite the anxious times. With many men 'called-up' for military service housewives were left at home with young children to bring up with little or no assistance and they had to cope with the use of 'coupons' and rationing. Queuing became a necessary part of shopping.

Air raid shelters were constructed in most homes and erected in schoolyards and in the streets around the village. They were a feature of everyday life for some years after the end of the war but were finally demolished.

On the outbreak of war one old resident recalled seeing Harry Billingham walking over the bridge from the coke works to join up for army service. As a reservist it is thought he was the first man from the village to be called up in September 1939

New housing became a priority after the war and in the late 1940s interest was being shown in the council houses that were being built in front of Ash Street and behind the Kings Cinema. Part of the estate was to contain prefabricated houses (Prefabs). These arrived in sections on lorries and were quickly assembled. In later years some residents were to comment that these prefabs were the best home they ever had. Intended as temporary accommodation they were occupied long after their 'sell by date' but were eventually dismantled and replaced by bungalows (Kingsway).

Ordinary life was very different. A young couple got together and 'courted' for some time before marriage was contemplated or affordable. Living together was unmentionable. Indeed anyone doing so risked being 'run out of the village!!!' And if parents did not approve of the match an unpleasant situation could present a problem for all involved. When marriage did take place the newly weds often 'lived in' with one set of parents until enough money was saved to make their own home a reality.

Some words were never used in everyday language. Sex, which comedian Albert Burdon referred to in a music hall joke is 'something the coals comes in'. Was there a word Lesbian? and 'gay', according to the dictionary meant frolicsome or festive. Swearing in public was not the done thing. The style of dress was formal. When the day's work was over and working clothes were discarded, men wore suits, ties and well-polished shoes and hats and coats for ladies were the norm.

Typical holiday photographs of the 1940s.

Holidays were a week at a boarding house at a seaside resort, often local, sharing a bathroom with other guests and being required to vacate the 'lodgings' each day by 10.30 a.m. and not returning until time for the evening meal. After the Second World War families often looked forward to spending a week at a Holiday Camp in the U.K. Butlins being a popular choice. Foreign travel and holidays abroad were in the future as was the casual dress that went with hot locations. The arrival of the bikini for the ladies in the post war years was considered shocking and women were yet to be seen wearing trousers.

In days gone by householders did not find it necessary to lock doors. Neighbours would wander in and out for a chat or to check on anyone who might not be feeling well. Taking a break from household chores residents took the opportunity to have a 'gossip' over the garden wall or the gate of the backyard, wearing a 'pinny' (apron) the appropriate uniform for housework. On Sundays and special occasions a smarter apron would be worn to receive visitors.

That was Langley Park some fifty years and more ago.

As Langley Park continued to grow during the early part of the last century, the 1914-1918 war intervened. Many local men were involved in the conflict. Recovering from the trauma of those days the 1920s saw the village coming to life. The colliery and coke works providing 24 hour employment for the men. (3 shifts 6 a.m. – 2 p.m., 2 p.m. – 10 p.m. and 10 p.m. – 6 a.m.) and these men along with energetic villagers and supporters (with the aid of the Consett Iron Company) were responsible for establishing the numerous sporting and social organisations which were to exist right through the life of the colliery and the coke works.

Now we can take a random look at some of the events that took place, sporting and social activities and meet a few of the people who lived, worked and were educated in the village.

Intro 4

WELCOME TO LANGLEY PARK
A railway bridge crossed the road at the point where the car on the left of the picture is shown. Until this was demolished high sided vehicles and double-decker buses could not enter the village from Kaysburn.

1914 – 1918 WAR PHOTO ALBUM

Top Left and Right: two local serving soldiers
Right centre: A group of three soldiers. It is known that at least one was killed during the war. Left centre: a Sergeant in First World War uniform and below right a medallion which was presented to the families of all servicemen who were killed during the war.
Bottom left; Home on leave with wife to be circa 1917

1939   THE SECOND WORLD WAR   1945

Airman Sgt. John Hayden son of Mrs. and Mrs. J. Hayden was awarded the Distinguished Flying Medal while serving as an air observer in Tunisia. Educated at Durham Johnston School he had passed the Cambridge examination.
The citation read: " During the last six months he has taken part in a number of operational sorties during which he got some excellent photographs. He has set a magnificent example to his comrades by his skill and devotion to duty" May 1943

A Northumberland Fusilier serving in North Africa .In civilian life employed as a bus driver on Tyneside.

During the war years lighting up times were also referred to as Blackout Times.

To take account of the blackout regulations by mid-September 1939 All Saints Church a.m. instead of 11 Sunday Evening Services were retimed to 3 p.m. instead of 6p.m. The Sunday School was to start at 10 a.m.

Between 1938 and 1941 The Durham Coalfield lost 23,681 from its mining industry through men joining H.M. Forces, taking up defence duties or taking up other employment.

Two Langley Park miners were fined for failing to cover hand lamps. They had lit the lamps in a cabin and walked 70 yards away from the pit when they were apprehended. William Hunter and John S. Dunn were fined ten shillings each at a court hearing in July 1940.

In the summer of 1940 a day tour to the Lake District by bus from Durham cost thirteen shillings and sixpence (67½ p). A single ticket to Blackpool was ten shillings (50p) and a return eighteen shillings and sixpence (92½p).

In September 1939 Langley Park Workmen's Club staged its usual Vegetable and Flower Show.

A.B. Albert Christian joined the navy in 1940 and had been a conductor on the Witbank buses based in Lanchester. He became a prisoner of war following the Java Bay battle during which he had served on 'The Exeter'. It took 18 months for news to come through that he had been captured and for a further two years his family at home received no cards or letters. In October 1946 he was free and had arrived safely in Singapore. His father died in 1943 but Albert did not know of this until he arrived home in November 1946.

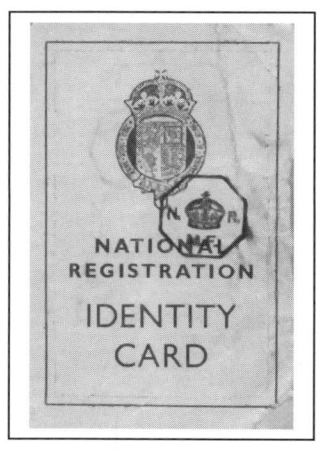

On 2nd June 1941 Gunner John L. Tomes R.A. of Lilian Terrace was reported as missing while on active service in Crete. It was later confirmed that he was a prisoner of war and had been taken to Germany. He joined the army at the age of 18 and was a reservist at the outbreak of war. Employed at Langley Park Colliery he was well known as a pigeon fancier. Sadly on 7 October 1944 he was killed by an aerial bombardment. He had been married for some six years and had two children. A brother saw service in the Sudan Signals Corps.

In August 1941 Quarter Master Sgt. George Newstead of Logan Street who had been reported missing since 29th. April 1941 had been located at Camp de Corinth in Greece where he was a prisoner of war. Aged 28 he had been ten years in The Hussars.

Twenty one year old Albert Williamson serving in the Royal Artillery in Malaya was reported missing in July 1942 and at that time it was thought he was a prisoner of war. He had worked at Malton Colliery having been earlier an apprentice with the mason E.E. Reed.

Gunner William Howard of Ivy Terrace was reported missing from February 1943. He had been in the army for four years before the war and was evacuated from Dunkirk

Logo for the N.A.A.F.I. An organisation well known to all servicemen providing refreshment for morning breaks and evening leisure facilities..

In July 1940 Corporal Thomas Kipling who had joined the Durham Light Infantry c.1937 was now a prisoner of war. Sent to France at the outbreak of war he had been at home on leave in February, 1940. His last letter home was dated 22nd August 1940. Before his military service he had been employed at Langley Park Colliery and was a keen ambulance worker.

Early in January 1942 P. C. Wood found a Langley Park man drunk in a burn near Wallnook Cottages. Appearing before magistrates the man was fined ten shillings.

Above: Two happy housewives enjoying a backyard break from daily chores

In September 1943 Mr. T. Naisbett aged 68 died suddenly. He had been caretaker at the Institute in Langley Park for 20 years and as a Special Constable had taken part in the Battle of Britain Parade earlier in the day.

In the early 1940s Langley Park British Restaurant was set up on land which is now occupied by the Derwentside Community Office.

Leading Stoker Arthur Attle of Davis Crescent, Langley Park and who came from a well known Malton Colliery family had been home on leave in February 1944 and told the exciting story of how, while serving on 'H.M.S. Duke of York', he was afloat when the action took place with the German battleship 'Scharnhorst', sunk on 26th. December 1943. At the time Attle was 27 and before joining the Navy had worked at Malton Cokeyard. One of five sons, four were in H.M. Forces. The other three were Fred, in the R.A.F., Ernest, in Kings Own Scottish Borderers in Italy and John in the Royal Engineers. The youngest was working in the mines.

A private in The Royal Pioneer Corps serving "somewhere in England". In civilian life he worked at Langley Park Coke Works.

A paratrooper, Pte. Jim Crozier who lived in Davis Crescent and had been a butcher before the war, was one of the first to be dropped in Algiers and was taken prisoner. In the autumn of 1943 he escaped. He hid underneath a bridge for a day and a night with enemy convoys passing over him. An Italian family have him shelter for over a week before he set out to treck 400 miles to reach allied lines.

IT IS AN OFFICIAL ORDER THAT YOU MUST CARRY YOUR GAS MASK IF YOU WISH TO ATTEND ANY CINEMATOGRAPH HALL. WITHOUT THE GAS MASK YOU WILL BE DENIED ADMISSION

Shortly after war broke out Verna Birbeck, daughter of Mrs. Birbeck, the secretary of the Women's Section of the British Legion, married Norman Buddle. Mr. Buddle was captain and had played for Langley Park Villa F.C. for seven years. He was also associated with Eden C.W., Crookhall C.W. and Shildon. His brother Raymond was also a footballer.

One night in September 1939 Matthew Russell Lyons aged 45 of South Street was walking from the Station Hotel area to Langley Park during the blackout when he was hit by a Gypsy Queen bus receiving serious injuries.

Linda Watson, whose brother Ernest spent the war years as a foreman in a Royal Ordnance factory in India, was the first young woman from Langley Park to join the armed services during the war. By the end of 1945 she was a Flight Officer in the W.A.A.F.

Playtime in the Recreation Ground with the Pavilion and Tennis Courts in the background (See 25)

Mr. and Mrs. R. Elwen of Quebec Street, Langley Park had, in July 1944, received a postcard to say their son L.A.C. Robert Elwen then aged 25 was fit and well but a prisoner of war in Japanese hands. He had served in Singapore for a year and his parents had not heard from him for eighteen months. Young Mr. Elwen joined the R.A.F. in 1938 and since 1940 was based in the Far East. Prior to joining up he was employed at Langley Park Colliery and played cricket and football for the village. By October 1945 he was safe in Sydney and back home in Langley Park in November 1945.

Prior to the start of the 1939-1945 war gas masks were being produced at the rate of 150,000 a week.

An ex doorman of Langley Park Workmen's Club Thomas Firbank Nicholson of Quebec Street died in October 1939 at the age of 70.

Elsie Lavinia Watson, daughter of Mr. and Mrs. Joseph Watson, Lilian Terrace, Langley Park who since leaving school had been employed in domestic service died in Durham County Hospital. Durham. She was working in the Estate Office at Brancepeth and had been putting paraffin oil on a fire when she became enveloped in flame. The incident happened in November 1939.

The retirement was announced in December 1939 of Mr. G.S. Watson who had been Superintendent of Sunday Schools at Trinity Methodist Chapel.

Three schoolchildren, Alma Erwin, Jenny Edmundson and lberta Garbutt raised £2 for The Lord Mayor Durham's Red Cross Appeal in September 1940 by holding a jumble sale in the backyard of a house in Elm Street.

In 1940 Langley Park Rovers were playing in Durham and District League.

Three films due to be shown in Durham on 4th. September 1939 the day when all places of amusement closed were 'Trouble Brewing' at the Regal, 'Let Freedom Ring' at the Palladium and 'Sword of Honour' at the Majestic, Sherburn Road.

1939 – 1945 War Medal.

In September 1939 the cost of travel to Leeds by bus was 7/- single and 12/- return. To Blackpool 10/6d single and 19/- return. A 7 day coach tour to the Isle of Skye was shown as £11 and a similar tour to Llandudno was £7.

At the end of 1942 Daniel Bailey then aged 23 of East Cross Street found himself in court and was found guilty of absenting himself from work without reasonable excuse on three days in October 1942. An official of Langley Park Colliery spoke up for him and as a result he was discharged following an undertaking not to repeat the offence. This was just one of a number of court cases in the area where mine workers were prosecuted for non-attendance.

A soldier in the Queen's Royal Regiment Private Kenneth Birbeck had been wounded while on duty in the Middle East. He was named as the son of Mr, and Mrs, Owen Birbeck. *Dec 1943*

In August 1942 it was reported that on the instructions of the Ministry of Supply 64 tons of iron railings had been removed from Langley Park.

EMPHASIS IS LAID UPON THE IMPORTANCE OF THOSE MEMBERS OF THE PUBLIC WHOSE EMERGENCY DUTIES DO NOT REQUIRE THEIR PRESENCE IN THE STREETS TAKING SHELTER IN THE EVENT OF AN AIR RAID. SUCH NEGLECT MAY HAVE SERIOUS CONSEQUENCES.

A worker at Durham Carpet Factory conscripted into the R.A.F. for wartime service.

Serving in North West Europe with the Royal Artillery (Anti Aircraft) Gunner Ernest Smith, Dale Street, Langley Park was killed in action in August 1944. At the age of 14 he went to London for two years and worked as a footman. Returning home he was employed at Lanchester Saw Mills and was also in the Home Guard. At the time of his death he was 19 and had been in the army for a year.

H. Garrod Serving with the R.A.F. in India

810 naval personnel were lost when on 14 October 1939 a German submarine sank 'The Royal Oak' in Scapa Flow. There were many fatalities in the region. Among them was A.B. Jack Wood son of Mr. Fred Wood a Langley Park butcher and Mrs. Wood who lived in Finings Avenue. Jack Wood joined the navy in 1938 and trained on 'The Caledonian' before transferring to 'The Royal Oak'. Educated in Langley Park he also attended All Saints Church Sunday School. He had worked at the Co-operative Laundries at Nevilles Cross and at the Kings Cinema, Langley Park. On the day his parents received news of his death his parents received a letter from their son.

Popular songs during the war years included 'A Nightingale Sang In Berkeley Square', 'Lili Marlene','White Cliffs of Dover' and 'We'll Meet Again. 'The Forces Sweetheart' was Vera Lynn and Glenn Miller contributed 'In The Mood' and 'Moonlight Serenade'.

In August 1946 Marion Hall aged 20 died in Lincoln Military Hospital. Serving in the A.T.S. she had been at home in Langley Park on ten days leave and had just returned to barracks at Welbeck Abbey, Worksop, Nottinghamshire when she collapsed and was taken to hospital. Prior to joining the forces she had worked in munitions at Birtley. The funeral service took place at Langley Park.

John Robson, a Langley Park man who had worked as a grocery assistant at Thompson's Red Stamp Stores served in the navy and had been a promising footballer. In December 1941 his home in Quebec Street, Langley Park received news of his death. Yeoman of Signals William B. Heppell R.N. was also reported missing in December 1941. Joining the navy as a 16-year-old boy he had completed almost 16 years service. Both men were serving on H.M.S. Bahran.

Leading Aircraftsman Thomas Pemberton who was married and lived in Garden Avenue missing after the fall of Singapore had become a prisoner of war of the Japanese in Java. The son of Mr. T. Pemberton he was born in Hartlepool and had joined the R.A.F. at the start of the war For eighteen months he had served in the Far East. An electric welder by trade he had been working in Essex and in June 1943 he had a two-year-old son. By 1945 he had been freed and had arrived in Colombo. Married to Susan Longstaff he had only been able to send three cards home in three and a half years.

ALL RANKS
Remember -Never discuss military, naval or air matters in public or with any stranger, no matter to what nationality he or she may belong.
The enemy wants information about you, your unit, your destination. He will do his utmost to discover it.
Keep him in the dark. Gossip on military subjects is highly dangerous to the country, whereas secrecy leads to success.
BE ON YOUR GUARD and report any suspicious individual.
(From 'Soldier's Service and Pay Book. Army Book 64

This Coldstream Guardsman was called up from his normal job at Consett Iron Works. Serving in the West Country he met the girl who was to become his wife and at the end of the war returned to settle in the area.

Leslie Preston, in 1942 aged 23 and the elder brother of Albert Preston (right) had been in the D.L.I. for three years, joining up just before the war. He had worked at Langley Park Colliery and played football for Langley Park Juniors.

He was posted abroad in 1941 and earlier had been involved in the Dunkirk evacuation. In October 1942 news was received that he had been missing since 27th June 1942 during service in the Middle East.

Younger brother Albert Preston spent two years as an apprentice joiner at Langley Park Colliery. In 1937 he joined the navy cadets training and in 1939 A.B. Preston was transferred to a destroyer 'The Bedouin'.

In July 1942 it was confirmed that he was a prisoner of war in Italy. His ship had been in action against the Italians and it had been sunk. Picked up by the Italian Red Cross he was taken to Pantellaria then to Sicily and eventually to Genoa and a prisoner of war camp. He spent 14 months there and when our troops landed in Italy he was to be transported to Germany. With two others he jumped from the train on which they were travelling and made his escape. On two occasions the three attempted to reach the British Lines and failed. They trekked for four days and four nights before they reached Switzerland. The Swiss authorities held them from 1st February 1943 and in October 1944 when the Americans reached the frontier they were released. Soon afterwards Albert was happily reunited with his family.

In December 1944 at Trinity Methodist Church in Langley Park, in a service conducted by the Rev. J.W. Kennedy, Albert married Jean Geddes of Witton Gilbert. After being apart for six years, Albert was reunited with his brother Leslie in June 1945. Their parents Mr. And Mrs. T.H. Preston were then living in Logan Street, Langley Park.

News reached Langley Park in September 1942 that Paul Yates had been wounded while on active service in Malta. Educated at school in the village he had worked in Walter Willson's shop in Front Street. Within seven months of joining the Royal Artillery Regiment he had become a Sergeant. Now two years on he had become a Second Lieutenant.

Aged 22½ Sgt. Gunner John Richardson R.A.F. and with 2 ½ years service was posted missing from operations over Germany in November 1943.

The death was announced in October 1939 of Mrs. Ann Penny (70) widow of the late Joseph Penny who died circa. 1927. A resident of South View she had lived in Langley Park for 60 years.

By the end of 1942 The Red Cross Prisoner of War Aid fund was being run by Mrs. W. Simpson, Mrs. Fred Agar, Mrs. S. Stephenson, Mrs. D. White, Miss Corcoran, Miss E. Bunn Mrs. William Woods and Mrs. Thomas Jupp. From one bazaar held in the premises of T.A. Coates in Front Street they raised £110.

During the war years travelling was difficult and often hazardous. Holidays away from home were virtually impossible for many resorts were 'closed' to visitors and beaches inaccessible. 'Holidays At Home' was the Government's solution. In Langley Park as elsewhere events were organised including sports days and walking. Quebec Street Methodist Church took the opportunity of inviting members to come along and clean the church.

In May 1945 Henry (Harry) Billingham who lived in Elm Street had, at last, returned home. Colleagues who worked with Mr. Billingham could recall him leaving Langley Park Cokeworks after his last shift in 1939. Being an army reservist he was called up two days before war was declared and so became one of the first Langley Park men to join the colours. On 21st June 1942 Gunner Billingham, Royal Artillery was captured at Tobruk and held as a prisoner of war in Italy. In September with about 100 others he escaped and for twenty months lived in the mountains until the British troops reached the area.

A second Elm Street man was Jack Wilson, who also worked at Langley Park Cokeworks. He enlisted in the R.A.S.C. in August 1940. Around about June 1942 he became a prisoner of war and was put to work in a pasteurised milk factory. Released by the Americans he too arrived home in May 1945.

Shortly after returning to England in January 1945 after six and a half years in India, Sgt. William White was posted to Western Europe where he was killed in action. Sgt. White who was the brother of Mrs. W. Sharp who loved in Oak Street had served in the Army Air Corps and had been a Company Sergeant Major in the East Yorkshire Regiment. Aged 29 he had been married a month – his wife was living in Manchester.

From September 1945 Leading Telegraphist Frank Harrison R.N. spent five months on leave at home in Ivy Terrace. Formerly he had worked in Malton Colliery offices. At that time he had been 3½ years in the navy and spent 2½ years overseas including periods in Mombassa, East Africa, Colombo and Ceylon. He had brought home with him bananas, lemons and oranges. His brother, Austin, was in Germany in the Royal Armed Corps.

An insurance agent before the war, Lance Corporal George Adamson whose home was in Laurel Terrace, Langley Park spent five years in the Royal Signals. He spent two years in the U.K. and then abroad in North Africa and throughout the Italian campaign. Home on four weeks leave he spoke of his experiences at a meeting in the Methodist Church of which he was a member.

Leading Aircraftsman Thomas Allison who came from Langley Park and had worked in Thompson's Red Stamp Stores before the war spent 5 years in the R.A.F., three of them in Italy. In May 1946 he married Gianna Lauzzano in Undine, Italy, the first British serviceman to be married there. At the reception an eleven-course dinner was served and The People's Committee bestowed on him the Freedom of the Town. In November 1945 he had returned to his home in Lambton Street for his parents silver wedding celebrations.

Towards the end of 1943 two brothers met in North Africa. They were the sons of Mr. And Mrs. W. Gregory who lived in West Cross Street, Langley Park. Their second son Pte James William Gregory (44) of the Northumberland Fusiliers had met their 5th. Son Sapper Thomas Gregory, Royal Engineers in North Africa. Thomas had been a miner at Askern, near Doncaster, and enlisted at the outbreak of war. Eighteen months earlier he had been posted abroad and served through the evacuation of Dunkirk. James joined the Royal Navy as a boy and served through the 1914 – 1918 war before becoming a miner at Langley Park for four years. He then enlisted in the army. At the time of the meeting he had been abroad for five months.

In the summer of 1943 another two brothers met in the Middle East. They were the sons of Mr. And Mrs. F .P. Burdon. For three years Frederick had been with the Queens Own Cameron Highlanders and was wounded at the Battle of the Mareth Line and had come across his brother Private Norman Burdon of the R.A.S.C. who was a cook in the officer's mess. Norman was married and his home was then in Wakefield. A few months later there was another reunion for another two brothers. The Henderson's, James F. and Charles L. of Dale Street also met in the Middle East.

Rumours circulated around the village late in 1944 as to why P.O. John Royce Elliott was being interviewed by the police. It turned out that the plain-clothes officers had only been asking for his assistance. P.O. Elliott was staying in East Cross Street while on leave from the navy. He had been 11½ years in the service and had vast experience of the Mediterranean and Pacific seas.

During the years of the 1939-1945 war many young women in Langley Park were conscripted into the armed forces. Others found themselves taken from their normal home life or employment to work in munitions factories. Locally the Royal Ordnance Factory at Birtley was their base and working 12-hour shifts was the norm.

LANGLEY PARK WAR MEMORIAL

World War One (1914-1918)

ADAMSON John Joseph Private
ATKINSON Harold Private
BARKER Harry Sergeant
BARKER James Private
BELL Fred Private
BELL John RN.D.
BELL John Private
BERESFORD John William Private
BEWLEY Isaac Private
BOWESFIELD Thomas Corporal
BRENKLEY Benjamin Sapper
BUCKHAM Thomas Sergeant
BURTON George R.N.D.
CALLAND Thomas
CAMPBELL Henry
CHARLTON Thomas Private
CLARK Arthur Sergeant
CLARK Harry Private
COULT Fred Private
CUMMINGS Edward Private
DODGSON John Corporal
ECCLESTONE Edward Trooper
ELLISON Percy Private
ELTRINGHAM Harry Corporal
FIDDLER George Driver
FISHER Arthur Private
FULLARD John Private
GARBUTT John Private
HALL David Private
HASWELL James Private
HIDDLESTONE Charles Private
HOPE Joseph Private
HUGHES Owen
HUNT Jack Private
HUTCHINSON Richard Private
JAMES Matthew Private
JOBLING Percy Private
KEENLEYSIDE Shield Ridley
MERRIGAN William
MOFFAT A
MORRISON Donald Captain
McGRATH William Private
McSHANE Dominic Private
NAISBETT David Gunner
NEWTON Richard Private
NICE Walter Private
NICHOLSON Nathaniel Gunner
NICHOLSON George Private
OGDEN Jack Private
OWEN Harry
PICKERING Jack Sapper
PIERSON George Gunner
POTTER George Corporal
RAPER Tom Private
REID W Private
RENNISON Joseph RN.
ROBSON Edward R.N.D.
SELLARS William Stoker
SHORTEN Charles R.N.
SHORTEN Richard Corporal
SIMPSON John Private
SMITH A.B. Private
SMURTHWAITE Thomas R.N.
SMURTHWAITE William R.N.
TAYLOR Tom Private
TEASDALE Leonard Private
TODD Ernest Private
WADGE Richard Private
WARDLE George Rifleman
WARDLE T
WARLOW Tom Rifleman
WATSON Walter Gunner
WHITE Nicholas Sergeant
WILKINSON Richard Corporal
WILLINS Jack R.N.
WILLINS John Private
WRIGHT Christopher
YOUNG John Stoker

Photo Courtesy of Mr D. C Rider and Esh Parish Council

World War Two (1939-1945)

BILLINGHAM Harry Gunner
BURDON James William
BRADLEY A.P. Private
COOK Thomas R. N.
COWLEY Thomas Sergeant
FLETCHER Frederick Private
HALL Marion A.T.S.
HALLIDAY Jack R. N.
HANNON Eddy R. N.
HAYSON Alec Private
HEPPLE William R. N.
HOWARD William Gunner
KING Ernie Gunner
MAWSON Eric R. A. F.
MONTGOMERY Thomas Guardsman
RICHARDSON Jack R. A. F.
ROBINSON Herbert R. N.
ROBSON John R. N.
RUTHERFORD Wilson Sergeant
SMITH Fred Gunner
SPROATS William Private
THOMPSON Fred Trooper
TOMES Jack Gunner
WOOD Jack R. N.
WILLIAMSON Albert Gunner
WHITE William Sergeant
WHITE William Private

Korean War (1950-1953)

TURNBULLL R.

Northern Ireland 1974

DAUGHTERY Alan Guardsman

Langley Park War Memorial was unveiled in April, 1921 by Col J.H. Ritson. Costing £750 the money for the monument was raised largely by colliery workmen and local people.

HE LIVES IN FAME AND DIES IN VIRTUE'S CAUSE

LANGLEY PARK COMFORTS FUND

By December 1939 British Legion Women's Section were already at work knitting comforts to send to the forces and had put together six parcels that included not only socks but also gloves, cigarettes and chocolates. Each member was contributing 2d. a week towards the cost of the knitting wool. The Women's Institute and others in the village were also taking an active part and were organising fund raising events such as whist drives.

In January 1940 a meeting was held in Langley Park Co-operative Hall. Workmen and officials from Langley Park Colliery had been looking of ways to help Langley Park men who had been called up for war service.

As a result of this meeting a motion was passed which resulted in the setting up of the Langley Park Comforts Fund. Its aim being to raise money to send gifts to Langley Park men serving in H.M. Forces at home and overseas. Colliery workers agreed to contribute weekly to the fund.

Councillor J. Robertshaw was elected Chairman with Mrs. R. Rutherford and Rev. E.S. Barnett vice-chairmen. Mrs. M. Johnson was appointed secretary and Mr. T. Proud treasurer. These officials held office until the fund was wound up with the exception of Mr. Barnett who was replaced by Mrs. R. Groves. A schoolteacher Margaret Johnson had served on the committee of a similar organisation during the First World War. Her husband died in 1932 and she died in March 1980 aged 85.

Money was raised by house-to-house collections and by various events organized by several organizations in the village including the A.R.P. and the Special Constables. Sunday night concerts held in the Kings Cinema were a source of income and, of course, the other organizations already at work joined in the scheme.

Among those associated with the Fund during the war years were E. Hemsley, Mrs. A. Sullivan and J. Craggs.

By mid 1945 over £4,500 had been donated and over 400 servicemen were receiving comforts.

When the war was over collections ceased as it was no longer necessary to continue the work of the fund and it was wound up. The last house-to-house collection took place at the end of November 1945. Money from the fund was used to give gifts to servicemen returning home from the war. Around £2 each was given and more to those who had been prisoners of war.

It was decided that any remaining money should go towards inscribing the names of the 1939-1945 war victims on the war memorial in the village. Mrs. E. Birbeck was asked to meet Esh Parish Council to discuss the matter.

THE UNKNOWN SOLDIER

Westminster Abbey, London and Langley Park churchyard have something in common. They both have in their care a grave of an unknown soldier and they are, it is believed, to be the only such graves in Great Britain.

The events surrounding the Unknown Soldier who has been laid to rest in a small mining village in County Durham is one of the great puzzles of the Second World War.

Events began to unfold following the famous evacuation of Dunkirk at the end of May 1940 and are centred on Trooper William Bolton.

Mr. and Mrs. Newrick Bolton had four sons and one daughter (some versions of the story say he was the third son and another the second child of a family of six). During the Great Depression that fell over the north-east William enlisted in the army. Firstly in the King's Dragoon Guards and then he served in the Fife and Forfar Yeomanry. On the outbreak of war he went to France with his unit.

On 1st June 1940 Mr. and Mrs. Bolton received a telegram to say their son William had died on a military hospital ship on 30th May 1940 and his body lay in a Folkestone hospital. They were given the option of accepting a travel warrant for two persons to travel south to attend a funeral service or to have the body sent home for burial in Langley Park – they chose the latter.

The coffin arrived in the village sealed and with strict orders that under no circumstance was it to be opened. It was placed in the Church Hall and members of the local A.R.P. held vigil over it until the funeral. It is said that one of the wardens on watch remarked, on seeing the coffin 'if that is William Bolton he must have shrunk since I last saw him'.

With full honours the funeral was held at All Saints Church. Mr. Bolton was very popular in Langley Park and hundreds of villagers attended, as did members of the local branch of the British Legion, The Services Comforts Fund and a military detachment. The coffin bore a plate with Trooper Bolton's name, age and regimental number and was draped with the Union Jack.

Three weeks after the funeral, Mr. and Mrs. Bolton's daughter, Edna Sample, was standing at the door of her parent's house when she heard and eventually saw a motor cycle approaching. She soon recognised the rider as her brother William. Dumbfounded and surprised she dashed inside to tell her mother. One report says that on coming face to face with the son she thought she had buried Mrs. Bolton fainted. There was cause for great celebration but Mr. Bolton's visit was brief and after a cup of tea and a wash he left the village. His regiment was passing through the area on the way north and William was given leave to pay a quick visit.
Where had he been? Again reports differ. One account says he was successfully evacuated from Dunkirk and another version of the incident says that he had never

been out of England!). It appears that just before the telegram reporting her son's death Mrs. Bolton had written to him and he had in fact received the letter.

The police were called to investigate the case but they were unable to throw any light on the extraordinary event.

A further twist to the story was to involve the Mayor of Durham. The strange affair attracted widespread publicity and a Mrs. Bolton of Arundel Street, Ashton under Lyne, Greater Manchester wrote to the Mayor asking if he could find out whether it was possible that the man buried in Langley Park churchyard could be her son Harry who had been reported missing. Despite the difficulties of wartime travelling and petrol rationing the Mayor set out to see Mr. and Mrs. Bolton. However, he mistook the address and finished up in Malton Colliery. The home of the Bolton's was in Malton Cottages, Langley Park. To reach his destination he travelled along cart tracks and uneven country roads to meet the Boltons. It was soon to be proved that the Ashton under Lyne man could not be the person who had been brought to Langley Park.

How did this case of mistaken identity come about? It appears that the only means of identification was an Army Education Certificate which was found on the body and bore the name and address of William Bolton together with his army number. How this certificate came to be in the possession of the dead man is still unexplained. Some reports which have circulated over the years have claimed there was also identity discs and other documents found but this does not seem to tie in with a letter that was sent to a local M.P. from Sir Edward Grigg, Under Secretary State for War following an enquiry. This letter stated that a letter of regret had been sent to the family and the cost of the funeral was refunded to Langley Park Comforts Fund who had paid for the funeral.

After his unexpected return to Langley Park, William Bolton rejoined his unit, which was en route for Dumfries. After a time north of the border he moved to Workington where he met and married Betty Porter Bethwaite. By the end of 1945 he was serving in Italy. The only injury he received during the hostilities was a damaged eardrum caused by a bomb that had exploded near to him while on duty in Italy.

It is said that when back in Langley Park Mr. Bolton visited the grave several times and looked wistfully at the mound. Mrs Bolton and her daughter continued to visit the churchyard. Initially they laid wreaths and as their income decreased they placed small bunches of flowers every two weeks or so.

Today over sixty years after the event the name of the soldier who is buried in Langley Park churchyard is still a mystery and it will never be known who he is.
At one time it was suggested that the body be exhumed and re-interred in the grounds of Durham Cathedral.

After a great deal of discussion The Fellowship of the Services adopted the grave in 1977 and a letter to the Commonwealth War Graves Commission in Berkshire brought the satisfaction of a headstone of the Commission's war pattern being placed on the grave. It was also stated that the grave could in no way be altered, as it is the

ONLY OTHER ONE in Britain apart from Westminster Abbey. A service of dedication took place on 6th June 1978.

The grave of the Unknown Soldier in All Saints Churchyard.
Photo Courtesy of Mr. D. C. Rider

Every year on Remembrance Sunday wreaths are laid on the War Memorial in Langley Park Front Street and there follows a service in All Saints Church. In the churchyard immediately after the service a wreath is laid on the grave of the Unknown Soldier.

Today members of the Women's Section of the British Legion endeavour to keep the grave tidy. As Mrs. Bolton said at the time "Whoever he is, he is someone's son".

The headstone itself is of sandstone and bears the following inscription:- A SOLDIER OF THE 1939 – 1945 WAR. KNOWN UNTO GOD. But the question still remains WHO IS HE? William Bolton lived until the age of 76 and died in 1997.

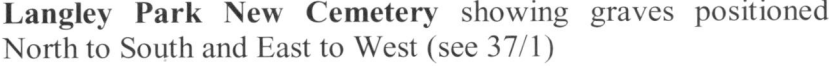

Langley Park War Memorial in earlier days

Langley Park New Cemetery showing graves positioned North to South and East to West (see 37/1)

4/1

THE HOME GUARD

When watching the highly amusing and often repeated episodes of the B.B.C. Television series 'Dad's Army featuring Arthur Lowe and his motley band of warriors it might be easily forgotten that, in the grim days of the Second World War, Langley Park had its own Home Guard. The village version of Captain Mannering was "Major" Joseph Penny.

Mr. Penny came to the village aged six months and at the age of 13 began work at Langley Park Colliery. He began as a coal hewer and was the first hand putter in the Brockwell Seam. During the 1914-1918 World War he joined the Green Howard's Regiment and eventually reached the rank of Sergeant. Wounded twice at the Battle of the Somme he returned home and not able to work underground became a timekeeper and for 35 years a colliery official.

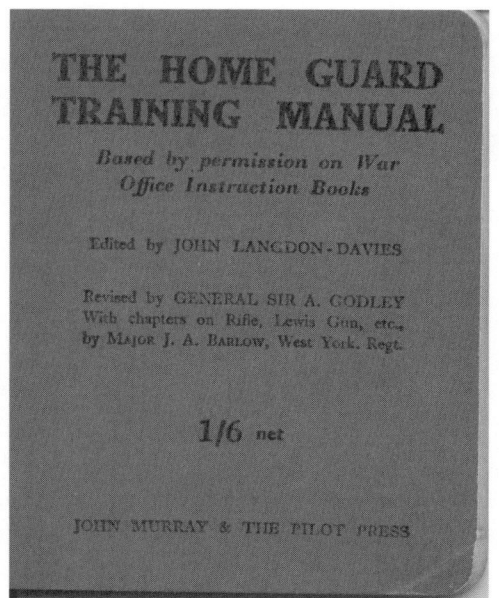

The coming of the 1939-1945 war saw him in 1941 take command of the local Home Guard (3rd Durham (Lanchester) Battalion). Older members of the community still have memories of him and his volunteers carrying out parades and exercises in the area with the most primitive of equipment. Although it would never have been possible for them to stop an enemy, no doubt with their enthusiasm and determination they could have caused any invaders a great deal of harassment.

At first there were two sections of the Home Guard in the village. One comprising men from the Colliery and the other from Tradesmen and other residents. Eventually the two merged. Early parades took place at various establishments including a blacksmith's shop near the Workmen's Club and at another shop in Quebec Street.

On Saturday 12 September 1942 the new Home Guard Headquarters was opened at the West End Social Club. Officers attending were Major Oliver and Lt. Hassett, (Lanchester), Major Wallace, Lt. Stoneman (Cornsay), Lt Holmes and Mrs. Smith (representing Colonel Ritson, Lts. Maggison, Reggie Nesbitt, Norman Holmes and Billy Graham and also Captain Brennan (Esh). The Imperial Dance Band provided the music for an evening of singing and dancing.

As time went on paper work increased. Records had to be kept and there was a large store of equipment, weapons and ammunition. To keep the books in order Mary (Mrs. Sid) Howe was appointed to look after the secretarial work.

In April 1952 Mr Penny was living in The Crescent and retired from the pit after 52 years. He recalled that after his first eleven days work he received for his first pay 10/-.

He was a keen sportsman and played cricket for Langley Park for thirty years and was one of the village's keenest supporters of Newcastle United.

In his latter days Joseph Penny was a resident of The Haven. He died in March 1959 at the age of 71.

Corporal Lawrence M. Yates of George Street was chosen to represent Durham County Home Guard in the London Victory Parade on Saturday 8th June 1946. Engaged on haulage work at Langley Park Colliery he had been with the Home Guard throughout the war and trained cadets. His brothers George and John were also associated with the Home Guard.

EVACUEES

5

With the coming of the Second World War Mr. N. M. Collingwood, headmaster of Langley Park Council School was appointed Billeting Officer for child evacuees coming to the Langley Park area.

In the early days of hostilities and coming mainly from the Newcastle-on-Tyne and Gateshead area 550 children aged between five and fourteen years arrived at Ushaw Moor Station and some 165 at Lanchester and other stations. Carrying little luggage the youngsters were accommodated in various houses in the village and surrounding area. Many found their way to their new wartime address in special buses. For some Langley Park was to be a permanent home.

> **A.R.P – RECOMMENDATIONS TO OUR PATRONS**
> You will be notified from the stage if an air raid warning has been sounded during the performance – but that does not mean that an air raid will necessarily take place. If you wish to leave for home or an official Air Raid Shelter, you are at liberty to do so. All we ask is that – if you feel you must go – you will depart quietly and without excitement. We recommend you to remain in the theatre.
> *Announcement in theatre programmes during the war years.*

At Christmas 1939 a special party was laid on for the evacuees at Langley Park Council School. Mary A. Smith, a teacher and Rev. E.S. Barnett were involved in the arrangements.

THE AIR RAID WARDENS

In October 1938 there was an A.R.P. meeting in the Church Hall at which the chairman, Councillor Mrs. R. Rutherford was appealing for volunteers to enlist. She also informed the gathering that the distribution of gas masks to villagers was on hold as they were awaiting the arrival of new containers.

By March 1939 eighteen villagers were passed out by the A.R.P. having attended classes under Mr. J. Ardley. They were Miss M. Hunter, Mrs. J. Halliday, Mrs. M. A. Emmerson, Mrs. J.A. Camsell, Mrs. J. Rutherford and Messrs. W. Trotter, T. Howard, G.R. Proud, A. Coxon, J.C. Johnson, A. Weighill, E. Lowdon, H. Hepburn, G. Craggs, T.H. Preston, J Ramsey, R. Atkinson and O. Birbeck.

During the ensuing war years, as well as carrying out their duties, the A.R.P. were working hard raising funds for Langley Park Comforts Funds. By August 1944 they had collected over £1,500. At this time their Secretary was Mr. F. Fletcher and their Chairman was Mr. J. Ardley. W. Wilkinson was Treasurer and on the committee were A. Gill, J. Kipling and J. Vickers.

THE SPECIAL CONSTABLES

During the war years the Special Constables carried out their duties and like the A.R.P. were involved in fund raising.

In 1941 Langley Park Band were engaged to play at a Field Day they organised on Langley Park cricket field. There were sports events for the children and in the evening villagers attended a dance. Prior to this the A.R.P. and the Special Constables staged a cricket match to raise money for the events. The A.R.P. scored 121 for 7 wickets then dismissed the Constables for 78 runs. The Special Constables also arranged a match with the Langley Park Bowling Club.

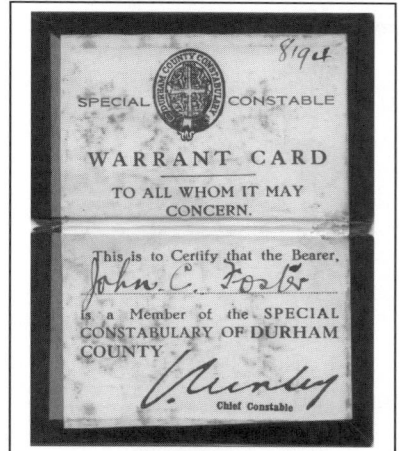

There were 200 prizes for children's competitions at the 1942 event and each youngster received two lollipops, a bar of toffee, two cakes and bottles of mineral water. Mrs. Angus won the baby show with her little girl. There was also a demonstration by the Langley Park National Fire Service and the Home Guard staged an exhibition of their guns.

Over 1,000 adults attended the gathering in 1943 when 700 children were treated to tea and cakes.

THE WAR IS OVER

The 1939-1945 war is over.

The Prime Minister, Winston Churchill spoke on radio at 3 p.m. on Tuesday 8th. May 1945 to inform the country that the Germans had signed an act of unconditional surrender of all German land, sea and air forces in Europe to the Allied Expeditionary Force. Hostilities had ended at one minute past midnight on Tuesday 8th May 1945.

An occasion of great rejoicing.

School children were sent home as part of a national holiday and Union Jacks of all sizes were suddenly displayed from the bedroom windows of many houses in the village. As everywhere else in the country Langley Park was very quickly in the mood for jubilation and celebration that lasted for about a week.

Nearly all the streets in the village organised street parties. Children were given tea, residents provided the food and a good time was had by all. It is said than any food left over was sold to adults for a charge of sixpence. Throughout the village there were games, sports and dancing. At one venue dancing went on till two o'clock in the morning from V.E. Day until Saturday. Everybody, young and old joined in the dancing and the road was also used as a ballroom. By some means a band was assembled. Out of nowhere there appeared a piano, double bass, drums and even a banjo player was found.

One of the events was a Fancy Dress Parade which was a great success particularly for Mrs. Court, Mrs. Allison and Mrs. Hutchinson who were prize-winners.

Most of the proceeds from the various events were divided between the Red Cross and The Welcome Fund. It was estimated £30 had been raised.

At this time of celebration the local cinemas were screening on the week commencing 7th May 1945:

Kings
- Mon-Wed William Bendix in 'Abroad With Two Yanks'.
- Thurs-Sat Maria Montez in 'Cobra Woman'

Hippodrome
- Mon-Wed Robert Newton and John Mills in 'This Happy Breed'
- Thurs – Sat Basil Rathbone and Nigel Bruce in 'The Scarlet Claw'.

A week before the announcement of the end of hostilities there was a fund raising event held in the Labour Hall. Councillor J. Robertshaw welcomed home four Langley Park men who had been prisoners of war. Aged 36 Private Robert Maddison had been five years in enemy hands. Captured at Boulogne he was taken to West Prussia and was involved in farm work. A resident of South Street Private James Worden, who in pre-war days had been a conductor on the Gypsy Queen buses, had also been held for five years. From Arras in France he was transferred to Poland. Eventually the Russian Army was marching on Poland and he was forced to march for many weeks with little rest or food and finally reached the Baltic. Later he was taken to South Germany. Signalman Stanley Wilson was a prisoner for five months in Greece and in camps in Italy and Germany for the rest of his long stay in captivity. In 1942 Private George Thompson was taken prisoner at Tobruk and soon found himself on the way to Italy where he spent fourteen months before being moved to Germany.

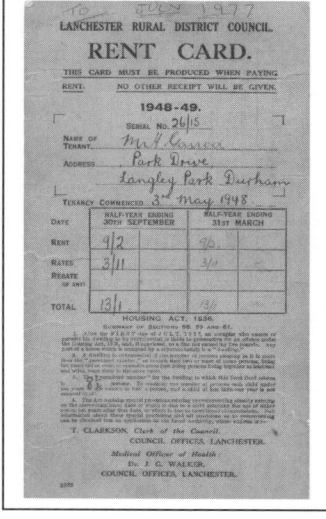

Rent card belonging to the first tenant of a new council house in Langley Park 1948

The four spoke very highly of the Red Cross who were able to get parcels to them while they were in captivity It is interesting to note that at this special evening in their honour each man received sums of money ranging from five pounds eight shillings to six pounds eight shillings and sixpence from the Langley Park Comforts Fund who organised the homecoming.

Around this time there were two couples enjoying a happy day. The weddings of Mr. J Gregory and Miss D. Cuthbert and Mr. Floyd Vincent of the Royal Canadian Air Force and Miss Dorothy Nicholson took place.

There was one sad occurrence during a happy week. The death of Mary Ann Stoker late of Elm Street. She was a widow who had died at the home of her daughter and son-in-law, Mr. and Mrs. Hogarth of Church Street. For the first nine years of her life she had lived in Burnhope. Coming to Langley Park she was for fifty-six years a member of Quebec Street Methodist Church. Her late husband had been a preacher on the Methodist Circuit for over fifty years. The Rev. J.W. Kennedy conducted the funeral service which took place on Saturday 12th. May 1945. Mrs. Stoker was aged 77.

One of the first men released from the Royal Air Force under the 'age and service', scheme was Sgt. E. Dennison of Wood View, Langley Park. During his war service he had spent nearly three years in India and had seen many areas of that country.

After the war military conscription continued as National Service (See 13). Typical group photographs of platoons during training

9

A WOMAN WITH A PAST

In May 1958 the sudden death was announced of Mrs. Irene Howe of Davis Crescent, Langley Park. She was 46 years old and worked at Morley's Factory at Langley Moor. Always a quiet, pleasant and friendly woman she had collapsed on arriving at work and soon it was revealed that Mrs. Howe was a woman with a past.

Before her marriage she was Mlle. de Rideaux, one of the heroines of the Belgian Resistance movement during the 1939 –1945 war. She was involved in many daring and dangerous missions behind enemy lines and was often smuggled into occupied France to collect funds.

She had been awarded two bronze medals by the Belgians for courage and fortitude and possessed a card issued by the Belgian authorities after the war. It bore her photograph with the awards a grateful country had given her written across it.

Mlle. de Rideaux met her husband, a Langley Park man Mr. J. Howe, in Brussels in 1945. He was with the liberation forces. She happened to serve him with a glass of beer at a hostelry during a brief rest period he was having. The couple corresponded for eight years and married in1953. Mrs. Howe went about her daily tasks normally and no one was aware of her adventures.

At the funeral held in All Saints' Church, Langley Park the coffin was covered with the Belgian flag.

10

CIVIL DEFENCE

Although the Second World War was over the political uncertainty in the world in the immediate post war years made Civil Defence a necessary requirement of life throughout the country. Everywhere there were volunteers prepared to carry out duties and attend training courses and lectures in preparation for any further outbreak of hostilities.

In 1960 Langley Park Colliery had a champion First Aid Team. Four awards for Civil Defence were won during that year, The Durham County Rally Trophy, the Northern Defence Tourney Cup, the N.C.B. Trophy and the No. 5 Area Industrial Shield. Each of the participants received certificates. These included R. Atkinson, W. Rose, W. Clegg, F. Weighill, L. Morland, J. Gleghorn and K. Wilson.

Robert Atkinson died in July 1968 aged 65. As well as a life long interest in first aid he held the Civil Defence Long Service Medal and held a Home Office Warden Instructors Certificate. In 1963 he was elected as an Associate Fellow of the Institute of Civil Defence and awarded the B.E.M. As a joiner Mr. Atkinson began work at Langley Park Colliery and when he retired due to ill health in 1967 he was a foreman joiner and shaftman.

11
A CHINESE INCIDENT

Chief Officer George Cyril Jones of Bridge Street, Langley Park then aged 41 was serving aboard 'The Glenearn', a 10,000 ton British cargo ship. In July 1950 a Chinese nationalist plane attacked the motor vessel and C.O. Jones was badly injured by machine gun bullets. The ship had been sailing in Far Eastern waters and was in the Straits of Formosa. Taken ashore at Nagasaki in Japan, Mr. Jones was transferred to a hospital in Fuyoka and later to Osaka.

C.O. Jones had been in the Merchant Navy since a boy and had served throughout with the Blue Funnel Company who owned 'The Glenearn'. During the war years he took part in Atlantic Convoys and later spent some time in Canada in charge of British built vessels undergoing conversion for the Canadian navy. Early in the war he had a narrow escape when his ship left Singapore two days before the Japanese entered the city.

Mr. Jones and his wife, Joyce together with their son Fred came to Langley Park around the time the Second World War was starting. At the time of 'The Glenearn' incident young Fred now 15 years old was attending Durham Johnston School.

Mrs. Jones was a grand daughter of the late Dr. John Wilson and was a fully qualified nurse before she was married. On coming to Langley Park she took up District Nursing and was known for her appearances with the local amateur dramatic club.
By August 1950 Nurse Jones was reporting that her husband was on the road to recovery.

12
ARMY CADET CORPS

In the immediate post war years youngsters were being persuaded to join one of the services cadet corps. For a time Langley Park had a well supported Army Cadet Corps and its uniformed members were often seen parading through the streets.

Early in 1951 the first annual party of the Langley Park No. 12 Platoon of Army Cadets took place in the Labour Hall. Under Officer Commanding Lt. T.B. Fishwick, the group were often referred to as 'Fishwick's Fusiliers'.

In May 1952 Langley Park Army Cadet Headquarters opened with Lt. Colonel Lamb, O.C. Durham Army Cadet Force, in attendance, as was Lt. Fishwick. At that time there were some forty boys in the platoon.

A big parade took place in Durham in 1960 when members of the 8th Cadet Battalion, D.L.I., Durham, Langley Park, Ushaw Moor and Esh Winning contingents took part in a service at Durham Cathedral.

The Langley Park hut, which was situated on land in the area of Rutherford House and Rutherford Court, remained in use for several years and was often used by other organisations. Young cadets often attended week-end camps at Stanhope and were taken to Bishop Auckland for boxing.

NATIONAL SERVICE

From 1948 conscription to the armed forces was National Service, which became a British Institution and a fact of life for young men. Initially the period of service was 18 months but with the coming of the Korean War in the early 1950s this was extended to two years. The last soldiers to be called up were enlisted on 24th November 1960 and in May 1963 the last man was discharged. Three men from Langley Park saw service in the D.L.I. Gordon Hammel, Malcolm Craggs and Mowbray Ward. They also became members of the D.L.I. Band (photo below). Some men saw overseas service in politically dangerous Kenya, Aden, Malta, Singapore Malaya and Cyprus. Others were given U.K. postings in various occupations.

Pte Coates F.
Kings Royal Hussars

Pte Kipling L.
R.A.O.C.
Prior to service in Belgium

Johnny Cuthbert 'gloves up' with British Army Boxing team.
Below: F Coates on parade in Northern Ireland.

Johnny Cuthbert and regimental boxing team out on exercise. Below: Pte Foster R.A.P.C. during basic training at Devizes

THE BRITISH LEGION
WOMEN'S SECTION

The British Legion was formed in 1921. Sixty years after the end of the Second World War there are still 11 million people eligible for support. 300,000 calls for help are received each year. It has to be remembered that since 1945 there is only one year (1968) that a British serviceman has not been killed in action somewhere in the world.

The first Poppy Day was held on 11 November 1921. A poem by John McCrae 'In Flander's Fields' was the inspiration of that flower becoming the symbol of the British Legion.

Throughout the country branches were quickly set up Langley Park among them.

Firstly it was The Men's Section that had a good following up to and well after the Second World War, but sadly it has now been disbanded. There are still a few old comrades living in the village who were associated with the organisation
.
By 1928 a Women's Section was formed but soon voluntarily closed down. In the spring of 1935 it was reformed. Miss Ainsworth Chairman of the North East Area addressed the opening meeting after which Mrs. Ross was elected branch Chairman, Mrs. Sherrington, Vice Chairman, Mrs. Johnson, Secretary and Mrs. Leeming Treasurer. These officials were confirmed in office at the first Annual General Meeting in the autumn of the same year. This group flourished up to and after the war and exists today. Some members clocked up years of service. In December 1950 Mesdames Dodds (23 years) E. Birbeck (15) B. Smith (15) L Smith (13) E.A. Birbeck (13). There loyalty being rewarded at a celebration at Dunelm Hotel, Durham where it was reported Mrs L Smith injured her wrist playing games.

In December 1936 a new standard was dedicated at All Saints Church. Mrs. Birbeck was the standard bearer and there was a parade lead by the Colliery Band from the Church Hall to the church. Representatives from other branches attended the dedication service. By 1937 Mrs. E.Birbeck was Secretary and Mrs. E. Smith Treasurer. Mrs. Bramley was President in 1943, Mrs. Watson Vice President and Mrs. O. Birbeck had become Chairman. Mrs. Richardson was Vice Chairman. Late in 1944 Mrs Dodds had been elected President.

Over the next few years all officials had deputies and as well as a governing committee there was a Benevolent Committee, sick visitors, a poppy organiser and a press officer.

In June 1953 The Women's Section held a 25th. Birthday Party in the Parochial Hall and in November of the same year there were 400 delegates at the Women's Section Conference in the Town Hall, Durham.

The minutes of a meeting held on Thursday 12 November 1959 records that Mrs. Birbeck had now retired after over 30 years as Hon. Secretary. A vote of thanks for her work over all those years was moved and it was agreed that a presentation be made at a future meeting. A month later good wishes were extended to Mrs. Birbeck who received a sea grass stool and a bouquet of roses. At this meeting which was a joyous occasion with games, songs and carols some of which were recorded and played back to members on a new fangled tape recorder to great amusement.

A meeting held in the middle of June 1960 was a sad gathering. Mrs. McEleavey, obviously well liked as Chairman had died. Tributes were made and sympathy cards sent to her family. The normal social aspect of the meeting was not in evidence, members preferring to spend the evening quietly together.

Vice-Chairman Mrs. L. Richardson presided at meetings until the autumn when Mrs. Johnson was elected chairman and remained so until her death in March 1972. At this time Mrs. L. Smith was President, Mrs. L. Fishwick (Secretary) and the treasurer was Mrs. Coulson who was still in post at her 70th. birthday in March 1972.

The branch continued to hold regular meetings, dealing with official British Legion business, arranging social outings, attending rallies and keeping the Langley Park Branch of The British Legion in the public eye.

In July 1961 it was announced that former Hon Secretary Mrs. Birbeck had died. Each year with the coming of autumn arrangements had to be made in conjunction with the Men's Section for The Annual Poppy Appeal it being essential that all areas of were covered for the distribution of poppies. It had also to be decided which members should lay wreaths at the War Memorial, The grave of the Unknown Soldier and at Esh Church

In June 1964 Mr Dodds, Durham County Chairman made a presentation to Mr Wade who had given long and devoted service to the Legion. The ladies provided a splendid supper. Later in the year the Branch standard was carried at City Hall, Newcastle Remembrance Service.

On Sunday 12 September 1965 the standard-bearer and members attended the 25th. Anniversary of The Battle Of Britain Service held at Durham Cathedral organised by the Air Force Association. Prior to the service members and standard bearers paraded from Old Elvet to the Cathedral.

In the summer of 1968 The Women's Section Standard Bearer, Mrs. Bailey, won a cup at Brandon Sports Day.

Throughout the 1960s and 1970s around thirty members regularly attended meetings.

Mrs. Fishwick continued for many years as Hon. Secretary but over the years membership has declined. The war-time veterans are becoming fewer in number and new members are not coming forward.

Today only a small number of faithful older residents keep the British Legion alive in the village.

14/3

Remembrance Day parades used to muster at the Parochial Hall, marching off with the church choir leading, followed by the Colliery Band playing, the British Legion standard proudly carried and representatives from The Boy Scouts, Girl Guides, The St. John's Ambulance and other organisations following. Stopping for the laying of wreaths at The War Memorial the procession progressed to All Saints Church for a service of Remembrance, the reading of names of men killed in action and finally the laying of a wreath on the grave of the Unknown Soldier in the churchyard.

Now few of the organisations mentioned exist or have very few members. The band last paraded in 2001. On Remembrance Sunday the British Legion banner is laid on the altar of the church and the few remaining members of the British Legion assemble at the War Memorial before walking up Quebec Street for the church service and the traditional laying of the wreath in the churchyard. House to house collections for the Poppy Appeal ceased some time ago. Collecting boxes are now placed in various establishments throughout the village and a substantial amount of money is still raised to help ex-servicemen.

So many young men and some women too lost their lives in the two world wars and other conflicts and the British Legion reminds us constantly of the sacrifice they made.

15

THE BRITISH LEGION
MEN'S SECTION

By 1933 Dr. R. Rutherford was President of the Langley Park Branch with G. Douglas as Vice President, H. Morgan Chairman and M. Parker Secretary. The Chairman in November 1934 was H. Morgan, J. Ward was Secretary and W. Smith was Treasurer. G. Jameson was running the Benevolent Committee. At the Remembrance Day ceremony that year Mr. Ward sounded the last post. Two years later Captain P. A. Ross was President and continued through until 1937. The Vice President was W.W. Smith Senior and J. Ward was Secretary. Three others were named as Vice Presidents in 1937 Rev. C. Blomely, Rev. E.S. Barnett and Dr. R. Rutherford.

This page and next page: Photographs of Langley Park British Legion outside the Labour Hut late 1940s/early 1950s

R. Atkinson replaced J. Ward as Secretary by April 1938 and later in the year Mr. M. Parker held the post continuing through to 1940. At this time Captain Ross had moved to Blackhill.

Officials in 1939 were T. Miller President with Rev. Blomely Vice President. H. Morgan remained Chairman and J. Wade was treasurer. Other members named around this time were T. Smith, C. Gregory, R. Atkinson, J. Charlton, A. Liddle and W. Sadden.

When the year 1948 came around J. Davison held the position of President, J. Wade was Chairman, J. Tait was Secretary and the treasurer was D. Shorten. During this time Messrs. Wadge, Evans and Wells were also involved with the work of the Legion. The President in 1951 was J. Wade. A Smith was in the chair with W. Chapman as Vice Chairman and R. S. Bradley as Secretary. Mr. Wade is shown as president in 1961 and through to the following year Mr. G. Fetcher was Chairman and J. C. Ewan was Secretary.

Thomas Byron Fishwick

Having been determined to attend the 1997 Remembrance Day Service Mr. Fishwick, who had been in ill health, died on 20th November 1997. He was 84 years old. He had been a Councillor on Esh Parish Council and on the Derwentside District Committee but was best known for his work in the village for the armed services and the British Legion. He had been happily married to Lily for many years and who was a great supporter for his work for ex-servicemen.

Sadly the Men's Section of the Langley Park British Legion was disbanded some time ago but there are still a few old comrades resident in the village today.

**One further memory of the Second World War
BEVIN BOYS**

Between 1943 and 1948 a number of men came to Langley Park Colliery having been conscripted as Bevin Boys. After their period of service some stayed on in the village, married and brought up families who still live in the area.

Courtesy: Bevin Boys Association

SCHOOL

In 1878 Consett Iron Company helped to support the first purpose built school in Langley Park, The British School, and this was in use until 1907. It eventually became The Church Hall sometimes referred to as The Parochial Hall. In 1964 it came into use as The Youth Centre. The school of 1878 opened on 10th March and the first Headmaster was George Henderson. In June 1883 Mrs. Helena Waistrell was Headmistress. From 1887 Amos Hollingworth was Headmaster and he remained in the village for 43 years eventually moving to the 'big school' where he remained until early in the 1930s when he was succeeded by Mr. Collingwood. Mr. Hollingsworth seems to have been a very popular teacher and it is said when Mr. Collingwood arrived for his first day at the school he came armed with an armful of canes which he distributed to the various classrooms. The British School was supported by grants from Consett Iron Company and Church Authorities. Initially there were 97 pupils and shortly after opening Mr. Henderson engaged a pupil teacher, Robert Lamb then aged 16. Fees were 2d or 3d and later 3d and 4d.

Within the new development in the wooded area near The British School a new infant school was built sited opposite Wood View (now The Wood View Community Centre). Three years later in 1910 the 'big school' opened opposite Lillian Terrace and near Ivy and May Terrace just off the main road. This became known as Langley Park Council and later Langley Park County School.

At one time children were starting work as early as 9 years old. During the period of this account the school leaving age had risen from 14 years to 15 and later still to 16.

In 1921 there were 335 boys and 300 girls attending Langley Park Council School. By 1938 the figures were 207 boys and 185 girls and in 1945 the figure had dropped to 190 and 155.

Youngsters began their education as 'mixed infants'.

In the mid-1930s Miss Stothard was Headmistress of the Wood View school. Teachers at the Infants School during the 1939-1945 war years were Mrs. Spirlet, a long serving member of staff, the homely Miss Mulcaster and Miss Hull who came from Cornsay and who also appeared much sterner in manner. Miss Mulcaster's sister ran the millinery department of the Co-operative Wholesale Society in the village.

Miss Hull retired from teaching early in 1956. She trained at Neville's Cross College and taught at Lumley, Washington and Cornsay before her long time residency at Langley Park. On the occasion of her retirement a former Headmistress, Mrs I. Harrison returned to attend a presentation made to Miss Hull from pupils and staff.
At that time the Headmistress was Miss E. McNay. Hundreds of pupils must have passed through the hands of Mrs. Spirlet who ended her career in teaching as Headmistress of the school. Other teachers remembered at the school included Mrs. Thompson, Mrs. Morpeth, Mrs Reay and Mrs. Angus.

In the summer of 1961 Mrs. M. Johnson retired from the teaching staff of the infant's school after twelve years. She began teaching in 1911 at Langley Park Girls' School where she remained until 1922 when she gave up teaching. In 1918 she married Mr. R. Johnson. He died in 1932 and she moved to her parent's house in the village. During the Second World War she was employed as master's clerk at Lea Hill Hospital, Lanchester but later returned to teaching at Cornsay. As Secretary she served the Langley Park Comforts Fund. (see 2). She then came back to Langley Park Infants School. On her retirement Miss McNay on behalf of the staff presented her with a transistor radio set and a coffee table. Mrs. Johnson died, aged 85, in April 1980.

After a year in Mrs. Spirlet's class the pupils left and progressed to 'The Big School' 'Mixing' ceased. Girls and boys were separated. The girls to the left of the building, coming under the watchful eye of the formidable Miss H.W. Dawson who held the post for over 30 years. She was succeeded circa. 1949/1950 by Miss M. Hunter who was already a teacher at the school On her retirement Miss Dawson moved to Wales.

The boys were housed to the right of the building under Headmaster Mr. Collingwood. There were no uniforms in those days but children were expected to dress reasonably well to attend classes. At infants school pencils were the writing tools. Pen and ink now became the new form of writing and woe betides any pupil who had a blotted copybook.

At the end of the First World War there were some 40–50 children to a class this figure reducing as the years went by. One teacher taught all subjects, English, Arithmetic, Geography, History etc. At one time it was necessary to pass an examination to move into a higher standard.

In the girls department teachers included Mrs. Campbell, Miss Moss, Miss Ward, Miss Boxall and Mrs Mitchell. Also named are Miss Crozier and Margaret Maggs.

Teachers entrusted to the boys' education were Mr. Heslop, who had part of one finger missing, Mr. Phillips who travelled from Chester-le-Street, Mr Black who took the 'eleven plus' class and who lived for many years after retirement, as did Mr. Russell and Mr. Ardley. Jack Ardley who was one of the longest serving members of staff and in younger days was a highly accomplished cricketer being notable as a wicket keeper. Mr Ardley was always associated with the top class in the school and in that final year he was often seen with the senior boys tending to the garden in school grounds. He retired in the summer of 1955.

In the late 1940s John Wigham arrived at the school for his first teaching post. In the autumn of 1948 Stan Lewis from Cornsay took up a teaching post at the boys' school having spent 18 months at Willington County Mixed School. He had seen war service in the R.A.F. in North Africa and Italy. A keen football player he had been associated with teams at Willington, Tow Law and Cornsay. He had been an amateur international player and was for a time on the books of Tottenham Hotspur.

The 'eleven plus' could be a turning point in education. Mr Black was responsible for preparing pupils for a two-part examination, the successful outcome of which being a scholarship to Durham Johnstone Grammar School. In the writer's year several lads made it to the Johnstone School for the second part of the test but only two were successful in obtaining places.

In earlier years the financial commitment made it impossible for some students to contemplate the attendance at a Grammar School. School uniforms, travel and schoolbooks had to be paid for by parents.

At one time boys were leaving school at 14 or 15 to start their working life at the colliery.

Facilities for sport were severely restricted. There was no playing field and games were played in the schoolyard but Langley Park still managed to produce a successful schools football team and achieved some success at athletics. A sports afternoon with the boys was organised, the school divided into four houses and this was held on the cricket field next to All Saints Church. (*See also 62*).

Another feature of the late 1940s/early 1950s was the introduction of school dinners. They arrived in a van in special containers and were served to the pupils by Mrs. Raper, wife of long time caretaker Bill Raper.

A new extension to the school had been planned and begun when the Second World War broke out. In October 1948 Councillor J. Robertshaw was pressing Durham County Education Authority to 'evacuate' the Ministry of Food from the incomplete building. It seems that during the Second World War they had been using the site as a storehouse. It was considered that it was now time for work to be restarted in order that the new school could open It took until 1952 for work to be sufficiently completed to allow occupation. A sports field became a reality and was first used for a sports afternoon in the summer of 1951 and on Saturday 23rd June 1951 Durham Central Area School Sports were held. Successful competitors would progress to County Sports at Houghton-le-Spring a week later and then to All England Championships at Southampton Allen Ferguson was a Langley Park lad who had success in the long jump. (*see 61*).

The official opening of the Langley Park Modern School, as it was now called took place on 27 November 1952 and the school hall and gymnasium were soon in full use.

In May 1954 it was announced that Mr. William Lynne Miller of Sacriston was to succeed Mr. N. Collingwood as Headmaster of the new mixed school for boys and girls. Miss Hunter continuing as Headmistress of Langley Park Junior Mixed School. Other teachers around this time were Mr. Brearley, Mr. Martin and Mr. Eastman who was in charge of woodwork.

A teacher for 42 years of her life Miss Hunter retired in December 1960. All her teaching had been at Langley Park. Mr. Stan Lewis succeeded her. At this time Mr. W. Black was deputy head. In the 1960s teachers remembered are Mrs. Brown, Mrs. Mitchell, Miss Ridley, Miss Blaycock and Messrs. Smart and Coates.

TEACHERS AND SCHOOLCHILDREN

*Above: Langley Park County School Class of girls 1951.
Below: Langley Park County School Boys Football Team 1950-1951 with Headmaster Mr N. Collingwood left and teachers Mr. W. Russell and Mr. J. Wigham right.*

Stan Lewis

Miss Doris Wilkinson

Mrs. Brown

Brian Smart

Ethel Ridley

Mrs. Mitchell with her class. Circa mid 1960s.

Mr Lewis retired in 1978. In May 1961 Jenny Buchan, who eventually became deputy head, directed the pupils of the Junior School in an operetta 'Alicia' based on a story by Charles Dickens. Frank Powell played Mr. Pickles, Chris Robinson was the King, Brenda Ardley, the Queen, Joyce Towns, Fairy, Pamela Gray, Alicia and Willis Joynes was The Prince. Others named included Gavin Eccleston and Peter Wadge. Mrs. E. Brown was pianist. Mr. Leach, music teacher, was to have considerable success with the school choir. In June 1980 the Junior School published its first magazine 'Juniorscope'.

The coming of Comprehensive Education in the 1960s involved many changes in education. The eleven plus ended and pupils were automatically transferred to Secondary Modern Schools around the area.

Eventually the Infants School closed and was re-housed in the old part of The Modern School. The old building became Wood View Community Centre.
The school continues today as Langley Park Primary School under the guidance of Headmistress Miss Brennan.

In the decade that followed World War Two further education was only available by attending evening classes in one's own time involving attending classes two or three nights a week. There was no Day Release from employment. Durham Commercial College offered courses for work in the secretarial world and in 1957 Durham Technical College at Framwellgate Moor came into being. It opened for classes on Monday 9 September 1957 enrolment taking place during week commencing 2 September 1957 and a new chapter in education was opened.

Infants School Headmistresses
Below are the names of some of the teachers who were Head of the infant's school in Langley Park together with approximate dates they were in post:

1890 Miss S.A. Walker
1894 Miss Margaret Haswell
1897 Miss Maria Gott
1902 – 1914 Helen Hogarth
1921 – 1925 Ida Greenheld
Pre 1920 Harriet Waldie Dawson is shown as **Headmistress of the Girls School***.*

Miss Margaretta (Etta) Hunter (pictured) who retired in December 1960 died in November 1963 aged 65. She lived in Front Street, Langley Park and had been associated with the Langley Park Branch of The Friends of The Hospitals, a non acting member of Durham Dramatic Society, a member of All Saints Church, a member of the Archaelogical Society of Durham and Northumberland and had been well known in the area as a teacher of folk dancing. She was also a past President of the Durham and District Head Teachers Association.

For over ten years Mr. N. W. Harbottle ran a popular history class at Langley Park School giving more than 200 lectures.

(See also under 'Sport') (Miss McNay: see under Langley Park People)

TRANSPORT

Signal box at Witton Gilbert Station

Can you imagine what it might have been like travelling from Langley Park to Durham in the days before mechanised transport? By horse? Or by pony and trap? Up to 1939 you could make the journey by rail but that meant a walk to Witton Gilbert Station. There were plans for a station in Langley Park that was to be behind Railway Street but the scheme came to nothing. In earlier days the North Eastern Railway began a bus service.

In November 1912 the North Eastern Railway had begun a bus service from Durham to Sacriston but with the advent of the First World War this was withdrawn. However in 1920 there was a service from Langley Park to Durham via Witton Gilbert and Sacriston again run by the North Eastern Railway.

The bus services caused a drastic reduction in railway passengers. In 1920 Witton Gilbert Station had 74,292 customers, a year later the figure was 39,982. The money taken had fallen from £5,117 in 1920 to £2,950 in 1921. The number of passengers in 1930 was 18,161 who paid £579.

By this date bus services were operating from Langley Park to Durham, Chester-le-Street, Newcastle, South Shields and Consett. The train service was reduced to five a day to Durham and four to Consett. The last train from Durham was 5.25 p.m. on weekdays and 9.55 on Saturdays.

Witton Gilbert Station had been the best supported station on the line attracting nearly three times as many passengers than Lanchester but on 1st. May 1939 passenger trains were withdrawn altogether. Goods traffic continued and on summer weekends excursions to seaside resorts were advertised.

THE GYPSY QUEEN

Originally a Mr. Benton who owned an off-licence had to convey his goods from Witton Gilbert Station using a horse and cart. Circumstances arising out of World War 1 (the horse was called up for military service) meant he had to find alternative means of transport. Getting possession of a motorised vehicle and removing seats he carried goods for himself and other tradesmen in the village. In 1920 he bought an open top bus with a canvas hood. This charabanc led the way to the creation of Mr. Benton's unique bus service.

Visitors to Durham have often been puzzled when seeing a bus with the name Gypsy Queen prominently displayed. Billy Benton took the name from a winning racehorse of that name that he had backed. He won £3,000 and as a result the name of the horse became a household name in the area and provided the bus link from Langley Park to Durham. Although the company no longer exists the name 'Gypsy Queen' still crops up from time to time in everyday conversation.

Before the new road (the direct link from Langley Park to Kaysburn) opened at the beginning of World War II vehicular traffic had to go via Wallnook and past Witton Gilbert Station to reach Kaysburn. It is said an eccentric old lady living in a cottage, long since demolished, used to throw obstacles on the highway in attempt to prevent motorised transport from passing.

Re the new road mentioned above, it will be noticed that there are wide verges on either side of the carriageway. It was intended to construct a cycle track but due to the war the work was abandoned.

In May 1937 a Gypsy Queen conductor, George Haswell, was in court giving evidence against a passenger who had been accused of disorderly conduct and using obscene language on a bus travelling from Durham to Langley Park. The culprit was fined £1

Garaged in what was once a Salvation Army Citadel, the Gypsy Queen set out on its journey from opposite the Co-op Buildings in Front Street picking up the first passengers at the end of Durham Street. The route went to Witton Gilbert where the only stops were near the Travellers' Rest and The Old Co-Op Store or old Village Hall near the Glendinning Arms. Up the Clink Bank and following the route into Durham which the present day Service 53 used to follow until recently.

The bus left Durham from a stop opposite houses in Milburngate later the departure point was moved to the waterside directly beside the river. If there was flooding you were likely to get your feet wet while waiting. The bus to Consett (the Witbank) occupied the first stop, then ' The Gypsy Queen' and behind that there was a bus to Stanley (The Diamond). For a while all these services were moved to Waddington Street. That is situated at the Viaduct end of North Road and below The County Hospital. When the new road complex was opened in the mid 1960s the bus services returned to Milburngate to a spot very near to where it was earlier. After a great many years residents living in the Stringer Terrace end of the village managed to get the service extended to that locality. The conductors on the Gypsy Queen were known to all, Lofty, Arthur Pinkney, Sadie, Chrissie, Muriel and Vera and so were the drivers. Before the Second World War James Worden was a conductor on the service. Serving in the forces he was captured and was a Prisoner of War for five years.

> *William Arthur Pinkney who lived in Finings Avenue died in May 1969. For 30 years he worked as a conductor on the Gypsy Queen. Away from work he was keenly interested in billiards and snooker.*
>
> *A conductor on the Gypsy Queen from 1941 until shortly before his death in September 1978 Norman 'Lofty' Richardson took a keen interest in greyhounds and whippets.*

You could always rely on catching the Gypsy Queen, if the driver or conductor saw you coming they would wait for you. And they never left anyone behind. It was not unusual for there to be more people standing on the bus than sitting with the conductor hanging perilously on the open door to keep passengers in. In these circumstances there was no way the conductor could get to the back of the bus to collect fares. Passengers passed the money down the bus to the conductor. Tickets and change were returned by the same method. If the bus was so overcrowded it could not always make it up the Clink Bank. All the men would respond to the request 'Everybody Off'. Off they would get and push the vehicle to the top of the hill get on board again and the journey would proceed – no doubt arriving at the destination on time.

During the years of the 1939-1945 war it was not unusual for passengers to find the bus on which they were travelling had wooden seats.

Reliability was the outstanding feature of the service and even today that reliability is still talked about in glowing terms. No matter what the circumstances or the state of the roads or through ice or heavy falls of snow or whatever the Gypsy Queen would struggle to get passengers to Durham or to get them home.

The former Gypsy Queen garage in Front Street.

In days gone by there was an hourly service to Newcastle (Service No 54) operated by the Northern General Transport starting at Esh Winning. Similar to today's service 725 but operating via Birtley and Low Fell and terminating at Marlborough Crescent, near the Central Railway Station. The Northern also ran an hourly service (No 62) which provided a direct route to South Shields all be it by a rather circuitous route.

Eventually after many years of trying the Northern took over the Gypsy Queen as it did the Bishop Auckland based O.K. service. These services continued for a while under their original names but these names were eventually lost to Go-Ahead Northern.

The building of the Arnison Centre at Framwellgate Moor led to a new service to cover that new amenity and with De-Regulation in the 1980s Bob Smith began offering an alternative means of travel to Durham.

One last recollection of the Gypsy Queen. In 1982 it was named 'Bus Company Of The Year'.

If you do not walk or take the bus or train why not take the motor car for a ride to the seaside or into the countryside for a picnic. No motorways and little traffic on the roads!!!. Date of the photograph of this summer outing is unknown.

DOCTORS

No National Health Service until the late 1940s so patients had to pay for the services of a General Practitioner. A knock on the door on a Friday night would herald the arrival of someone collecting on behalf of the doctor. The cost of the weekly contribution being 6d. (2 ½ p).

Some families were registered with Dr. Brown or Dr. Wilson who had a surgery at Bearpark.

Before and after World War 2 the village G.P. was Doctor Robert Rutherford. While he was away on war service Dr. Melrose deputised. Dr. Rutherford lived at The Firs, near Witton Gilbert Station and next to The Station Hotel which eventually became 'The Centurion' and later a house.

As well as being his home Dr. Rutherford had his surgery at The Firs in a building separate from the house and to the right as you entered the gates.

This was where all patients in the village had to go to see their G.P. (and bear in mind vehicular transport was in short supply in those days). Here you would not only consult the doctor but he would also dispense the medicine he considered you needed. A vast array of jars and bottles surrounded the shelves around the consulting room. No need for a prescription or a pharmacist. And something had to be seriously wrong before it was deemed a hospital visit was needed.

Also, in those days, it was very rare for a mother to be to go to hospital to have a baby. The birth would take place at home with a neighbour who was well versed on such matters in attendance and probably the local midwife.

Nurse Higginbottom *(see also 19)* was a well-known figure, pedalling around the village on her bicycle, a most convenient form of transport. In later years Nurse Robertshaw is remembered.

Dr. Rutherford was also well known in the village for his involvement in many organisations *(see no 20)*.

In January 1948 Dr. Rutherford wrote to Esh Parish Council asking that Gypsy Queen buses run past the surgery at The Firs during evening surgery hours. The Council wrote to Lanchester Rural District Council asking for a surgery to be provided in the village. (In the late 1930s there was a morning surgery at 28 Front Street).

After the war a Polish doctor came to the village to assist Dr. Rutherford and later Dr Robert Graham came to the practice.

Eventually the surgery was moved to Prospect Villa now a residence. The upper floor contained the consulting room of Dr. Rutherford while Dr. Graham occupied the lower half. Mrs. Bunn was a long serving receptionist.

Dr. Rutherford was the 'old type of doctor', rather abrupt in manner and straight speaking which did not always go down too well. So often there was a great demand for the services of Dr. Graham.

Dr Robert P. (Bobby) Graham 1927-1990

On one occasion, it has been noted, Dr. Rutherford arrived for Monday morning surgery and surveyed a crowded waiting room of mostly workers. He asked:-
'Was the beer good at The Club last night or were you drinking at The Blue Star. If any of you men are in need of a sick note, forget it'. Some of the men got up and left and with a sly wink in the direction of the receptionist the doctor went on his way to the upper floor.

Another patient made a painful journey up the lino-covered stairs to see the doctor. On entering the room Dr. Rutherford did not look up to identify the patient. 'There's something very wrong with you' he said. 'How do you know that?' 'You came up those stairs very slowly' the G.P replied 'If you'd run up there couldn't be much wrong with you'.

Old age eventually overtook Dr. Rutherford and he retired, ceasing to practice on 30th April 1972

A new surgery was built on land behind the Church Street Community Centre and was named 'Rutherford House'. Rutherford Court also stands in the same area. A group practice was established. Dr. Graham remained for a time but eventually moved into private practice in Newcastle. Dr. Nagi another member of the group left and set up his own practice at Browney House.

In May 1967 Jack Gray who from 1932 was part-time handyman for Dr. Rutherford retired. He went to the Firs initially in 1919 and had been with the two Dr. Wilsons (father and son). Mr Gray had been employed at Langley Park Colliery until he retired in 1964. Older residents can still remember how well Mr. Gray attended the garden at The Firs.

Note: Another Dr. Wilson, Dr. John Wilson of Park House, Lanchester died in June 1926.

According to Kelly's Directory from circa. 1879 – 1890 'The Firs' was occupied by John Francis Bell and in the early 1900s by Frederick Octavius Kirkup who became manager of Langley Park Colliery. Named from around 1903 – 1926 Thomas Watson Wilson M.B. Ch.B. Glas was the local doctor living at 'The Firs' He died in April 1926 aged 48   He was the son of The Rev. T. Wilson of Lanarkshire and married the daughter of R.S. Fell of Crook He was succeeded in Langley Park by one of his two sons, Thomas Alexander Wilson L.R.C.P, L.R.C.S. Edinburgh and L.R.F.P.S. Glasgow. It is believed that the young Dr. Wilson died as a result of contacting a disease from one of his patients.

THE LANGLEY PARK AND WITTON GILBERT NURSING ASSOCIATION.

The Langley Park and Witton Gilbert Nursing Association was founded early in 1930. Langley Park curate the Rev R. Richardson was President and Mr. and Mrs. Goodenough were Treasurer and Secretary. A nurse had also been appointed.

Before the advent of the National Health Service nursing had to be paid for by private means in the same way as doctors. To use the service villagers had to be members of the scheme.

Prior to the Second World War W. Forster was Chairman for seven years. He died in 1938. Others concerned were J. Rogers (treasurer), Councillor Mrs. R. Rutherford, Chairman from 1938, Dr. Rutherford and Councillor J. Robertshaw. In 1946 J. Brighton was treasurer. Mrs. M. A Groves was secretary for most of the Association's existence and others served for 17 years.

The 18th Annual General Meeting was held in June 1948 and the Association was disbanded when new National Health Service Act came into being on 5th July 1948.

UPROAR AT MEETING

There was uproar at a meeting in the Co-operative Hall at the end of 1940, a meeting chaired by Frances Richardson, which lasted for two hours.

The meeting had been called because of a dispute over Nurse Higginbottom although she was not personally involved in the controversy.

For nine years Nurse Higginbottom had been general nurse and midwife in the village and had been very popular in the community. Following an Act of Parliament of 1936 a Queen's Nurse had been appointed, in conjunction with Durham County Council, to act as midwife. Nurse Higginbottom was continuing as District Nurse and her duties had been extended to take in Hill Top and Witton Gilbert. People in the village resented the change and by the outbreak of war the new nurse had been withdrawn.

Later in 1940, for financial reasons, the Langley Park and Witton Gilbert Nursing Association had decided to hand over control of the midwifery service to the Health Committee of the Durham County Council retaining Nurse Higginbottom for general nursing.

After a long battle of words the meeting was ended with the Nursing Association adamant that at the end of the day it was their decision that mattered.

At the next meeting of the Association it was decided that, in despite of the protests, to hand over the midwifery to the County Council.

Throughout it all Nurse Higginbottom was perfectly happy whatever the outcome.

DR. ROBERT RUTHERFORD

Born in Blyth, Northumberland Dr. Rutherford was educated at public school and Durham University. He qualified as a doctor in 1928 and became a house surgeon/house physician at the Royal Victory Infirmary, Newcastle. From there he went into an assistant-ship partnership at Sunderland. He came into the practice at Langley Park as assistant to Dr. Wilson in 1931 and succeeded him the following year taking up residence at The Firs. He also joined the Mid Durham St Johns Ambulance Brigade as Divisional Surgeon and Superintendent of the Langley Park Division. He was also Police Surgeon for the district.

In 1934 he joined the Territorial Army and received a commission as a medical officer in the 9th Battalion of the Durham Light Infantry (50th Division).

In October 1938 Dr. Rutherford was summoned to Langley Park Colliery to attend to a miner who had been seriously injured in a fall. After giving medical treatment down the mine the patient was conveyed to Durham County Hospital. A week later he was called to an accident near the Langley Park War Memorial when a motorcar had hit a 5½-year-old boy riding a tri-cycle.

In February 1947 Dr. Rutherford himself was involved in an accident when his car collided with a Witbank Bus on the Witton Gilbert to Durham Road near Half Way House. He received slight bruises.

Sixty years ago he was one of the few people in Langley Park to own a car and was in possession of several. *(See note on 20/2)*.

In June 1939 he was appointed a Justice of the Peace.

On the outbreak of war in 1939 he joined the Royal Army Medical Corps and as a Regimental Medical Officer was posted to France. A distinguished army career followed. Posted to France he was mentioned in dispatches during the Dunkirk evacuation. In 1945 he was demobbed with the rank of Major.

In September 1951 at St. Bartholomew's Hospital in London he received the Insignia of the Order of the St. John's Ambulance Brigade. At this time he was County Surgeon for the Mid Durham Group and later became Area Commissioner for the South Durham Area.

In 1958 he was appointed County Superintendent.

It was announced in December 1959 that he was to succeed Sir Myers Weyman as County Commissioner of the St. John's Ambulance Brigade.

For well over 20 years he served as a Magistrate in the Durham, Consett and Stanley Division.

He served on the Durham Hospital Management Committee and was involved in many social and sporting organisations in Langley Park including President of

Langley Park Villa and later Langley Park United football clubs, and associated with Langley Park Farmers and Tradesmen's Association, Langley Park Cricket Club, The British Legion, the Angling Club and the Langley Park and Lanchester Nursing Association.

He retired from medical practice on 30th April 1972.

He was a good friend of the actor Sir Michael Redgrave. If Sir Michael or any of his family were appearing at a theatre in the area they would stay at The Firs.

The new group practice surgery Rutherford House and Rutherford Court close by honours his name.

Dr. and Mrs. Rutherford

MARJORIE B. RUTHERFORD

Marjorie B. Rutherford died after a long illness in July 1965. The daughter of Mr. T. B. Tilley who was a former Director of Education for Durham County, she was brought up in Gateshead and attended Gateshead Grammar School. When her father became Director of Education she moved to Durham and attended St. Mary's College where she was an Honours Student. Gaining an M.A. she went to Northern Counties Domestic Science College in Newcastle and qualified for a diploma in Domestic Science. For a time she was a teacher at Whinney Hill School and in 1933 married Dr. Robert Rutherford and came to live at The Firs. During the 1939-1945 war, while her husband was in the R.A.M.C. she took over the management of the practice. Mrs. Rutherford was described as being quiet, retiring and charming and was keenly involved in charity work.

Langley Park St. John's Ambulance Cadets – 1950s with Dr. Rutherford pictured second left.

Note: Retired school teacher Lydia Pearson who lived at Fern House died in February 1978 aged 90 was a lady who loved travelling. It is claimed she was the first person in Langley Park to own a motorcar.

ST. JOHN'S AMBULANCE BRIGADE

In July 1931 a new division registered at Langley Park of Mid Durham Corps. Dr. Wilson of Langley Park was Divisional Surgeon/Divisional Superintendent.

One of the main figures in the St. John's Ambulance Brigade in Langley Park was, of course, Dr. Robert Rutherford.

Another was Mr. Frederick P. Agar. Mr Agar, up to 1954, had been associated with the Brigade for 26 years. After being Superintendent of the Langley Park Brigade for some years he was promoted to Corps Officer. The new Superintendent was Jim Davison. In December 1954 Mr. Agar was admitted as a serving brother of the Order of St. John of Jerusalem.

In October 1945 Mr. Davison, then Sergeant Davison, had returned to the United Kingdom after three years overseas of six spent in the Royal Army Medical Corps. He had been in Algiers working with the 95th General Hospital in North Africa and also in Italy in military hospitals.

He had been in the St. John's Ambulance Brigade for eighteen years and while overseas was awarded a long service medal having spent most of the time with the Sacriston Brigade. Prior to the war he had worked at Kimblesworth Colliery. After the war he became Superintendent of the Langley Park Pit Head Baths. He was also made a serving brother of the Order of St. John of Jerusalem. This was in January 1957 when his years of service now amounted to over 30 years. A third Serving Brother, honoured 1968, following 28 years in the Brigade was J. J Gleghorn.

In July 1957 Ann Morland had received the Grand Prior Badge from the Brigade, the highest award a nursing cadet can achieve.

In the early 1960 the St. Johns Ambulance Brigade was an important part of village life with a great deal of interest being shown in the organisation particularly in the cadet section. Fred Agar was Divisional Superintendent and Ann Morland was very keenly involved in the recruitment and training of nursing cadets in both Langley Park and Witton Gilbert. Dr. Rutherford was reporting that the local brigade during the year 1962 had put in 250 hours attending events not only in the village but also in the surrounding area. The cadets were also scoring notable successes in competitions and in the mid 1950s took part in sports days with notable success.

One of the events in which they regularly took part was the village's Remembrance Day parade and the local Brigade often organised flag days to raise funds for the branch.

From time to time Langley Park Corps was host to other brigades from around the area who met and marched to All Saints Church for a service.

At a presentation in the King's Cinema in February 1947 Fred P. Agar and Thomas W. Gardner received the Order of Industrial Merit for rescuing a fellow worker who had been overcome with blackdamp at Langley Park Colliery.

THE ISOLATION HOSPITAL

Langley Park was chosen as the site of a new Isolation Hospital which was built in 1895 and was located on ground away from the centre of the village, Known as an emergency hospital for infectious diseases it was well kept and maintained. The new hospital cost £5,000 to build.

The first Master and Matron of the hospital were William and Caroline Halkier. They held the positions for nine years. Mr. Halkier died circa. 1909. Mrs. Halkier lived until the age of 79 and died in December 1935.

Mrs. Davis, who was associated with Langley Park Post Office, was well known as the matron in early years. During her time school-teacher Jack Ardley met and married Lily Gibson who was on the staff. The matron in 1910 was Agnes Dempster and in the early 1920s Charlotte Clark. By 1929 Lavinia Wilson was in charge. In 1935 Miss Elaine Brench was Matron and staff named include Sister Gallagher and nurses Proctor, Todd and Paxton who then was a probationary nurse. Jennie Haswell trained as a nurse for three years in Langley Park from circa. 1930. Matron Bowyer is also mentioned in connection with the hospital in the years leading up to the start of the war in 1939. She was later at Maiden Law. In 1944 Gladys Paxton had been on the staff for ten years and had married Lance Corporal Ernest E. Elliott who was serving with the Royal Army Service Corps.

During the Second World War the site was used as a barracks. Eventually it was kept open as an emergency hospital in the event of an outbreak of smallpox. It was one of only two establishments in the country maintained for this purpose.

In May 1957 a full-scale emergency did take place. At short notice the building was put into use to accommodate an 11-year-old boy from Stockton on Tees who had suspected smallpox. It was also thought two ambulance men, one from Durham and the other from Framwellgate Moor may contact the disease and they were detained in the hospital.

The hospital opened on 8th May but closed again after six days when it was found the boy was not suffering from the disease.

Miss M. Davison who was responsible for the care and maintenance of the hospital and the staff who moved in from Chester-le-Street were very highly praised for the way in which they had quickly put the hospital into operation. It was the first time since 1948 that an emergency had arisen. In 1972 a boy from Penrith arrived at the Isolation Hospital with a genuine illness. He remained there for about three weeks.

Eventually the building closed as a hospital and was converted into Rookstone Nursing Home and later Linden Lea. After a time both these enterprises ceased trading and demolition took place to make way for a new housing development.

LANGLEY PARK ISOLATION HOSPITAL

22/2

Left – circa 1907   Right – a group of nurses and below on the ward circa 1915

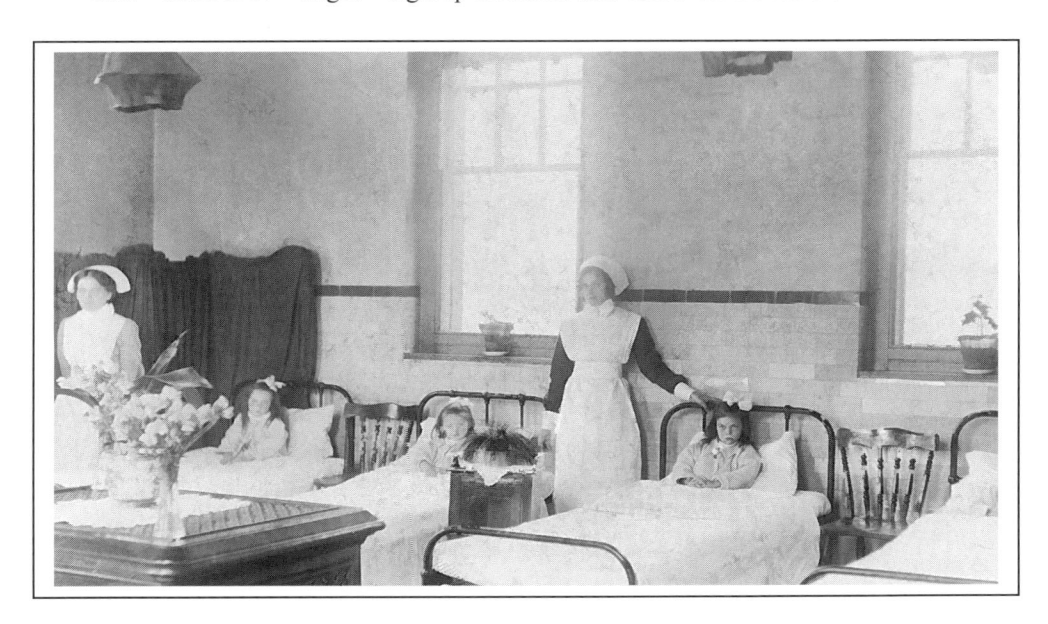

Presentation made to Mr. Thomas Preston on retiring as boilerman at the Isolation Hospital, Langley Park. He served there for nine years taking up the post after leaving Langley Park Colliery. He was also involved in the activities of the football and cricket teams in the village and was both referee and umpire. Mr. Preston died in December 1970 aged 79.

THE FRIENDS OF DURHAM HOSPITALS

Prior to the Second World War there was a very active support in the area for the Friends of Durham County Hospital (Dryburn Hospital did not exist in those days). Some of this support came from an enthusiastic group of Langley Park residents who included Mrs. Sarah Eccleston, mother of Enid.

In June 1954 a new organisation was born following a meeting at Dryburn Hospital, Durham that was to become The Friends of The Durham Hospitals. Throughout the country a national league had been formed to advise and organise volunteer help. Among those attending this inaugural get together were Miss E. Eccleston, Miss H.W. Dawson and Mr. J. Davison. Enid Eccleston was President of the local branch of the National League for some time.

In March 1955 a branch of Friends of Durham Hospital was formed in Langley Park, Mrs. R. Bowers of Stringer Terrace being appointed secretary and the group were soon organising beetle drives, whist drives and a flag day. The first money raised went to equip one hospital ward with wireless headphones.

In 1958 a flag day raised the sum of £27 10 shillings. £25 was the income from a house-to-house collection in 1959 and in 1960 it was reported that £827 had been raised by various means. Gifts to the hospitals including funding of work to enable services to be relayed from the chapel to the wards of Dryburn, a Paediatric Cystocops to the Department of Surgery, wardrobes and chests for The Dunelm Ward. Also Datames hearing aids and a tumble dryer for the Day Unit at St. Margaret's Hospital, Durham.

In 1962 Enid Eccleston and friends were responsible for the establishment of the chapel at Dryburn Hospital. This enterprise was always close to Enid's heart and it was a sad day when it had to be demolished following the building of the new hospital.

Since that time T.V. sets, wardrobes, curtains, toys and a patient controlled Analgesic Pump went to Dryburn Hospital, birthday gifts for patients at St. Margaret's, £4000 towards an estate car for the Bowburn Unit of Earls House Hospital and donations to the Baby Monitor Appeal and The Hospital Broadcasting Service.

From 1969 friends were also helping to run Dryburn Coffee Shop however, this came to an end with the opening of the new University Hospital. Fund raising for the Durham Hospitals continues.

From its formation until she died Miss Enid Eccleston was an enthusiastic supporter and Chairman of the Langley Park Friends and for some time Mrs. Nellie Facey, although in poor health herself carried out secretarial duties. Mrs. Facey died in March 1991.

A trolley shop at the Bowes Lyon Unit of Earls House Hospital is run by local volunteers from Langley Park, Christmas Gifts are given to patients at the hospital and annual donations have been given to Hospital Radio since its inception Langley Park Friends raise an average of £600 each year.

ENTERTAINMENT

"The Stage Year Book" records that the Hippodrome, Langley Park opened on 27th. March, 1911. The new theatre staged variety and plays. A famous melodrama of the time "The Face At The Window" was a popular attraction. Until the mid 1920s Dixon and Winter were proprietors/managers then Jack E. Dixon is named. Mr Joe Hately and then James Stephenson were the proprietors in the mid 1930s and before the Second World War Ernest Little became licensee/manager. Mr. Little also owned the Empire Cinema, Willington and the Comedy Theatre, North Shields. *(see - 24/5)*.

In the early days seat prices were 2d, 3d and 4d and as well as a variety turn pictures were shown. Children's Saturday afternoon matinees were popular providing excitement on the screen and often mischievous and rowdy behaviour from the wooden benches which provided the seating in part of the cinema. The matinee performances cost children one old penny.

After the 1914-1918 war silent films were shown. Playing the piano accompaniment to this entertainment was Fred 'Tibby' Burdon. It was not unusual for younger members of the audience to throw apple cores and similar missiles at the unfortunate Mr. Burdon. Later Mr. Burdon was well known at the local public houses in the Durham area for his piano playing. *(see - Langley Park People)*.

In later years Mrs. Wilkinson could recall some of the antics of the children. On one occasion she noticed a youngster with a mousetrap firing matchsticks at the screen. On another occasion a small boy or girl staggered to the pay-box carrying another child who was bigger than they were and asked for one admission ticket (on the concessionary basis of 'babes-in-arms' were free!). One evening the heating system at the Hippodrome broke down and it was extremely cold in the hall. One patron who was clad in a heavy thick overcoat with scarf, motorcycle helmet and gauntlets came rushing out of the cinema saying to Mrs. Wilkinson in the pay box 'I'm going! Its warmer on me motor bike'.

Before the arrival of the talkies the theatre experimented with the much talked about new medium starting records and film at the same time in an attempt to achieve the desired effect.

In May 1944 two men appeared in the magistrates court and were fined £5 for stealing, while under the influence of drink, 2 pairs of scissors, a torch and two films ('American Number One' and a trailer). They also admitted trying to steal from a fish and chip ship in Front Street. W. Beadnell was cinema operator for Mr. Little at this time.

The auditorium at the Hippodrome was all on one level with the rear seats, under the projection box, being raised.

The outside access to the projection box at the Hippodrome known to the staff as the 'operating box' was by means of an iron ladder that ran up the side of the building adjacent to the Catholic Church. This was a rather hazardous and cheerless means of entry in winter and icy weather particularly during the hours of darkness. The 'operating box' could also be accessed from the back of the auditorium in the cinema by a trapdoor and ladder during the daytime when the hall was not in use by the public. On one occasion some one had inadvertently left the trapdoor open and one of the staff working in the box and oblivious to this fell through the trapdoor void! Fortunately he was a young and fit person and apart from a few bruises was uninjured.

Dorothy Ward (later Mrs. John Hattam) worked as an usherette at the Hippodrome during the early 1940s. From time to time she had the backbreaking job of scrubbing the Hippodrome out. With kneeler bucket and scrubbing brush she carried out the hard work for which she was paid about one shilling and sixpence (7½p).

In the forties and fifties programmes were shown Monday to Wednesday, then a change for Thursday to Saturday. In those days there were two houses on a Saturday night. Audiences attending the first house could leave the cinema and dash home and listen to "Music Hall" or a "Saturday Night Theatre" play on the wireless.

At the end of each performance the National Anthem was played. Curtains were swished back and all exit doors flung open. Many people respected the playing of the Anthem but others had gathered up their belongings and were off well before the final notes were played.

A few years after the end of the 1939 – 1945 war films were allowed to be shown on a Sunday evening, a policy which did not find favour with some sections of the community. On Sunday 4 April, 1948 the Hippodrome screened 'Home In Indiana' and the Kings ' That Night in Rio' – the first time films were shown in Langley Park on the Sabbath (?).

For two whole weeks (7th and 14th June 1943) the Kings screened 'Gone With The Wind'.

For many years Thomas Victor ('Tommy') Wilkinson was projectionist. He came to the Hippodrome in 1939 but later left to go to Newcastle News Theatre and to a hall in Sacriston. In 1949 he returned as Manager, his wife Elizabeth being cashier. Later Mr. Wilkinson was employed by a large Bingo Organisation.

From Whit Monday, 18 May, 1959, there were two changes of programmes in the week and in its latter days a wide screen was installed to enable Cinemascope films to be exhibited.

Now owned by Hyco Cinemas, Newcastle on Tyne (Mr. Hyman and Mr. Cohen) who had succeeded Mr. Little (he retired to run a farm) the Hippodrome finally closed its doors on Saturday 6 February, 1960 after the showing of "Idols On Parade".

The expansion of the television service and the astonishing popularity of Bingo (it used to be "Housey Housey") was blamed. Mr. Wilkinson commented at the time that there were four venues holding Bingo sessions in the village -
   The King's Ballroom, The Parochial Hall, The Workmen's Club and
   The Green (a wooden structure erected on the land behind the Hippodrome being used) Bingo could also be played at The Catholic Hall.

Admission to the cinema was 1/- (5p) and 1/6d (7½p) at the rear but it was possible for pensioners to get in for 3d. Strange as it seems the public were prepared to pay 5/- (25p) for a night at the Bingo. Mr. Wilkinson was convinced that the craze would not last and people would eventually return to the cinema and the Hippodrome's fortunes would revive. A forlorn hope. Incidentally away from work Mr. Wilkinson was a keen Bingo player himself. For a time during the 1960s 'Stan's Prize Bingo' was played at the Hippodrome.

After the closure Mrs. Wilkinson ran a shop in one of the two small buildings at the entrance to the Hippodrome selling sweets cigarettes and small grocery items. Circa. 1965 she went to the Palladium Cinema in Durham as cashier. Mr. Wilkinson who by now was not in the best of health ran this shop for a short time. It was only open during the evening.

In the late 1930s a new purpose built cinema The King's opened. (Proprietors W. and M. A. Dunn – later Mr. Little ran both cinemas). With a prominent frontage the new amenity had a downstairs and an upstairs. The policy of this cinema, the programming and the price structure was similar to that of the Hippodrome.

During the Second World War concerts were held in aid of The Langley Park Comforts Fund (formed to provide help to servicemen). The writer recalls attending one of these concerts and being highly

Mrs. Wilkinson in the pay-box at the Palladium Cinema, Durham Circa 1966.

amused on hearing for the first time "There's A Hole In My Bucket, Dear Lisa" performed by Fred and Betty Goodyear. This comic song was to become their party piece for many years afterwards. The Sunday night concerts at the Kings were quite a novelty in the days when 'the Sabbath 'was more strictly observed. The programme would usually include a duet by a couple in the Anne Ziegler and Webster Booth mode usually singing Ivor Novello's singing 'We'll Gather Lilacs', a baritone singing 'Bless This House' and someone reciting a monologue 'Albert's Horses Head Handle' All good fun!

After these concerts a 'Silver Collection' was taken. This was because the performance took place on a Sunday evening and there could be no charge for admission. Donations of probably 6d (2½p), -1/- (5p), 2/- (10p) or half-a-crown (12½p) were the norm but there was a great deal of whispering as the audience left the building when someone put a ten shilling note (50p) on the plate – such generosity.

During the years 1939-1945 cinemas were obliged to show a certain percentage of British films and no option was given in this respect. Whilst there were undoubtedly some very good British Films there were many produced with a background of heavy depressive music usually supplied by a Symphony Orchestra and they were not particularly popular with the viewing audience who preferred the more light hearted nature of American films.

For the showing of Ivor Novello's 'The Dancing Years' in 1951, a very popular musical film in its day, Mr. Wilkinson prepared a handbill and had it distributed prior to the opening night.

A disastrous fire in March 1953 brought an end to the King's as a cinema.

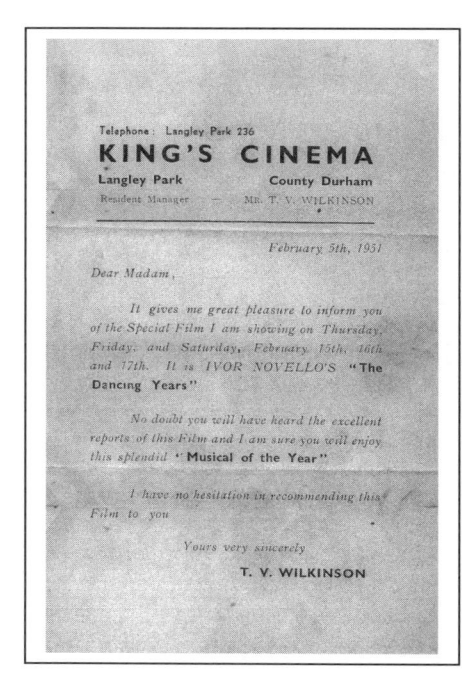

Handbill distributed by Mr. Tommy Wilkinson prior to the showing of 'The Dancing Years' at the Kings Cinema, Langley Park in 1951.

Local people would remember many happy nights "at the pictures". At the end of the war escapism was very much in demand. Large-scale musicals ('White Christmas' starring Bing Crosby was around in those days) and films starring Hollywood legends were popular as were well-made versions of classics such as "Great Expectations". British stars such as Margaret Lockwood, Richard Todd, John Mills and Jean Kent attracted large audiences. Then along came the Ealing Comedies that are still shown regularly on television today. One of the most popular films of the early 1950s was 'Genevieve' the story of a veteran car on the London to Brighton run. In Newcastle this comedy had a record breaking run at the Grainger Cinema.

The Saturday evening showings at both cinemas were always well attended and Mr. Wilkinson usually stood in the main entrance of the Kings and welcomed patrons. He also effectively controlled the flow of people to the pay box through the foyer making it easier for the cashier to issue tickets. On many occasions large queues formed which stretched well down Esh Terrace in the main street.

When the Hippodrome cinema was about to start the evening showing the electrical equipment used in starting up affected the electrical supply in the streets around about and locals knew what was happening when their lights dimmed. The Kings Cinema had its own generator at the rear, housing the generator which had a hinge wheel which when spinning shook the whole of the generator house. The vibration and the noise could be quite frightening for anyone being nearby.

The old King's Cinema took on a new lease of life when on Saturday 16 April, 1956 it re-opened as the King's Ballroom. Described as County Durham's Luxury Ballroom many people had to be turned away on the opening night. In the early days there was a visit from Ray Ellington (May 4), Teddy Foster and his Band with Vincent Hill and Brenda Hayes (June 16) and Sid Phillips and his Band with Frank Nelson, Kay McKinsley and trombonist Norman Cave. Eventually the programme settled down to regular sessions Monday, Wednesday, Friday and Saturday – the latter advertised as a non-stop dance. The orchestras appearing were those of Tommy Davis, Bob Fawcett and Joe Frame. Very quickly popular demand brought in jazz, teenager's nights, skiffle and soon rock-n-roll reached the Langley Park Hall. The Venture Orchestra, The Cadilac Rockets and The Wearside Ramblers appeared in the latter days of this type of entertainment. The final dance was announced for Easter Monday 18 April 1960.

By 1960 there were Bingo Sessions at the King's but the building was then closed for three years and re-opened in August 1964 presenting wrestling. £4,000 was spent on refurbishment and on the opening bill Digger Powell, Tom Loughton, Rob Roy, Peter Mackley, John Price and Barry St.John appeared. J. Maddison was referee and the compere was P. Barclay.

Tom Burns of Kingsway Coaches took over the building followed by Fultons and, until its demolition in April 2006, was the depot for Bob Smith Travel.

MR. LITTLE'S PONIES

Mr. Little had three show ponies that competed at local gymkhanas, which were stabled at the rear of the Kings Cinema. They were pretty successful and were accompanied to many events by a number of villagers. Mr. Little's son Brian was a keen rider. Tommy Wilkinson used to ride one of the ponies which was a descendant of 'Barnum' a classic winner. This particular pony, Lady Purdy' had a fiery temperament but Mr. Wilkinson seemed to have the knack of controlling it although he never had a riding lesson in his life. He was often seen riding around the village on this pony. The exercise and jumping practice for the ponies was carried out in a field adjoining the Kings Cinema. This entailed the 'roping in' of Daisy, a small but aggressive little pony who was the occupant of the field. The lads to whom the task was delegated were apprehensive of this undertaking and tackled it with a degree of reluctance. For the spectators it provided great entertainment as the usual scenario was that the lads chased the pony to 'rope her in' and having cornered her would endeavour to put a halter around her neck at which point Daisy having decided she'd had enough would advance towards them baring her teeth with a wild look in her eye and would start chasing them!

The Hippodrome, Langley Park was demolished during the week commencing 19th. December, 2005. Former projectionist Ossie Towns, aged 75, visited the site before the bulldozers moved in.

'THE GREEN'

"The Green" was the ground behind the Hippodrome and the R.C. church (now St. Joseph's Hall) also behind Fred Teasdale's workshop, a garage and a building that was occupied for a time by Jean Richardson, the hairdresser.

Periodically the "shows" would come The Green. The traveling fair opened for a few days each visit and villagers enjoyed rides on "The Moon Rocket", "The Shuggy Boats" or children's roundabouts. There were round stalls for "Roll-The-Penny", Slot Machines and "Hoop-la" and side entertainments including Cocoanut Shies and Rifle Shooting. The music and noise created by these visits must have caused some discomfort to the residents of Thomas Street. One of the features of these fairs was the beautiful caravans in which the show people lived.

In the 1960s there was also a wooden structure on The Green that staged regular sessions of Bingo.

24/6

GYMKHANA

A new event for the village was introduced in 1949 when Langley Park Farmers and Tradesmen's Association organized a Gymkhana. This was held in a George Wallace's field on the edge of the village adjacent to the Recreation Ground. A big success it was again staged the following year. In 1950 it was estimated over 2,000 people attended. The Langley Park Band played and the chief officials of the organizing committee were Dr. R. Rutherford (President), Mr. S. Hoggart (Chairman) and Mr. T. A. Coates (Treasurer).

The 1951 event provided seven hours of entertainment and attracted a crowd of 5,000. There were 180 entries in the pony classes. T.D. Dixon had joined Mr. Hoggart in the secretarial duties and Dr. Rutherford was on hand to present the prizes. Norman Richardson was the popular compere. Entries were slow in coming in for the 1952 show but nevertheless on the day of the gymkhana almost matched the previous years figures in entries and attendances.

1954 was the sixth year of the event but it coincided with appalling weather and underfoot conditions. The field was a mud bath and it was only with an enormous effort by the organisers and helpers that the day went ahead.

25/1

RECREATION GROUND

Like so many clubs and organisations in the village the Recreation Ground (or 'The Rec') owed its existence to the Colliery.

Situated on the very edge of the village close to the houses in Bridgeway and off the footpath that leads to Witton Gilbert Station, the site covered a huge tract of land on a graduating slope.

Entering the gate at the lower end, the first section was devoted to a children's playground with a large expanse of grassland and swings, a slide and roundabouts. Walking up the slope there was a wooden shelter. Proceeding up the gentle rise or if approached from the top of this area by the centre a short flight of steps led to tennis courts. At the far end stood an imposing pavilion with a verandah again reached by steps where spectators could watch play. The pavilion had a small central room where people could have tea and on either side there was a ladies and gentleman's dressing room. At the rear there was a pleasant half circle patio. A tennis club was a popular feature of sporting life.

This patio overlooked a 9 hole pitch-and-putt golf course. In creating this recreation area £9,000 was spent.

By May 1930 Mr. J. Abbs had been appointed caretaker of the grounds in time for the summer opening. The following month the tennis courts were in use.

The pavilion was built by Gradon and Sons and cost £1,200. It was opened in June 1938 by P.R. Smallwood, Chief Mining Agent for Consett Iron Company, during a heavy thunderstorm. Financed with grants from the Central Welfare Fund, London, it was described as the finest building to be erected in the county under the Welfare Scheme. At the time the secretary of the Welfare Committee was Mr. N. Brown and Mr. R. W. Dixon was treasurer. At the opening of the new pavilion villagers were urged to 'take great care in the use of it'.

On a fine summer night visitors to the Recreation Ground could find themselves entertained by a concert given by Langley Park Colliery Band.

Proceeding up hill to the top of 'The Rec' there was a football field.

A gate leading from behind one of the goals on the right gave access to a footpath which, in days before an open cast mining project altered the landscape, led to a pleasant walk either up the bank to Esh Hill Top or along the top of 'The Rec' to join an existing footpath which again led up to Esh Hill Top or down to Witton Gilbert Station.

The walk could be continued over 'The Heights' towards the river.
In 1936 proposals were being made regarding a swimming pool for the Welfare Ground. However, in some quarters, the scheme was not seen as practical and by the autumn of that year the plan had been quietly put to one side.

In March 1950, A Ministry of Education grant of £500 was awarded to Langley Park Miners Welfare Committee for restoration work to be carried out on the tennis courts.

With the closing of the colliery, changing times and changing ways of life and vandalism also Health and Safety Regulations, the Recreation Ground fell into a sad state of repair. This leisure facility was a great loss to the village.

For many years Mr. Abbs, (appointed May 1930) was the groundsman who was devoted to the amenity and later Mr. Herbert ('Herbie') Taylor. The grounds were always beautifully maintained and villagers could enjoy an afternoon or a summer evening enjoying the flowering shrubs, watching the children and adults play and, with many seats what better place for ladies to bring their knitting which was always a popular pastime and often an essential means of equipping the family wardrobe or making scarves in the colours of the football team supported by male members of the family.

LANGLEY PARK COLLIERY BAND

After the first World War Daniel Oakley and his three brothers, Joseph, Harry and Jim formed a jazz band and later one had a bright idea. What about a colliery band? However, they had only a slight knowledge of brass band music but into their lives came W.L. 'Bill' Casson who was to become bandmaster, an excellent tutor and a founder member of the Durham Brass Band League. When he died in January 1949, aged 71, he had had a twenty-five years association with the band.

The first meeting of the proposed band was held in the home of Mr. G. Britton in Durham Street. George Britton died in January 1938 aged 75. Still resident in Durham Street, this gesture was never forgotten by the band. Mr. Britton was born in Carrville and began work aged nine at Broomside Colliery. He worked at various collieries but chiefly at Bearpark where he was foreman overman for 16 years. He came to Langley Park circa. 1906 and eventually retired at the age of 67. Married for 53 years the Brittons had a daughter who went to Australia and had four sons. The eldest was, in 1938, Managing Director of Hugh Woods Ltd., Newcastle.

A band concert in the Recreation Ground. (Date unknown).

To form the band approaches were made to the Miner's Union and it was agreed that 1d. a week be deducted from the wages of each man working in the colliery, the money to be used for the purchase of equipment. Once they had collected £500 it was possible to buy a complete set of instruments and later £124 was spent on uniforms. By 1920 (10 months before the 1921 strike) the band was established and instead of contributing 1d a week miners could now be asked to subscribe 1d a month. In 1922 the musicians proudly played at Durham Miners Gala for the first time. Most members were Langley Park people. (*Some accounts of the band's early days quote 1924 as the year of formation*).

In January 1926 the band held its first 'annual social'. 70 people attended The President Robert Bewley and N. Potter, J. Adamson and R. Wilson praised the achievement of the conductor Mr. Casson who was presented with a tobacco bowl and an ash tray. There was a musical entertainment and dancing. In June 1927 the band obtained new instruments. Made by Beeson and Co. of London the cost was £530. At the same time a silver mounted baton was presented to W. L. Casson.

Daniel Oakley was treasurer of the band from its formation until he died. At his funeral in January 1956 the coffin was carried by four of his colleagues. Bandmaster at the time Mr. G.B. Dover, Mr. S. Maitland (Chairman) Mr. W. Ward and Mr. R. Dixon.

The mother of the brothers was Mrs. Sarah Oakley who, at the time of her death in January 1937 at the age of 85, lived in Railway Street. She was born in Stafford and lived for 22 years in Quebec before moving to New Brancepeth. She came to Langley Park circa 1907. Mrs.Oakley and her husband (who died circa 1912) had 6 sons and one daughter. Five of the sons were to be the mainstay of the band over many years. They were Joseph (born circa 1886 – bass) and who before the war lived in Irene Terrace, Daniel (born circa 1888 -euphonium) (Durham Street), John (born circa 1890 – side drums (Front Street) Harry (born circa 1893 – drums) (Logan Street) and James (born circa 1895 – soprano cornet) (Railway Street).

All except John were coal hewers at Langley Park Colliery. John and his nephew Arthur (Daniel's son) joined the band circa 1934 playing trombone. The remaining brother of the musical quintet was Jabez. Born circa 1872 he was living in Dinnington, Northumberland before the start of the Second World War. He left his home in Quebec in the late 1920s and was also a brass band enthusiast having been a member of Quebec Colliery Band.

Langley Park Colliery Band with bandmaster George Dover. (Date unknown).

At the Annual General Meeting of the Band held in January 1930 the President was Robert H. Bewley and the Treasurer was, of course, Dan Oakley. Secretary and Bandmaster was W.L. Casson and Norman Brown was Financial Secretary. Medals were presented to H. Oakley and George Dover for the highest attendance at practice.

Immediately prior to The Miners' Gala in 1932 the band received new uniforms and first paraded in them at a concert held in the Recreation Ground on the Sunday before the big event.

In the years immediately prior to the 1939 – 1945 war the Chairman of the band was Mr. R. Robinson, Secretary and Bandmaster Mr. W. Casson, Financial Secretary Mr. M. Indian, Treasurer, of course, Mr. D. Oakley, Librarian Mr. A. Oakley. Others named on the committee were Mr. N. Brown (who became Secretary). Mr. R. Coates, Mr. P. Robson, Mr. J. Oakley, Mr. T. Ward, Mr. J. Clayton and Mr. W, Dowson.
Following W.L. Casson, George Dover was the bandmaster in the 1950s having previously been principal cornet player.

A new band-leader, Gilbert Brown of Chopwell, was in charge of the music by December 1961 when the Langley Park Old People's Treat was held. During that year the Junior Section won the Manchester Spring Festival. Dr. Rutherford was President, H. Owens, Secretary, G. Holden, Treasurer and T. Donkin, Vice President.

26/3

Valued at £2,350 the band was presented with new instruments in time for the 1962 Miners' Gala. The presentation was made by Mr. Norman Nattrass, N.C.B. Industrial Relations Officer for Durham Division. Harry Smith of Spennymoor is named as bandmaster. Bandmasters of the band over the years included Barry Holden, George Holden, Derek Scollard, Richard Thompson Minns, Keith Short, John Weirs, Frank Graham, Steven Smith, Dave Kirby, John Baxter, David McClean and Edward Layton. In 1968 Dr. Rutherford was President, Vice President; E. Young Chairman A. Oakley, E. Young, Secretary: G. Morrow, Treasurer: M. Lynn, Bandmaster: D. Collins and Assistant Conductor: M. Ward. There were 21 youngsters under tuition. Two families long associated with the band were the Joiceys and the Walkers. Nichol Joicey was in the band from 1925. He and Thomas W. Ward were members for over 50 years. Mr. Ward died in May 1985 aged 80.

Other names associated with the band included Mark Hewitson, Martin Indian, Martin Rynn, Dick Bewley, Bill Jewitt and various grand and great grand children of the Oakley family and relations of other band members. Audrey Schofield, who played trombone, was at one time secretary and in 1996 David Greene's niece Kelsey was the youngest member learning to play the cornet. Over the years the band took part in various competitions with varied degrees of success.

In the village older residents can recall pleasant summer Sundays sitting in the Recreation Ground enjoying the music of the Colliery Band.

Late risers of the morning of Durham Miners' Gala would hear the enthusiastic playing of the band as it marched either from Stringer Terrace or from The Langley Park Hotel (The Blue Star) accompanying the colliery banner to Witton Gilbert Station to board a train for Durham. Re-assembling in the city they would march through the streets to the racecourse. If fortunate enough members of Langley Park Colliery may have been able to go to Durham Cathedral for an afternoon service After all the speeches and festivities they made the return journey. Accompanying their own banner, marching through the vastly overcrowded thoroughfares was the only way people could make progress. They were proud to be able to do this, greatly enjoyed the band playing and were happily singing and dancing all the way back to the railway station and home.

On a shopping expedition to Durham on a Saturday morning or afternoon in the summer, one would pass through the Market Place and would not be surprised to find Langley Park Band entertaining the crowds. (In December 1981 the valves of the instruments froze during a concert in Durham Market Place. Despite the problem £162 was raised that day).

For a great many years part of the entertainment at the annual Aged Peoples' Treat in the village Church hall was provided by these musicians and Christmas would not be Christmas without the band touring the streets and playing carols at almost every gable end. On Remembrance Sunday they provided the music for the parade which began at the Church Hall and were in the forefront of the march to the War Memorial and from there onward to All Saints Church.

After the colliery closed in 1975 circumstances changed and the band had to become self-supporting.

From their formation, all those years ago, they practised in the Band Room (an old engine room behind Irene Terrace) but by the 1980s, they could be heard playing in the Co-operative Hall in Front Street. There enthusiasm was still apparent but some twenty years later the band was no more.

There were probably many reasons why it had reached the end of its life but the outcome was terminal. It died. Perhaps some day in the future someone else will come along with the enthusiasm and commitment of the pioneers of the 1920s and give Langley Park another 70 – 80 years of brass band history. Or is it a pipe dream?

Finally, from a souvenir programme for a concert at the Wood View Community Centre, Langley Park in April, 1996 celebrating 21 years as a self supporting organisation, a look at the contribution made by four members of the band:-

Derek Bell
Derek Bell was the longest serving member of the Band in 1996. He joined the band in 1946 and learned to play the Flugel Horn at the age of 11. His father was killed at Langley Park Colliery in 1944. Derek was born in Langley Park and lived there until his marriage to Shirley. He then moved to Sacriston where he worked at the Colliery. For well over 30 years Derek travelled from Sacriston to Langley Park. Over the years he was asked to join many Bands but chose to stay loyal to Langley Park Colliery Band. In 1996 Derek Celebrated 50 years continuous service with the Band

Ken Scurfield
Another long serving Member with 35 years service in 1996 was Ken Scurfield principal Cornet Player. Having learnt to play at home through a friend of his dads he started going to Langley Park for Junior Practice with George Holden who at that time along with brother Barry played in the Band. Ken who joined the Band under the direction of Harry Smith in the 1960's shared a few successes with the Band being runners up in two Coal Board Area Contests and winning at Belle Vue Manchester. He has qualified for National Finals on numerous occasions and also qualified for National Finals at London.

David Gent
David Gent, Baritone player, first joined the Band in 1979 having first played with Esh Winning Band for 7 years. David played Baritone, moved on to the Euphonium and then the Bass. During David's time with the Band he helped out on different instruments. He became involved with teaching youngsters to play on Friday Evenings, one of these youngsters eventually became Bandmaster. After David was married in 1989 his commitment to the Band had to relax a little due to the considerable travelling and pressure of work. He still continued playing with the Band on engagements. By 1996 David was a regular player with the Band.

Edward Layton
Bandmaster in 1996 Edward Layton joined the Band in May or June 1982. Spending two years practicing on Friday Evenings as part of the Junior Band. The first engagement he recalled doing as a fully fledged member of the Senior Band was at Castle Chare Community Centre in Durham. Mr. John Weirs, at this time, being Bandmaster. After a year playing 3rd Cornet Edward moved on to 2nd Horn from here he eventually reached the Solo Horn Spot. Around 1988/89 Edward himself started teaching people to play Brass Instruments. From this point his role in the Band became more active taking on Librarian then Secretary in 1991 and finally Bandmaster in 1995.

PUBLIC HOUSES

The oldest public house in Langley Park is the Langley Park Hotel known locally as 'The Blue Star'.

27A

THE LANGLEY PARK HOTEL

Dating from mid 1875 it was built using the same sort of stone as that used in the old terraced houses nearby. Originally managed by the Consett Iron Company, in 1909 Newcastle Breweries took possession and as the company logo was a blue star the name became familiar to local people. In 1879 Timothy Lakey is named as Landlord and from 1890-1897 Edward White followed by James Frederick Gray. Walter Smurthwaite is shown as Landlord in 1902 and in 1910 John Brannan. From 1914 to 1925 Thomas Clark is named. In 1925 Newcastle Breweries gave Mr. Clark notice to quit. They claimed he had been found several times drunk and unfit to manage. Not leaving willingly Mr. Clark found the owners had had all his furniture removed into the street and a near riot resulted. Frederick James Gray of Gateshead was installed as temporary licensee. From the mid 1930s leading up to the Second World War, William Spivan Berriman was landlord.

At Langley Park Hotel In October 1902 Mr. Smurthwaite and local villagers celebrated the return to the village of Private John Turnbull. He had at first enlisted with the First Durham's in 1891 and later served in the 2nd Battalion. He spent 6 years in India and, on leaving the army came to Witton Gilbert and worked at Langley Park for Consett Iron Company. Re-called for military service he served in South Africa returning to the village in September 1902.

At one time women did not enter public houses. It was not the done thing. In pubs like 'The Blue Star there would be a side door through which women could slip in carrying an empty jug and with it filled with ale by the management could go quietly away to the seclusion of their own homes for their tipple. And there was a 'Snug'.

Viewers of 'Coronation Street' on television may remember the three women characters, Ena Sharples, Martha and Minnie being frequenters of 'The Snug' in the 'Rovers Return' that was set apart from the men.

THE BALL ALLEY

Langley Park has a Grade Two Listed Building. At one time the men of the village enjoyed a game of hand-ball which was played against a wall mainly using the hand. The game was sometimes called 'fives' and it is believed to have had its origins in a sport dating from the 18th Century. The game was very popular in many parts of the region watched with great enthusiasm by local miners who placed bets on the outcome of games. The Langley Park wall survives today and is now preserved under listed building status.

LANGLEY PARK WORKMEN'S CLUB

Eventually the local men could go to The Workmen's Club situated at the entrance to village coming from the Kaysburn direction. For many years after it's opening definitely a 'men only' establishment.

The suggestion that a workmen's club should be formed in Langley Park was first mooted in 1902. Those involved were J.W. Cousins, newsagent, Jack Eland, George Lawton, William Elwick, Albert Cook, Isaac Miller, William Eccleston, William Dodgson. The first meetings took place in Mr. James's house, Mr. Dodgson's fish shop, Mr. Forster's and Mr. Rutter's joinery. Finally they met in a field that was to be the venue of the present Club.

In July 1902 enough money had been raised and the Club was registered as a friendly society.

On 10 February 1904 they entered into a mortgage for the sum of £1,000 with Robinson Brothers, a well-known brewery firm in Durham.

The Langley Park Workmen's Club opened its doors for the first time on Saturday 28th May 1904 with a short speech from the President and then the first committee met. They placed an order for Scotch and Irish Whisky rum and other spirits provided it cost no more than eleven shillings a gallon.

Within a year the Club was paying a dividend of 1/2d to 250 members.

In the year 1935 the Club had re-elected A. Burdon as President, J. E. Newell as Secretary and W. Haswell as Treasurer. On the committee were M. Cavanagh, W.E. Sproats, T. Charlton, J. Watson and G. Shorten. Later in the year Fred Proud, William Steadman, William Birbeck, William Wardle and Herbert Elliott were elected. The first of two elections in 1936 saw W. Birbeck, D. Foster, T. Wright, J. Carney and J. Cooper on the committee.and in August O. Birbeck, J. Teasdale, J.H. Layton, R. Smith and B. Howe are named with H. Kirkup as Librarian.

Early in 1939 T. Charlton, T. I. Golighly, T.J. Milner, W. Moralee and A. Todd were serving on the committee. In September 1939 William Newman left Langley Park Club retiring after 31 years service as Steward. He received a dining room table suitably inscribed and a wallet containing £11.

In January 1940 the Club hosted a smoking concert and social evening for 66 veteran members and following elections for the committee M. Cavanagh, J. Birbeck, E. Shorten, N. Richardson and T. Wright are named. In August 1940 Langley Park Club decided to give £400 as an interest free loan to the Government. The leading officials were the same as those named in 1935 and on the committee were O. Birbeck, J. Wilkinson, J. Watson and J. Reed. The Librarian was now F.Proud. The following February T. Golightly, W. Moralee, T. Charlton, J. Smith and A. Todd are named. Early in 1944 J. Birbeck, J. Elliott, H. Morgan, T. Miller and E. Shorten were elected.

27B (cont)

By February 1951 M. Appleby, W.E. Moralee, A. Todd, W. Ludbrook and E. J. Milner were serving on the committee.

In 1954 there were 800 members and a healthy balance of £13,006 in the bank. The Club spent £2,500 on a dividend for members, a tea for 150 older members and club officials and an evening concert.

Celebrating 50 years of existence in 1954 the secretary at that time was Thomas Jupp, who had a club management diploma. The President was Mr. B. Howe and the Treasurer W. Haswell. The Committee members were S. Maitland, W.S. Hunter, R Proudlock, S. Williamson, T.H. Cooper, J. Nattrass, J. Carney, M. White, R.W. Dixon and H. Morgan. Sid Lavers President of the Northern Clubs Federation Brewery attended the Jubilee tea. Original members who attended this tea were Jack Eland then 75 and Jim Hall 70. Robert Moreland then 91 was unable to attend.

In the grim days of the 1920s, The Club proved its great value to the community; it not only survived the hard times but also grew in strength in spite of them. In time for the fiftieth anniversary the building had been redecorated, had new rubberised flooring, a giant television set, a grand piano on stage in the large concert room and it had a ladies room.

B. Howe was Chairman in August 1956, T. Jupp, Secretary and W. Haswell Treasurer with elected members A. Abbs, C. M. Fletcher, F. Smart, N. Wadge and R. Waggott serving. In 1957 the leading officials continued in their posts alongside J. W. Williamson, T. Milner, A. Todd, C. A. Gregory and D. Dunn. A. W. Dixon, J. Carney, W. Layton, S. Maitland and R. Proudlock successfully contested elections early in 1958 as did A., Abbs, E. Milner, F. Smart and N. Wadge later in the same year.

For many years Chairman of Langley Park Club Mr. A. Burdon, who lived in South View, died in April 1958. He was 77.

Committee members elected later in the year were E. Milner, F. Smart, A. Abbs and N. Wadge and in February 1959 M. Fletcher, W. Hunter, R. Markham, W. Moralee and R. Wilkinson are named. Two years later serving members were M. Fletcher, R. Hunter, E. Hall, R.T. Gordon and J. Gregory. In August R. S. Bradley, R. Cave, D. Christian, T. Miller and R. Wilkinson are serving under President W.G. Mason Secretary Mr. Jupp and Treasurer S.B. Williamson.

William Haswell of Elm Street died in April, 1964 aged 80. He worked at Langley Park Colliery for 42 years and retired in 1938 due to ill health. In 1907 he joined the Workmen's Club and in 1915 was elected to the committee retiring as Treasurer in August 1961. He held the post for 25 years and had been responsible for over a million pounds of cash. Looking back to 1914 he could remember the price of a glass of brandy being 6d a glass.

The Workmen's Club is affiliated to the Club Institute Union. Members pay an annual fee (no payment for pensioner members) and additional subscription allows them to visit other C.I.U. establishments throughout the country.

27B(cont)

The Steward of The Club lived in the house next to the club in Hawthorn Terrace. Eventually The Club purchased the house next door to the stewards. The steward moved into that and The Club was extended.

In recent years, of course, the membership situation has changed and women can now become members. However, there is still controversy as to how much say they should have in running the affairs of Clubs run by the C.I.U.

Whether for a drink or a chat, concert entertainment or to play bingo the club provides an ideal venue. And now members can sit and watch football games on large screen television. Darts, dominoes, snooker, billiards are played and teams play regularly in competitive matches. Football is a popular attraction. One of the big events is the annual Leek and Produce Show. At one time there was an experiment season of 'striptease' shows.

The old members of pensionable age are well provided for. They are taken on an outing to a seaside resort for a day in the summer with a money gift to buy a lunch and given entertainment in The Club on their return in the evening. At Christmas they are served a dinner. All free. Likewise, children of members receive similar treats.

27C

THE RAM'S HEAD

In 1939 the population of Langley Park numbered 4280. After World War 2,198 new houses were built and 100 more were planned. So by 1953 there were 5472 residents and only two establishments with full drinking licences and two with off-licences. (The Board Inn and The Station Hotel not included)

The population of Hamsteels was declining and there were moves to transfer the licence held by The New Inn at Hamsteels to an ex butcher's shop at 29-30 Quebec Street (there was already an off-licence on the premises). In the early days of Langley Park the site had been an hotel but there had never been an application submitted to obtain a full licence.

The first application for a full licence was made in March 1939 and plans for a tea-room on the premises were proposed. However, at Lanchester Brewster Sessions, the Chairman Basil Sadler said, on behalf of the magistrates, that the application had been refused. Further applications were made in 1951 and 1953 when there was considerable opposition including representations from The Baptist Chapel and the local branch of the British Abstinence Union. By early 1952 it was confirmed that T.A. Coates had sold 29, Quebec Street to Westoe Breweries and had moved his butchery business to adjacent premises.

A meeting on Monday 9 February 1953 of the Annual Brewster's Sessions held at Consett considered the transfer request which was submitted by Westoe Breweries. After a short deliberation the Chairman of the Justices, Sir Andrew Common, declared they had turned down the application on the grounds that the premises, which were opposite The Institute in Church Street were unsuitable. Young people

27C (cont)

frequented The Institute and it was not considered that a drinking establishment should be situated so close to that location. The matter came up again in 1954. There was vociferous opposition from some sixteen members of the public, 13 women and 3 men representing the British Women's Temperance Association, The Baptist and the two Methodist Churches. Likewise there was enthusiastic support. Finally after a short period of deliberation the Chairman of the Justices announced that Dora Brown had finally been granted a licence. The Ram's Head opened on 4th September 1954. The first customer was said to be Mr. John Clark of Finings Avenue.

In the summer of 1955 a scheme, which was originally the idea of Mr. J. Coult resulted in the formation of the Goodwill Club which met at The Ram's Head. Set up to help the aged and infirm, the success of Mr. Coult's scheme had seen 123 residents being taken out on outings by car or by coach attended by a nurse. The new Club was placed on a more firm footing and announced that its principal officers would be Organiser: Mr Coult, Chairman: R, Robson, Secretary: Miss D. Barron and Treasurer: A Scott. In 1957 Mrs. Benton was Secretary and T. Robson, Chairman and in the summer of that year there was an excursion to Seaton Carew organised. Activities in 1960 included a social evening. Mr. B. Brenkley was Chairman, Mrs. Nicholson, Treasurer and Mrs. Benton was continuing as Secretary. R. Robson was Chairman in 1960 with Mrs. Knowlson, Treasurer. Mrs. Donnelly is also named. Connie and John Openshaw were associated with the Goodwill in the 1970s.

Today The Goodwill Club still operates and raises money for the benefit of residents. Out of the funds of the Club pensioners are taken on a day trip in the summer.

Early in 1979 The Ram's Head was given a new look. At the same time George and Josephine Welch ex The Three Tuns, Easington Lane took over the running of the establishment from Norman Georgeson and his wife.

Mrs D. Nicholson died at Eastgate in March 1961 aged 55. She came to manage The Ram's Head and married R. Nicholson. In 1960 they moved to an hotel in Eastgate.

WHY 'THE RAM'S HEAD'?

When the butcher's shop with an off licence existed a shed at the rear was used as a slaughterhouse. In the days of 'the long bucket' beer was taken by the bucket into this shed. Local slaughter men sat around a brazier drinking to their heart's content. In one of the lighter moments, the butchers considered their premises should have a name. One worthy settled the issue by nailing above the door the head of a ram that had been slaughtered that day. The name caught on and from long distant days had been known as 'The Ram's Head'. When eventually a full licence was granted to the premises in the 1950s it was suggested that the public house should be called 'The Greyhound' but this was very firmly rejected.

27D

THE BOARD INN

There are two other hostelries in the vicinity of Langley Park. Climb the 'silly steps' and you come to The Board Inn, which is in a commanding position overlooking Langley Park and with a spectacular view of the valley. This building is thought to

27D (cont)

date from the 1500s and pre-dates Ushaw College which is just down the road. Hunting was an important part of life in olden times and the venue was a popular meeting place for riders and supporters. At the Board Inn in the 1870s/1890s Landlord Thomas Waugh was in charge and from the late 1890s Mrs. Elizabeth Waugh. From the early 1900s Miss Mariah Jane Waugh, Frederick Callan and George Dodds are named. In 1921 Mrs. Bertha Dodds is shown as landlady and a few years later Alexander A. Dodds was 'mine host' followed by Mrs. Jane Dodds. In 1938 T. Meegan was landlord.

27E

THE STATION HOTEL

The other is The Station Hotel next to Witton Gilbert station in the Wallnook area. It became The Station Tavern and for a while The Gay Tavern. Landlords named in the latter part of the nineteenth century are Abraham Peacock (1879) Thomas Suddes (1890), Joseph Hodgson (1894) and Mrs. Isabella Hodgson (1897) In the early part of the twentieth century the landlord was John R. Gascoigne and leading up to the First World War Joseph Lawson. By the mid 1920s John William Bradley was in charge and in 1934 R. D. Cresswell is named and in 1938 Joseph Hodgson was landlord. Nicholas Anderson, in later years, was associated with the establishment. He was also involved in The Cross Keys at Esh. In 1974 a military gentleman, an army major, took over the establishment and renamed it The Centurion (after a tank or a Roman soldier?). It was a popular stopping off place for motorists touring the area at weekends or on an evening drive on a summer's night. With the opening of the Lanchester-Bearpark Trail, cyclists found it a convenient resting place. The building has now been reconstructed as a private residence.

27F

LANGLEY PARK SPORTS AND SOCIAL CLUB

The sports activities that took place on the Welfare Grounds next to All Saints Church are documented in later pages. The grounds were also used for other activities including school sports – the local school not having a playing field until the opening the new Modern School. In earlier years this site also included tennis courts and in recent times the Langley Park Sports and Social Club has emerged. Outside the grounds today a board announces Langley Park Cricket, Football and Bowls Club under the sign of Newcastle Breweries.

27G

THE UNION JACK CLUB AND INSTITUTE

An organisation that was well established in the early 1920s was The Union Jack Club and Institute and sometimes referred to as The West End Social Club. It had in those early years Mr. James Newall as Secretary. Around 1921 Mr. R. Jones was caretaker and four years later Mr. Michael Cavanagh is named. The Ex-Servicemen's Club was taken over, renovated and became the Headquarters for the local British Legion. It was opened in late January 1928 by Col Headman M.P. The Chairman of the branch at the time was Mr. F. W. Rutter. The building was eventually used for other purposes and for some time A.L. Holmes West End Bakery occupied the site.

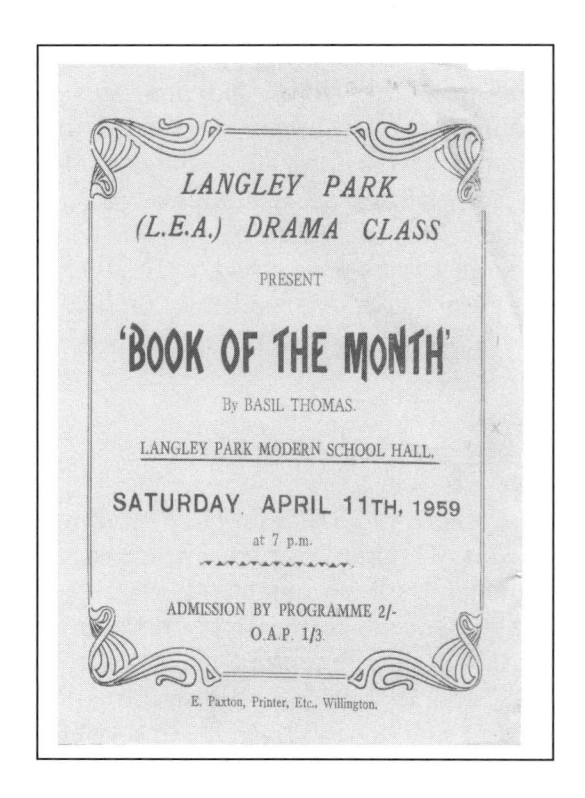

LANGLEY PARK (L.E.A.) PLAYERS

LANGLEY PARK PLAYERS

Present

"THE DAY'S MISCHIEF"

A TWO ACT PLAY

by Lesley Storm

on Friday, July 9th, 1954

in the

New School Hall, Langley Park

Commencing at 7 p.m.

ADMISSION — 2/-
OLD AGE PENSIONERS 1/3

LANGLEY PARK (L.E.A.) DRAMA CLASS

PRESENT

'BOOK OF THE MONTH'

By BASIL THOMAS.

LANGLEY PARK MODERN SCHOOL HALL.

SATURDAY, APRIL 11TH, 1959

at 7 p.m.

ADMISSION BY PROGRAMME 2/-
O.A.P. 1/3

E. Paxton, Printer, Etc., Willington.

LANGLEY PARK (L.E.A.) DRAMA CLASS

PRESENT

'WILD GOOSE CHASE'

BY DEREK BENFIELD.

In Langley Park Modern School Hall,

FRIDAY, NOVEMBER 25th 1960

AT 7 P.M.

ADMISSION BY PROGRAMME 2/-

O.A.P. 1/30

E. Paxton, Printer, 76, High Street, Willington.

LANGLEY PARK DRAMA CLASS

.....PRESENTS.....

"THE SHOP AT SLY CORNER"

A Play in Three Acts

by EDWARD PERCY

In LANGLEY PARK MODERN SCHOOL HALL,

ON FRIDAY, MAY 26th, 1967.

at 7-15 p.m.

TICKETS........2/- EACH

E. Paxton, Printer, Willington.

O.A.P. 1/6

Drama

LANGLEY PARK PLAYERS

The religious organizations in the village had for a long time staged concerts, sketches and other entertainments also oratorios. 'The Messiah' was always a favourite with chapels. In February 1939 All Saints Church was forming a drama group with the Rev E. S. Barnett as producer and with W. E. Cooper, Miss E. Eccleston and her two brothers actively involved. Through the Women's Institute Miss Westhorpe was getting the ladies of the village into dramatic mode and as a result of her efforts things moved on and the Langley Park Drama Class was born taking in men and women.

In January 1937 the Drama Class made its public debut with four one-act plays. 'Little Glass Houses' by Philip Johnson, 'Pandora's Box' by Rosalind Valence, 'Altar Piece' by Emmanuel Levy and 'Other Times and Other Manners' The class was proving very popular with Langley Park residents indicated by the large number of players involved – Ethel Mulcaster, Miss L. Watson, Miss H. Hunter, Mrs M. Harron, Mrs. E. Gerry, Enid Eccleston, Miss E. Gibson, Miss E. Swainston, Miss D. Weatherall, Miss B. Emmerson, W. Sharp, C. Shaw, G. Proud, I Dover, Miss M. Sherrington, Mrs. M. Sherrington and Miss F. Harvey.

In April 1937 Miss Westhorpe produced 'The Barretts of Wimpole Street'. Florence Harvey played Elizabeth Barrett Browning and Charles Shaw was Robert Browning. The role of Edward Moulton Barrett was acted by William Sharp. Others participating were Elizabeth Swainston, Elizabeth Emmerson, Minnie Sherrington, William Wood, Thomas Ather, W. Ross, W. Jennings and D. R. Shaw.

In the same year, as part of an evening's entertainment in aid of Durham County Hospital, the drama class presented the trial scene from 'The Merchant of Venice'. On stage were C. Shaw, W. Sharp, G. Sharp, D. Shaw, G. Holmes and Misses E. Gill, M. Sherrington and R. Thompson. Mrs. G. Sharp and Mrs. Linsley also took part.

An ambitious choice but in late 1937 Miss Westhorpe worked miracles on the small stage of the Church Hall by staging 'The Scarlet Pimpernel'. Charles Shaw was Sir Percy and Linda Watson his wife, Lady Blakeney. William Sharp was cast as Chauvelin and others in the large cast included Mrs. Sherrington, secretary of the group, Charles Cornell, Gilbert Holmes, Mrs.Linsley, D. R. Shaw, James Abbs as The Prince of Wales, George Sharp and Mrs Gerry. It is not surprising that a play demanding a great many costumes and complicated settings was not a financial success. In March 1938 the drama class staged an entertainment in aid of an outing for the Old People of the village. Many of the people mentioned above took part.

The following month the group made a presentation to Miss Westhorpe who was getting married and giving up her duties as producer. Sadly in November 1938 Miss Westhorpe, now Mrs. Lonsdale died. Early in 1939 plans were being made to stage 'I Have Five Daughters' (Pride and Prejudice) directed by Miss Stevens of Newcastle.

In the Spring of 1940 the Langley Park group (associated with the Durham County L.E.A.) had Edna Willis of Houghton-le-Spring as producer and were preparing some one act plays to be performed in aid of local Comforts Funds and the N.S.P.C.C.

In March 1941 Langley Park Drama Club (usually known as Langley Park Players or Langley Park L.E.A. Class) presented three one act plays produced by Edna Willis who came from Hetton-le-Hole. 'Red Wax' featured Mrs. Newman, Mrs. Hewitt, Mrs. Dixon, Mrs. Lindsley, Mrs. Humphrey and Mrs. Barrett. J. Abbs, W. Hewitt, and C. Shaw were in 'In Port'. The third play was 'Mirror To Elizabeth' with Mrs. M. Ridley, Mrs. Hope, Mrs. Gray, Mrs. Sherrington, Mrs. Reay, Mrs. B. Emmerson, Miss Wright and Miss Morland.

The following year Edna Willis produced 'In Waltz Time' as an entry in Durham County Drama Association Festival.

Following a dance held in the Church Hall in. April 1944 it was announced that Langley Park were again to act as host for plays staged in the Durham County Drama Festival

Demanding a large cast and a great deal of versatility and effort Langley Park Drama Class tackled their first pantomime in January 1946. Produced by John R. Humphries whose first association with the group was in 1942. He was to continue producing plays in the village until just before his death in the autumn of 1959. The pantomime subject was 'Aladdin'. Sets were by Max Bergner and Ernest Todd, Costumes by Sally and Audrey Shorten who were also responsible for the children's dances. Solo dancer was Maureen Davis then a pupil at the Durham City School of Dance. Joyce Coulson who was planning a career as a dancer was an attractive Aladdin. John R. Humphries was Dame and others in the large cast were Audrey Shorten (Princess), Wilfred Hewitt (Abanazar), Edna Lindsley (Grand Vizier) Ella Hodgson, (Emperor), Sally Shorten (Pekoe), Gordon Coulson and Donald Maitland (Mule), Eva Shorten (Fatima and The Oracle), Laura Hepburn (Slave of the Ring), Mary Howe (Slave of the Lamp), Joyce Jones and Amy Shorten (Imperial Attendants), Olive Hewitt and Beryl Gray (Maids), Marie Humphrey (Shopkeeper) Eva Rutter, Ella Hodgson and Mamie Emmerson. Edmund Shorten and Donald Maitland were Chinese Boys and Ella Hodgson and Marie Humphrey were also cast as Abanazar's Servant). The girls were Brenda Rutter, Maureen Davis, Beryl Hepple, Miriam Hodgson, Betty Atkinson, Avril Kipling, Marjorie McGuire, Joan Skelton, Jean Snowball and Janet Ramsay.

March 1946 saw the production of 'Charity Begins'. The cast was Eva Rutter, Wilfred Hewitt, Sally Shorten, Amy Skelton, Laura Hepburn, John R. Humphries, Alan Murrie, Marie Humphrey and Beryl Gray.

In April 1947 Langley Park Players were presenting 'Once A Gentleman' in the Church Hall and later took the play to Coxhoe, The players were Laura Hepburn, George Collinson, Olive Hewitt, Wilfred Hewitt, Amy Skelton, Joyce Jones, Brenda Hope,

Mark Ferguson, Eva Shorten, Sally Shorten, Eva Rutter, Stan Shaw, Mark Bergner and John R. Humphries who also produced.

Mrs. Hepburn chaired an annual general meeting in the autumn of that year. Brenda Hope succeeded Mrs. Emmerson as secretary and Mrs. Rutter was elected treasurer. On the committee were Mrs. Emmerson, Mrs. Shorten, Mrs. Humphrey, Mrs. Skelton, Mrs. Jones, Mrs. C. Birbeck and Misses Shorten and E. Sunter.

Gordon Glennon's play 'Gathering Storm' was seen in February, 1949 and featured Laura Hepburn, Harold Eilles, Amy Skelton, Derrick Allison, John R. Humphries, Eva Rutter and J. Sunter.

At St. Oswald's Institute in Durham the group took part in the Durham. County Drama Association Central Festival of One Act Plays. With a cast comprising Laura Hepburn, Marie Humphrey, Joyce Jones, Brenda Hope, Don Elsdon, Derrick Allison and George Butterfield they performed 'Fire Below'.

By the autumn of 1949 they were rehearsing 'Lover's Leap' and 'Give Me Yesterday'. The cast of four in 'Lovers Leap' was Betty Warner, Brenda Hope, George Butterfield and Harold Eilles who produced. Mr. Humphries was indisposed.

In September 1950 'Tony Draws A Horse' provided the entertainment. This popular play gave acting opportunities to Eva Shorten, Colin Brown, Brenda Hope, George Butterfield, Laura Hepburn, Don Elsdon, Brenda Rutherford, Norman Lowden, Alan Monks and Amy Skelton. John R. Humphries was in the producer's chair.

A couple of months later came the production of 'Give Me Yesterday'. John R. Humphries joined the cast on stage which comprised Eva Rutter, Don Elsdon, Joyce Butterfield, Anne Hepple, Joyce Jones, Alan Monks and Brenda Rutter.

The spring of 1951 saw the same members of the group holding office as in previous years. H. Guildford was assistant secretary and Mesdames Birbeck, Shorten and Emmerson were serving on the committee.

'Rookery Nook' the famous Aldwych Theatre farce of the 1920s provided ideal entertainment for the dark evenings of January 1952. Tom Walls, Ralph Lynn and Robertson Hare had enormous success with this play one of a series first produced in the post World War Two years. At Langley Park the fun was in the hands of Norman Lowden (his second role with the group), Don Elsdon, Alan Monks, Beryl Gray, Laura Hepburn, Joyce Jones, John R. Humphries, Joan Summerside, Nora Dixon, Emily Birbeck and Walter Joynes.

In complete contrast Langley Park Players chose for presentation in February 1953 'Bonaventure' by Charlotte Hastings, a clever murder mystery set in a convent in a remote part of Norfolk. Joyce Jones, Brenda Hope, Laura Hepburn and Don Elsdon were in another John R. Humphries production. Also seen were Nora Dixon, Derrick Allison, Norman Lowdon, Eva Shorten, Joan Summerside, Jane Buchan and Beryl Gray. Brenda Rutter provided the set with the help of Colin Brown. Norman Lowdon and F. J. Jones.

Laura Hepburn was still Chairman of the group in November 1953 and Brenda Stoker (formerly Hope) secretary. After many years in the post Mrs. Rutter relinquished the treasurer's job and was succeeded by Marie Humphrey. Plans were made for two future productions. The first of these was Kenneth Horne's comedy 'And This Was Odd' This gentle play had in the cast Laura Hepburn, Joyce Milburn, Morrison Milburn, Freda Gray, M. Swinbank, George Butterfield, Brenda Stoker, Amy Skelton and Jane Buchan. John R. Humphries producing.

This play was staged in the School Hall of the newly opened Langley Park Modern School, as were all future productions.

Mr. Humphries produced Lesley Storm's play 'A Day's Mischief' in July 1954. Lena Smith and Dorothy Crosby joined regulars Morrison Milburn, Joan Summerside, Beryl Gray, Marie Humphrey, Don Elsdon, Nora Dixon, Jane Buchan and Eva Shorten.

Among the productions staged during the 1950s was a popular family play with a Christmas theme 'The Holly and The Ivy'. W. Lynne Miller, (headmaster of the Modern School) played the role of the clergyman in whose vicarage the play is set and Jane Buchan was his daughter.

A play popular with professional repertory companies and with amateurs 'Off The Deep End' staged in October 1956 saw producer John R. Humphries using a real mirror on stage an unusual occurrence at that time. W. Lynn Miller, Don Elsdon, Stanley Lewis, Alice Cave, Amy Skelton, Edward Leggatt and Edith Bellinger appeared. Laura Hepburn and Edward Leggatt had the leading roles in Emlyn Williams famous play 'Night Must Fall'. Jane Buchan had an important role and Marie Humphrey, Edna Hill, Robert Dargue and Don Elsdon supported. Mr. Miller designed the set. This was presented in February 1957 and in May 1957 there came 'Job For The Boy' by Denis Driscoll. Alice Cave, Edith Bellinger and Beryl Gray had the female roles while the men in the company were Don Elsdon, Stanley Lewis, W. Lynne Miller and Norman Lowdon.

As well as playing a leading role W. Lynne Miller designed the set for 'Book of the Month' (April 1959). Beryl Gray, Edna Hill, Doreen Watson (later Mrs. Michael Hill), Alice Cave, Lewis Plummer, Stan Lewis and John Foster made up the rest of the cast. In the autumn of 1959 John R. Humphries, who came from Shincliffe died.

On his death Elsie Craig Shaw from Sacriston, a relative of actress Wendy Craig, took over running the Langley Park Players. She was an accomplished actress herself with a keen eye for detail and an infectious enthusiasm. In January 1960 she brought to the village the big comedy hit of the day 'Sailor Beware' in which Stan Lewis, a teacher at the school, scored a success as the Scottish sailor Carnoustie Bligh.

The Durham County Advertiser gave a glowing review of a hectic farce 'Wild Goose Chase'. Suits of armour that moved, a sinister man, an ancient castle, a mad Earl and a Romeo and Juliet type of love affair Between a village girl and a local policeman combined to make an exhausting evening for the cast and a laughter filled hall. Headmaster Mr. Miller and the pupils of the school provided excellent sets for many of the plays performed in the Modern School Hall and the castle setting for this play was much praised.

In June 1963 Jimmy Collinson was seen in the Arthur Askey role in. 'The Love Match'.

Other productions were 'Hobson's Choice' with Emily Collinson and Jimmy in the leads with John Foster as Willie Mossop and no amateur group would miss out in putting on J.B. Priestley's 'When We Are Married'. Emily Collinson played Miss Marple in 'Murder At The Vicarage' produced in April 1964. In this Stan Shaw, husband of Elsie, and a capable stage manager made a rare stage appearance as the body of the murdered Colonel Protheroe.

Joe Armstrong from Sacriston played the lead in 'The Shop At Sly Corner' in May 1967 then after a couple of productions of farces, which were not of the best quality, the Langley Park Players disbanded.

Emily and Jimmy Collinson continued to put on plays in the village at St. Andrews Methodist Church School Hall for some years. (See Methodist Drama).

Your night's entertainment at a Langley Park Players production cost 2/-.   Old Age Pensioners 1/3d.

Throughout their existence Langley Park Players were run under the auspices of Durham County Council hence the L.E.A. Players.

Laura Hepburn who was a popular lady in the village died in June 1965 aged 76. She was made an Honorary Member of the Langley Park Players and had a long association with the Women's Institute. Shortly after the death of her husband in late 1942 she moved to Durham. Keenly interested in handicrafts, she was well known as a teacher of embroidery.

Since the 1980s villagers have had the opportunity to appear as extras in a number of films for television including 'Days Of Hope' and 'The First World Cup – A Captain's Tale'. Using the streets around Railway Street and the site of the old colliery for period locations. The makers of the film 'Billy Elliott' also spent some time in Langley Park

28/6

CURTAIN CALL

Langley Park Players (LEA)
"WILD GOOSE CHASE"
1960
middle
"THE LOVE MATCH 1963
with Jimmy Collinson left
bottom
"WHEN WE ARE
MARRIED"

Emily Collinson
who with her husband Jimmy had
a long association with the
Methodist Drama Group

76

METHODIST DRAMA

As well as the various activities within the chapels in the village – Women's Own, The Sisterhood, Christian Endeavour and The British Women's Temperance League there were concerts and entertainments by the choirs. The Methodists supported a football team and a drama group. At Quebec Street Mr. William Sharp was a producer and at Trinity Douglas Graham occupied the chair.

At the end of March 1938 Quebec Street Methodists staged an operetta 'Sherwood's Queen'. Taking part were R. Roberts, R. Groves, F. Clayton junior, L. Dover, S. Wright, T. Gardiner and Mesdames A. Indian, S. Wright and Penny.

At Christmas time 1945-46 Quebec Street Sunday School Teachers and Scholars presented 'The Stained Glass Window' directed by William Sharp.

William Sharp had, in 1937, appeared with the Langley Park Drama Class in the trial scene from 'The Merchant of Venice' and had played Edward Moulton Barrett in 'The Barretts of Wimpole Street. In February 1948 he was in charge of a production of 'The Other Carpenter' at the chapel. In the cast were Ethel Mulcaster, Sarah Cummings, Colin Brown, Fred Clayton, Alan Monks and Norman Lowdon. This was staged along with 'White Magic' which featured Pearl Wiseman, Jenny Spoors, Margaret Kennedy, Jean Lowdon, Thelma Coates and Margaret Curry.

Over the following years their productions included:

May 1950 'His Mother' with E. Mulcaster, A. Monks, W. Sharp, F. Clayton, S. Watson, M. Keeping, P. Wiseman, M. Curry, N. Lowdon and C. Brown. William Sharp producing.

Two years later Quebec Street staged a 'Passion Play' with a large cast. Among the players were W. Sharp, N. Lowdon, M. Ward, J. Lowdon, F. Clayton, Alice Hogarth, Dorothy Fawcett, Stanley Watson, Bobbie Herron, G. Hammel, H. Watson, Joan Garrod, Thelma Dodgson, Margaret Curry, Agnes Hogarth, N. Wright, A. Brown, Audrey Reah, Joan Elgey, The Rev. H. Johnson, who had been received into the local church in April 1952, and J. Standring.

A play by E. Eynon Evans entitled 'All Through The Night' was presented in October 1955. William Sharp appeared in this and others involved were Alice Hogarth, Margaret Curry, Mrs. F. Beattie, T. Trotter, N. Lowdon, G. Hammel, A., Nicholson, F. Clayton and Mrs. S. Watson.

1956 was a busy year for the players. In February came 'Forced Landing' with T. Trotter, F. Clayton, W. Sharp, Mrs. Beattie and Misses M. Curry, A. Reah, W. Hogarth and J. Elgey.

A month later there was 'Not This Man But Barabas'. Winnie Hogarth was stage manager for producer Douglas Graham's thespians: Audrey Reah, Thelma Dodgson, Alan Cartmell, Thomas Trotter, Mowbray Ward, Gordon Hammel, Mary Hogarth and Douglas Graham himself. Mavis Beattie played the music.

29/2

In the autumn at Trinity villagers were entertained by 'What's Cooking' by Joan Brampton. Thomas Trotter played Bill, Mary Hogarth was Gladys and others on stage were Thelma Dodgson, Mary Kirtley, Alan Cartmell, Alma Sharp, Florence Beattie, Alice Hogarth and Mowbray Ward.

'The Offending Hand' was the production in February 1957. Written by R. F. Delderfield in the cast were Alan Cartmell, Norman Lowdon, Florence Beattie, Margaret Curry, Alma Sharp and Stanley Watson. Producer was Douglas Graham.

Douglas Graham was again producing in March 1958. This time the play was 'For Heaven's Sake' His performers were Stanley Watson, Mowbray Ward, Alma Sharp, Emily Collinson, Winnie Ward, Arnold Brown, Florence Beattie, Jimmy Collinson and Alan Cartmell.

In the autumn the choice of play was ' The Camel's Back' The parts were played by Florence Beattie, Alice Hogarth, Agnes Hogarth, Muriel Sharp, Emily Collinson, Jimmy Collinson, Malcolm Craggs and Alma Sharp. William Sharp produced and took a part..

Two months later Douglas Graham staged 'Release' by Alfred Shaughessy. Most of the regulars were in the cast again. Jimmy Collinson, Agnes Hogarth, Alan Cartmell, Thelma Dodgson, Winnie Ward, Mary Hogarth, Tom Trotter, Mary Kirtley and Mowbray Ward who was also stage manager.

Early in 1959 Armitage Owen's 'Once A Gentleman' was advertised In the cast Muriel Sharp, Fred Clayton, Florence Beattie, Alan Cartmell, Thelma Dodgson, Alma Sharp, Arnold Brown, Emily Collinson, Mary Hogarth, Eleanor Hudson and Stanley Watson. Mowbray Ward was stage manager for William Sharp.

'The Crooked Road' by Janet Allen a popular playwright of the time gave parts to Alice Hogarth, Thelma Dodgson, Florence Beattie, Janet Sellars, Jimmy Collinson, Norman Lowdon, Mary Hogarth and George Cartmell. The producer was Douglas Graham and Jimmy Collinson and Mowbray Ward were the hard working stage managers.

Jimmy Collinson, Mary Hogarth, Mary Kirtley and Kitty Golightly were in Douglas Graham's production of 'The Young In Heart in October 1959.

In May 1960 'They That Saw Tears' was produced.. Audiences at Quebec Street School Room in February 1960 saw 'Such Things Happen' by Wilfred Massey and enjoyed the performances of Alma Sharp, Alan Cartmell, Eddie Catton, William Sharp (also the producer) Emily Collinson, Margaret Donnelly, Agnes Hogarth, George Cartmell and Thelma Dodgson. Jimmy Collinson and Mowbray Ward were involved in the stage management.

In September 1960 there were performances of 'Till Further Orders' On stage were Agnes Hogarth, Florence Beattie, Enid Chapman, Alan Cartmell, Janet Sellars, Jimmy Collinson, Thomas Trotter, Muriel Sharp, Alma Quinn and Thomas High.

29/3

Early in 1961 at Quebec Street School Hall the cast assembled by William Sharp for 'Murder In Mind' by Rex Hartley was Alan Cartmell, Muriel Sharp, Thelma Mitchell, Eleanor Hudson and Eddie Catton, Emily Collinson, Florence Beattie, Mary Hogarth, Norman Wright, Agnes Hogarth, Jimmy Collinson who with George Cartmell was also stage manager.

At the Quebec Street venue in March 1963 'One Of Those Days' was presented with a cast including Anne Collinson. Agnes Hogarth, Kitty Golightly, Emily and Jimmy Collinson, Carol Preston, Clifford Brown, Terry Bell and Jean Hogarth. The producer was William Sharp and stage management was in the hands of Jimmy Collinson, George Cartmell, Malcolm Preston and Arnold Elgey.

Wilfred Massey's play 'Leap In The Dark' was staged in Trinity Schoolroom in November 1963. Produced by Emily Collinson those taking part were Agnes Hogarth, Terry Bell, Catherine Golightly, Joyce Keenlyside, William Sharp, Angela Burdon, Stuart Watt, Ann Collinson, Florence Beattie, Clifford Brown and Mary Hogarth. Mr. G. Cartmell and Mr. J. Collinson were stage managers. In January 1964 the young people of the Methodist Church presented a pantomime in the same location. 'Cinderella' was the subject and joining in the fun were Avril Leeming, Pauline Bird, Denis Guildford, Eileen Markham, Joyce Keenlyside, David Hepplewhite, Maureen Johnson, Jean Hogarth, Stuart Watt, Malcolm Preston and Joyce Maddison.

The young people of the Methodist Church staged the pantomime 'Cinderella' in January 1964.

In January 1965 Emily Collinson produced the play 'The Time Of Your Life'. The players were T. Bell, K. Golightly, F. Beattie, A. Hogarth, C. Brown, S. Watt and M. Hogarth. J. Collinson, A. Elgey and G. Cartmell provided the stage management.

November 1966 saw the presentation of 'The Feminine Touch' by Wilfred Massey. In the cast were David Bottoms, Brenda Ardley, Clifford Brown, Florence Beattie, Joyce Keenlyside, Stuart Watt, Kitty Golightly, Joyce Towns and Maureen Johnson.

Emily Collinson was again in the producer's chair for 'Spring and The Oakleys' staged in May 1967. Stage managers were Jimmy Collinson and George Cartmell. On stage were Clifford Brown, Florence Beattie, Maureen Johnson, David Bottoms, Stuart Watt, Dianne Johnson, Brenda Ardley, Joyce Towns and Pauline Bird.

'The Mystery at Abbots Mead' by Wilfred Massey was staged in November 1967 by the same group with most of the players named in the Spring production appearing.

In 1969 J. B.Priestley's 'An Inspector Calls' and a version of Dicken's 'A Chrismas Carol' were presented. Into the 1970s Emily and Jim Collinson continued to be involved in the staging of plays.

Langley Park,
Wesleyan Methodist Church
1882 – Jubilee - 1932
Chapel Anniversary

Anniversary Celebrations
ON GOOD FRIDAY, MARCH 25th, 1932,
REV. T. H. KIRKMAN of Newcastle. SERMON at 3p.m. - PUBLIC TEA at 4 p.m. Price 9

PUBLIC MEETING
In the Evening at 6.30. Chairman, Mr. E. HEDLEY, Ushaw Moor.

EASTER SUNDAY, March 27th, Preachers
REV. H. T. ASHBY (Superintendent.)
APRIL 3rd, REV. H. V. SPROSON, B.A. (Sacriston.)
APRIL 10th -, MR. H. E. RAMSEY (Annfield Plain.)
Collection at each Service.

ON SATURDAY, APRIL 2nd, at 7 p.m.,

A GRAND CONCERT
will be given by the CHOIR, entitled

"FROM OLIVET TO CALVARY"

ductor: Mr. J. Hepburn. Organist-Mr. L. W. Johnson. Admission 6d.

MARCH 26th, A FREE TEA will be given to all Sunday School Scholars by the Trustees

---

Langley Park Quebec Street
METHODIST CHURCH.

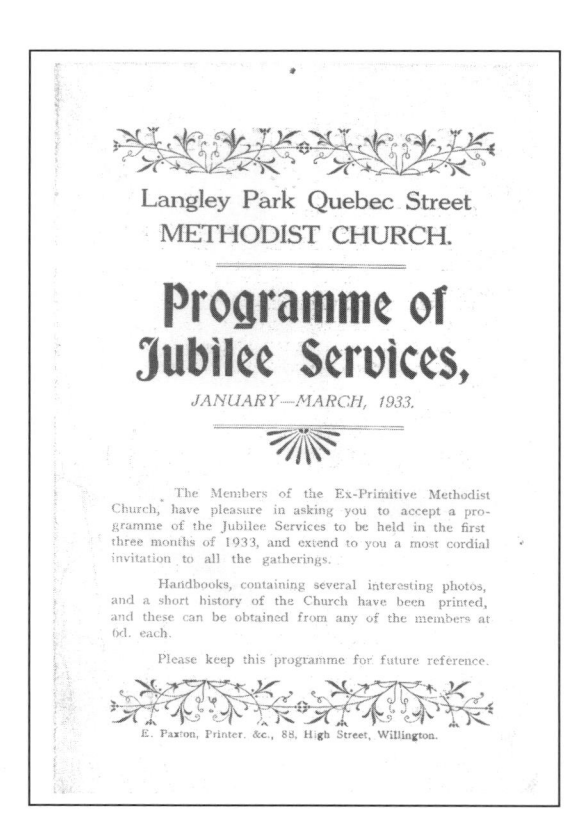

Programme of Jubilee Services,
JANUARY—MARCH, 1933.

The Members of the Ex-Primitive Methodist Church, have pleasure in asking you to accept a programme of the Jubilee Services to be held in the first three months of 1933, and extend to you a most cordial invitation to all the gatherings.

Handbooks, containing several interesting photos, and a short history of the Church have been printed, and these can be obtained from any of the members at 6d. each.

Please keep this programme for future reference.

E. Paxton, Printer, &c., 88, High Street, Willington.

PRIMITIVE METHODIST CHURCH
GROUP OF TRUSTEES 1932
Back Row: John Stoker, Jas. Johnson, John Hutchinson,
Wm. Puckering.
Front Row: Wm. Hall, Wm. Sharp, Thos. Barker, John Morland

LANGLEY PARK PRIMITIVE METHODISTS
QUEBEC STREET METHODIST CHURCH

Before 1874 the Methodists of Browney Valley had to travel to Lanchester or Witton Gilbert to worship. In that year Consett Iron Company started sinking operations for coal and a new village was coming into existence. Eventually there was a migration of new families to the locality bringing with it among other things, the teachings of John Wesley.

It was inevitable in a village growing in population that Methodism should establish a firm foothold.

By 1907 The Primitive Methodists claimed to have 4905 churches and preaching houses throughout the country, 17,300 Ministers and local preachers and 210,173 members.

In the years before 1883 the Primitive Methodists in Langley Park held their meetings in a house in Durham Street. They then moved to a miner's dwelling in South Street and later found accommodation in an off-license. The cellar was a beer house, there was dancing on the ground floor and upstairs was used for worship.

As the membership grew fund raising became easier which was a great incentive to those who dreamed of erecting their own church. Quebec Street being a favoured location. On 4 November 1876 a deed was signed for the conveyance of land. At that time the circuit minister was the Rev. T. Greenfield and the first trustees were named as Thomas Shipley, Matthew Buckle, William Bell, Joseph Bones, Mark Rutter, George Chalder, John Fawcett, William Wearmouth and James Jacques. John Taylor was Secretary and John C. Dixon was Treasurer. The new building, according to Kelly's Directory cost £800, (one source says £650) seated 150 people and opened in 1883. Above the building in Quebec Street, now a non-religious establishment, one can still read 'Primitive Methodist Church 1883'. Church members provided the labour for the new building work and Mr. Ritchie loaned a horse and cart.

This served their purposes for 25 years and was so popular that early in 1908 the trustees had drawn up plans for a larger church. £2,000 was needed for the development, furnishings and an organ. Attached to the existing structure the new church was opened in 9th January 1909, the foundation stone being laid on 8th June 1908. By 1923, when the circuit ministers were the Rev. G.B. Richardson and the Rev. A. McDonald, the debt had been cleared.

In January 1930 Luke Gardner and chapelgoers arrived for a Sunday service to find the fusing of an electric cable was starting a fire in the roof. Ladders were found and the men were quickly attending to the blaze. Using fire extinguishers and a chain of people with buckets of water the fire was put out Soon after the drama Westgarth Adamson conducted the scheduled service in the adjoining schoolroom.

In 1932 the Methodist Churches united but the two chapels in Langley Park continued as separate places of worship until 1977. The Primitive Methodists taking the name Quebec Street Methodist Chapel and In January 1933 original members Thomas

Barker and John Morland were still around to join in the special Jubilee services and events that were held.

A well-known member of the Quebec Street Church was John Hutchinson who in 1941 had served for 30 years holding several posts.

The Quebec Street Church celebrated its 75th Anniversary in 1958. One of the special events was the unveiling of a Tree of Memories painted by Mr. W. Standring, a miner, who was a member of the church. Past members of the Church had been written to asking for their memories of their home church. More than 100 replies were received from all over the world, some asking for a verse of their favourite hymns to be sung at the unveiling and there were many memories of the early leaders of the church, Mr. G. Chalders, Mr. Christter, Mr. Stoker and many others. At the unveiling a trustee of the Church, Mr. A. Indian, introduced the Chairman Rev. T.W. Bevan of Manchester and Mrs. M. Johnson, a trustee, who unveiled the tree. The project had been a great success.

In September 1961 a silver trowel used at the laying of the foundation stone of the original church building was presented to the church. It had been in the custody of a bank and was inscribed;
'Presented to J. Coward, Dunelm Mount, Durham on the occasion of his laying a memorial stone at the Primitive Methodist Church in Langley Park'.
This trowel is now in the safe keeping of Linda Kirby who in 1977 was the youngest member of the Church.

In 1951 Reginald Foort the well-known B.B.C. and cinema organist delighted a gathering at a concert playing the splendid pipe organ which was a feature of the church.

In 1977 The Quebec Street Methodists merged with the Trinity Methodists and formed St. Andrews Church using the Front Street Church for their worship.

Popular organisations within the Methodist Churches were The Women's Own and The Sisterhood.

One of the main events of the Methodist year was The Methodist Big Meeting that was held one Saturday in the summer in Durham City.

Two pioneer members of the Primitive Methodist Church were John and Betsy Morland. John Morland was one of those who helped to hew stones from Hill Top Quarry to build the 1883 church. Born in Edmondsley he had lived in Langley Park for 60 years. He began work aged nine at North Biddick Pit, Chester-le-Street and was to spend 63 years working in the mines, forty of them as a deputy overman at Langley Park. He and his five brothers had 250 years service with the Consett Iron Company. Mr. Morland was associated with the Quebec Street Methodist Church for 54 years and had been a trustee. He died aged 77 in February 1937. Mrs. Elizabeth (Betsy) Morland died in November 1944 aged 82. In her working days she had been involved in nursing and maternity work. Mr. and Mrs. Morland's son Tom served the church as organist and choirmaster for over 30 years.

Thomas Barker died mid 1934 aged 81. He had been a resident of the Aged Miners' Homes.

LANGLEY PARK TRINITY METHODIST CHURCH
ST. ANDREWS CHURCH, LANGLEY PARK

On the outside of St. Andrews Methodist Church in Front Street Langley Park one can clearly read Wesleyan Church 1881 and on the building which is attached to it there is the inscription Sunday School 1907. Stone built, Kelly's Directory notes that it cost £700 to build and seated 150.

Around the same time that the Primitive Methodists were becoming active in Langley Park another group who were enthusiastic Wesleyans were meeting in a house in North Street then later in another residence in South Street. These streets were demolished some years ago. The site is in the Browney Court area. The Superintendents of these places of worship soon established a Sunday School despite the difficult environment. Progress had to be made. Great efforts were made in fund raising, as a sum of around £700 was needed to erect a permanent chapel. All kinds of events were organised and eventually the money required was safely in the bank and work could begin.

The triumphant opening took place on Good Friday 1882 practically free of debt. The Rev. S.T. House of Newcastle preached in the afternoon and in the evening gave a stirring address. Thomas Hepburn, the colliery manager at the time was treasurer of the new enterprise. The total collections on the opening day were £19 - 11 - 1d while the proceeds of a tea amounted to no less that £20 - 6 - 5d.

Two colliery managers were Methodists, the other being Mr. Ralph S. Swallow. Mr. Swallow was enthusiastically involved in plans for a new and separate Sunday School building. The Superintendent Minister at that time the Rev. Hemingway Shaw and hard working fundraisers successfully raised £1,100 and in 1907 the new project became a reality. Dr. Haigh, Chairman of the District, conducted the opening services.

The next objective was a scheme to provide a new pipe organ. Circuit Superintendent Rev. H.P. Boase carried this through to completion. In April 1923 Charles Bowes gave an evening recital. For many years Mr. R. Peel was organist and Mr. H. Hepburn choirmaster. Mr. E. Winspear succeeded the latter. One of the features of a Methodist Chapel is the singing of the congregation and when coupled with that of the choir enhances any service. In 1932 choirmaster John Hepburn was wielding the baton and true to the traditions of the chapel was conducting a very fine performance of a well established and well loved work Handel's 'Messiah'.

Celebrations took place in March 1932 when the Wesleyan Methodist Church reached its Golden Jubilee.

Up to 1954 Mr. P.H. Hall of Esh Terrace had the longest service of any local preacher on the Methodist Circuit.

Sunday Schools were an important aspect of Methodism. A medallion produced in 1880 depicts Robert Raikes who 100 years earlier had set up the first of these well-supported institutions.

Another important and popular feature of chapel life were the Anniversaries. After the merger of the Quebec Street and Front Street chapels they both continued to celebrate separately. In the month of May the first and second Sundays were allocated to Quebec street and the third and fourth to Trinity.

Before the Second World War the three chapels in the village, Trinity, Quebec Street and The Baptists came together to organise the Sunday School trip. A day at the seaside had the added excitement of the journey itself. Children, parents and teachers walked to Witton Gilbert Station to board a specially chartered train. Passenger trains stopped running a regular service in 1939. Only on Miners Gala Day and the Sunday School Trip could one enjoy travelling on a steam train from Witton Gilbert.

Both Trinity and Quebec Street had well supported women's organisations, youth clubs etc. After the war the Methodist Youth Club had a football team playing in a local league and often dramatic plays usually with religious themes were staged in the school room

By the 1970s congregations were dwindling and finance was coming a major problem. In 1977 The Minister, The Rev. David Collinson had the task of bringing the two chapels together in one building.

From that date St. Andrews Church came into existence on the Front Street site.

Today the Rev. Paul Wood has responsibility not only for Langley Park but also for Witton Gilbert and North Road, Durham.

At Trinity Methodist Church in May 1950 Pastor D. F. Naumann dedicated church furnishings to the memory of John Hepburn and an altar desk to the memory of the three sisters of Mr. G. Peel.

In September 1959 after five years as Minister for the two Methodist churches in the village, The Rev. K. D. Bearsley left for Keighley. Mr. W. Adamson, the oldest member of the church, made a presentation.

Methodists and Sport:

(see 60 and 65/5)
Left: The Wesleyan Cricket Team 1930s.

LANGLEY PARK BAPTIST CHURCH

Over the door of the Baptist Church, situated in Front Street, Langley Park, opposite the War Memorial, the year 1895 is clearly visible. The church cost £600 to build and there were seats for 200.

For 14 years prior to the opening of this building services had been held in people's homes or in hired halls.

Early in 1935 the Church was actively involved in raising money for a new organ. By September 1936 a new pipe organ with an electric blower – the first of the kind the church had had - was a reality and was played for the first time on Saturday 31st October 1936. Soon members were enjoying organ recitals and the money needed for the new instrument -£300 – had been raised.

An ex-organist and choirmaster at the Church William James who lived in Front Street with his daughter Mrs. Tatters died in March 1940 aged 80. Born in Somersetshire he began working in the mines at the age of seven at Timsbury. Four years later he was at Houghton-le-Spring. He came to Langley Park Colliery in 1880 and worked there for 40 years. For a while he became a farmer and contractor and worked at Wallnook Mill Farm until he retired in 1928. Two years before his death he took up rug making, a hobby he greatly enjoyed. Mrs .James died in 1934. They had four sons, (one was killed in the 1914 – 1918 war), and two daughters.

Late in 1945 special services were conducted to celebrate 50 years. J. S. Iles preached and there was a tea and a rally. At the tea Mrs. Suttersfield, one of the church's oldest members cut the cake. Ten years later in 1955, The Baptists Celebrated the Diamond Jubilee of the opening of the Church. Church members made a tremendous effort and the result was that they had the finance to go ahead and build a new church hall for their activities. On Saturday 26th December 1955 The Robert Cooper Memorial was opened as a Sunday School Hall. A long time serving member as well as Superintendent of the Chapel, Mr Cooper then 91 years of age was due to perform the opening ceremony. However illness prevented him attending and Mrs. G. E. Tatters deputised.

Mrs. Tatters, who lived in Langley Park for over 70 years, was well known through the fruit and vegetable business in Front Street. (see also No. 54). When she died in 1957 she was the oldest member of the Baptist Church and had been a Sunday School teacher for over 40 years. Closed for a period in 1957 the Front Street Church re-opened on Saturday 10th. March. Mrs. Donaldson unlocked the door and after a procession from the Sunday School the building was soon packed to capacity with over 300 people inside and also standing in the vestry. A visiting minister has described the refurbished Church as 'The Baptist Cathedral of The North.

1995 was another notable year in the history of Langley Park Baptists. The Centenary Year. During the period 16 – 18 December there was an open day, a historical information display, video, literature and tea and coffee. There were special Sunday morning and evening services. Another open day followed and on the Monday evening a thanksgiving service was held the preacher being Rev. T. Hutter of Newcastle.

ALL SAINTS CHURCH

In the early 1880s Dr. Lee the vicar of Esh was conducting Divine Worship for members of his flock at a house in South Street, Langley Park using the same room that the Wesleyans were having their meetings. (*The Rev. Edmund Lee D.D. LL.D was vicar of Esh for ten years. He died on 6th March 1884*).

Probably built on the site of an earlier church, All Saints came into being and was consecrated on the 8th. October 1887 by Bishop J. B. Lightfoot. Costing £1,304 it seated 150 and it came under the jurisdiction of the Vicar of Esh.

From 1891 to 1902 Walter Stuart White was Vicar of Esh and in 1905-1906 the Rev. Henry Davies. During The Rev. White's time ladies and gentlemen of the village started a scheme to raise money for the building of a house next to the church in Langley Park to accommodate a curate. From 1909 – circa 1925 the vicar was the Rev. William Wilkinson Dibb Firth M. A. During those early years the living was in the gift of the Bishop of Manchester. In November 1928 The Rev. Harold Newport was welcomed to the parish. Educated at Egerton Hall Theological College near Manchester he first became curate at Todmorden. After two years he became a chaplain to the Armed Forces serving from 1915 – 1918 being attached to the 15th and 16th Cheshires in the 35th Division and later with the London Rifles in the 63rd Division. Wounded during hostilities he spent most of his service in France. He left the parish in May 1935 to become vicar of Eighton Banks.

> *Sextons.* From the opening of All Saints Church to circa 1897 the first sexton and parish clerk was Richard Shorten (see People 4) His successor was George Weldon.
> From 1906 – 1914 John T. Oliver was sexton and from circa 1921 – 1925 Timothy Thompson.

1937 was the Golden Jubilee year for All Saints Church. In November special services were held. The Bishop of Durham attended and there was a concert in the Church Hall organized by Mr. W. E. Cooper.

> *In January 1923 Nelson and Sons of Durham installed a new organ in the church. It cost £640 and was dedicated by the Bishop of Jarrow, The Rev. T. H. Walters a former curate who was then at Bishop Auckland attended and C.T. Craven played the new instrument.*

Leading up to the 1939 - 1945 War the Rev C. H. Blomeley was vicar of Esh and Langley Park. Cyril Blomeley was inducted in July 1935. Educated at Warminster (Wiltshire) Theological College he had been curate at Deane Parish Church near Bolton since 1927 and also at nearby Horwich Parish Church. Prior to that he had served in the Indian Army. In October 1939 Mr. Blomeley was proceeding on active service as a Major in the armed forces. At one time at Bearpark and later vicar of St. Peters, Monkwearmouth, the Rev. J. K. Hawkes who had retired to Cornwall came to Langley Park as a wartime replacement.

In July 1940 the curate the Rev. E.S. and Mrs. Barnett left Langley Park. Mr. Barnett became vicar of Chopwell (Mr. Barnett's father was vicar of Eggleston). His successor was the Rev. J. P. Inman who had been at St. Andrews, Roker and earlier, in 1936, had been at Crook Parish Church as curate. In addition to her church duties Mrs. Inman became a prominent member of the local Women's Institute. Mr. and

Mrs. Inman were at Langley Park for three years. Mr. Inman was appointed Vicar of Cleadon in April 1943. September 1945 saw the departure of the next curate and in February 1946 the Rev. Mark Ferguson M. A. from Morpeth was appointed. He had held a similar post in South London.

The Rev. Blomeley had by now returned to the parish. In all he served 13 years in the living until April 1949 when he and Mrs. Blomeley moved to Garveston.

> *The Rev. W.W.D. Firth retired in June 1928. He had been ordained 48 years earlier by the Bishop of Manchester. He received an M.A. degree following studies at St. John's College, Cambridge and as curate he served at Lancaster and Leicester. Following a period as vicar at Patricroft he became Commissioner for the Northern Province of Perth, Western Australia.*

Inducted in September 1949, the Rev. E.N.O. Gray became vicar. Mr. Gray had worked in the Diocese at Durham and had been a chaplain to the forces. He had also been associated with worship on Holy Island.

The Rev. C. L. Barron was in the parish at the beginning of the 1950s. Another clergyman associated with Langley Park was the Rev. E. Beevers. In July 1953 he moved on to Peterlee.

Ordained in Darlington in 1949 and serving three years as curate at Winlaton (In charge of High Spen), the Rev. William G. Payne succeeded Mr. Gray. His appointment was announced in January 1954.

In the spring of 1956, the Rev. Martin Robert Talbot who was born in Ireland and had been chaplain and lecturer at Queens College, Birmingham took over as Vicar of Esh and Langley Park. Later in the year saw the arrival in the village of James Ratnanayagam who was to be curate for a year before returning to his native Ceylon.

A ladies choir was formed early in 1958 with **W.** Rose as conductor, Mrs. Morland secretary and the pianist was Mrs. Belgin.

In April 1958 for the first time in the 700-year history of Esh and Langley Park churches there was a woman officer appointed to the Parochial Church Council. Mrs. Rutter.

In January 1959 Marjorie Preston was appointed organist succeeding W. Hocking who had moved to Chopwell. In more recent times another lady, Mrs. Birbeck was known for playing the organ at services. By 1961 the vicar was the Rev. M. R. Talbot, W.E. Cooper was Secretary of the Church Council, Councillor Stockdale Vice-Chairman and the Treasurer was A. Scott.

As choir-master, Dan Gregory served the parish for over thirty years. (See 'Langley Park People').

In April 1967 The Rev. Charles Lovell, formerly a chaplain in the Argentine was welcomed to the parish. Holding degrees in philosophy, politics and economics, he was ordained at Lichfield Cathedral and trained at Wycliffe Theological College. Four years were spent in Walsall, he was then at St. Giles In The Field, London and Holy Trinity, Cambridge. He and Frank Richardson organised trips from Langley

Park to the Oberammagar Passion Play in 1970 and a week in Zeefeld, Austria.

Various events were organised in the autumn of 1987 when All Saints Church celebrated its centenary.

The Rev. Peter Hood who had been in charge of the parish took up a new assignment in Stockton. The Rev. Paul Tyler came to the village in August 1989 as Priest in Charge of Esh and Langley Park in plurality with Hamsteels.

In 1990 Gillian Pocock came to Esh as Deacon. Mr. Tyler was here until 31st.August 1992 when he went to Durham University to train as a teacher. Mrs. Pocock then became Priest in Charge. On 28 May 1994 she was one of the first women to be ordained and continued to work in the village until her retirement in 1999. In 1998 Langley Park became its own parish.

The Rev. Michael Peers succeeded Mrs. Pocock and he was now responsible not only for Esh, Langley Park and Hamsteels but from 2000 St. Paul's, Waterhouses. At first he was Priest in Charge but in 2001 was appointed Vicar.

> *Phyllis Birbeck for a long time organist and Parochial Church Council member at All Saints was also well known for her needlework. At the beginning of the 1980s she was responsible for a new Mothers' Union banner and made new vestments for the church. Among her other interests was the Women's Institute and she also compiled a book of recipes to raise money for church funds.*

> *Long serving members of the Church included Mr. J. W. Rutter, Mr. M. King and Mr.. W. E. Cooper. (See People 1)*

The Rev. Richard Ireland B.A. L. Th. was curate at All Saints Church for seventeen years in the early part of the 1900s.

(The residence of the Vicar of Esh was at Esh Village. In Langley Park there was a curate who lived in the house next to the church).

THE CHURCH HALL, (THE PAROCHIAL HALL) LANGLEY PARK YOUTH CENTRE

When the new Infants School was opened in 1907 the old British School was no longer required and was put to good use as All Saints Church Hall, often referred to as the Parochial Hall. Not confined to church use, in addition to the weekly Sunday School, the building was booked by many organizations. The adequate facilities were used for dances, parties, meetings and plays were often staged. The Over 60s Club had a permanent booking and the Aged Peoples Treat was an annual event.

Closed in 1963 The Church Hall underwent a major refurbishment costing over £40,000. Saturday 21st, March 1964 was named as the re-opening date and the building became known as Langley Park Youth Centre. Secretary of the new

33/4

enterprise was Mr. W. Cave and William Rose, a fire officer, was the Youth Leader. The Bishop of Jarrow performed the opening ceremony and soon the Youth Club was the focus of attention for many of the young people of the village and one of its early achievements was raising two enthusiastic football teams (junior and senior) who competed in league competitions.

The Youth Centre continued to be used by various organisations for their social events. The Over 60s Club were still regular users of the hall and the venue was the only place in the village that could accommodate the annual Aged Peoples Treat.

By 2005 the building had been subjected to a great deal of vandalism and this was a major factor in the decision to close and dispose of the building.

34

THE MOTHERS UNION

Mary Sumner founded the Mothers Union in 1876 to meet the needs of women in those times. Over the years the society has broadly mirrored the current social outlook and works in many fields. Three things unite all members. 1. Their concern for Christian marriage and family life. 2. Faith and 3. Fellowship. It is a worldwide fellowship and the largest women's organization within the Anglian Church.

Daily around £1,000 is given from the central fund to the work of the Mothers Union overseas. In 1986 £300,000 was raised by members in Britain to support 140 overseas workers all of them nationals of the countries in which they worked. The Mothers Union works in most of the African countries south of the Sahara Desert, Australia, Papua New Guinea, the islands of the South Pacific and Indian Ocean, Korea and the West Indies, Canada, New Zealand and the British Isles.

Having 413,000 members in 35 countries it is controlled by Central Council, under the chairmanship of the Central President.

In September 1937 Langley Park Mothers Union held a party to celebrate the tenth anniversary of their separation from Esh. Mrs. Richardson, wife of a former curate gave an address and Mrs. Barnett and Mrs. Emmerson played the piano for dancing.

Then resident at South Kelsey, Lincolnshire, The Rev R. Ireland who was curate here for 17 years returned to address the Mothers Union in October 1938.

The Langley Park Mothers union had some 100 members in the year 1956.

1990 was the centenary year for the Mothers Union in the Durham Diocese.

At one time the curate's wife usually chaired the Langley Park branch of the Mothers Union and the banner was regularly carried by members to an annual service in Durham Cathedral.

Today the banner, which has been housed in All Saints Church, still exists to promote the continued existence of the Mothers Union in the area.

THE GIRL GUIDES

The Girl Guides movement was founded in 1910.

In September 1924 Dorothy Hall was appointed Captain of the local Girl Guides succeeding Mrs. Williamson who had resigned. May 1929 saw the re-establishment of the Langley Park Girl Guides with Dorothy Foster Captain and Lt. Lena Anderson. Fund raising events were organised to provide new uniforms.

In April 1933 The Girl Guides staged an operetta 'May Day In Well-A-Day'. In October 1933 Captain Lena Anderson is in charge and with the Brownies are Miss K. Hunter, Miss D. Wilkinson and Miss N. Carpenter.

In January 1936 The Girl Guide Badge was awarded to Guide Captain Lena Anderson who had seven years service, the first three as Guide Lieutenant and four as Captain. Mrs. Clear a former Captain was, in 1935, living in Wellfield.

Lt. Mary Black of Sacriston succeeded Lena Anderson as Guide Captain in January 1936. Nancy Carpenter became Guide Lieutenant. Nancy Carpenter, who was also a member of the Civil Nursing Reserve, was the daughter of Mr. and Mrs. T. Carpenter of Quebec Street. In August 1942 she married Corporal J.N.W. King of Wingate, a wireless mechanic in the R.A.F. In October 1937 Miss Kate Hunter was Brownie Owl. In May 1939 she married Cecil V. Rowell of Alton, Hampshire. She had been at Hedley Hill County School and had also taught at Langley Park Infants School.

In May 1939 the local guides gave a display and Miss. E. Wright and Miss B. Emmerson are named as taking part. At Christmas 1939 The Brownies had made a doll's house out of matchboxes. It raised one pound ten shillings (one pound and fifty pence) for Durham County Hospital.

During September 1943 Miss E. A. Kirkup who was an ex Girl Guide married C. E. Crozier who was in the Langley Park National Fire Service.

In the year 1947 Lieutenants under Guide Captain Mary Black, (who became Mrs. Yates) were Alma Andrews and Jean Ludbrooke. In March 1955 Miss M. Holmes and Miss E. Proud were with the brownies.

1985 was the 75th anniversary a light lit initially at a national ceremony was spread throughout the country so that individual guide and brownie were able to have a light from it. On Tuesday 25th June 1985 this light was brought to All Saints Church in Langley Park. In August 1988 with the Langley Park Guides having existed for 60 years Carol Carney, (now Mrs. Surtees) and Liz Dawson were organizing a re-union.

At the beginning of 1990 Louise Dover after four years hard work gained the highest award available to a guide 'The Baden Powell Trefoil'. This award must be gained before the guide's 15th birthday and Louise succeeded in this with thee weeks to spare. She was the first Langley Park guide to gain this award. There was a presentation in All Saints Church in March 1990

CHURCH PARADE

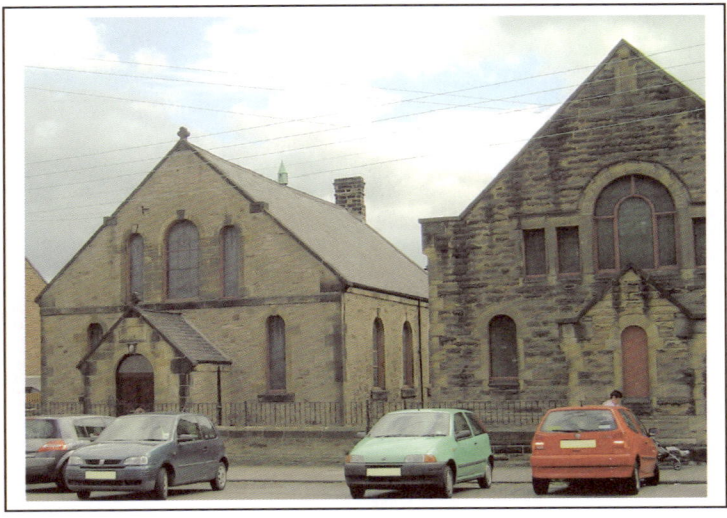

Top: All Saints Church.
Middle (left) Baptist Church
Middle (right): St. Joseph's Roman Catholic Church. and Quebec Street Primitive Methodist Church (now a business establishment)
Bottom (left) St. Andrews Methodist Church.

SCHOOL DAYS

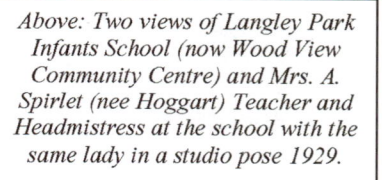

Above: Two views of Langley Park Infants School (now Wood View Community Centre) and Mrs. A. Spirlet (nee Hoggart) Teacher and Headmistress at the school with the same lady in a studio pose 1929.

Three views of Langley Park Modern School at its opening in 1952

PUB CRAWL

*Top: The Board Inn, Hill Top.
Below: The Ram's Head, Quebec Street.
Also shown: T.A. Coates and Sons, Butchers shop that was originally situated to the left of the archway.*

*Above: Langley Park Sports and Social Club. Bottom left: The Langley Park Hotel (The Blue Star).
Bottom right: Langley Park Workmen's Club and Institute, Front Street.*

VILLAGE SNAPSHOTS

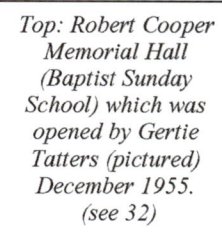

Top: Robert Cooper Memorial Hall (Baptist Sunday School) which was opened by Gertie Tatters (pictured) December 1955. (see 32)

Left: Rutherford House behind Church Street Community Centre (The Institute). The Doctors' surgery named after Dr. Rutherford (see 20)

Above: The Pavilion at Langley Park Welfare Ground beside All Saints Church. Above right: Annfield Plain Co-operative Society building, Front Street. Bottom: E. Hedley outside his shop in Quebec Street and Leslie and Ina Jopling at their shop that stood on the same site and closed in 1977.

ROMAN CATHOLICS IN LANGLEY PARK

The main centre of worship for Langley Park Roman Catholics is St. Michael's Church at Esh Laude that has been long established.

Schooling for Catholics is also at Esh and children from infants upwards have to make the journey up the hill and back again. Until the motorcar achieved its popularity this meant that all children had to walk up the steep bank and proceed to Esh Village no matter what the weather, rain, sunshine or in heavy snowstorms. This continued until they were of an age to go to St. Leonard's School, Durham to complete their education and is the school they progress to today.

For the people in Langley Park a church (St. Joseph's Chapel of Ease) was eventually established on a site next to the Hippodrome Cinema. After many years of fund raising a new church was built on land between the Langley Park Hotel and the Langley Park Nursing Home. This opened in 1969 and the old building became St. Joseph's Hall and used for social activities associated with the church. The first wedding in the new St. Joseph's Church was that of Robert Cave and Mary Bernadette Bailey in August 1969. The Rev. Father Kerr officiated.

A well-known and popular parish priest was The Rev Canon Samuel Harris. He died in 1933 having served the community for many years. For the next twenty years The Rev. Monseigneur Cogan D.D. was leading local Catholics and another remembered name is the Rev. Martin Holohan. In July 1963 Father Gerard McElhahnon celebrated 25 years as a priest. In later years Father Cain and Father Brice held office. Father Brice served as parish priest for roughly 20 years until his sudden death in 2000. He was a full cousin of Sir Jimmy Saville and celebrated his Golden Jubilee as a priest shortly before his death. A very popular priest at St. Josephs, Langley Park in the 1980s and 1990s was Father Michael Mahon. He left the area in 1995. He died tragically from a heart attack on 21st January 1996 at the age of 65 while serving in Madras, India. Today two priests cover all services at Langley Moor, Ushaw Moor, Esh Winning, Esh and Langley Park.

> Two notable events in the Roman Catholic world occurred at Ushaw College. In August 1951 the 13th Centenary of the death of St. Aiden was marked by celebrations that attracted a crowd of some 50,000. In July 1958 the 150th. Anniversary of Ushaw College was marked by a Thanksgiving Rally. The establishment being at that time the largest Roman Catholic Seminary in England. Over 40,000 people from Langley Park and many miles around converged on the college to take part.

On the social side the Catholic Women's Guild was a popular feature of life for many years and bingo has attracted good attendances since it first came on the scene. Today the Ladies Club that is open to all denominations continues to meet.

Doreen Cummings who died in September 2004 was a stalwart of the Catholic Church being involved in many of the social activities. She was also a long standing member and ex-Chairman of Esh Parish Council, helped to form a voluntary organisation 'Soapbox' and twice a week was a helper at the Luncheon Club in the village. Mrs.Cummings, who was a native of Crook, was also known for the trips she arranged to Lourdes, Rome, Austria, Germany and Switzerland. One of her last campaigns was for a bus service to run from Langley Park to Consett and Stanley. The service eventually came into operation shortly before she died.

FUNERALS

In a collection of memories of village life it is inevitable that funerals should have a place. Up to the end of the Second World War and much later they were very sombre occasions.

The death of a loved one, particularly a husband, meant deep mourning. The widow was obliged to dress in black immediately and continued to do so for some considerable time after the death. In the case of older villagers black would be worn for the remainder of their lives.

There were no Chapels of Rest and the deceased would remain in the home until the day of the funeral, the curtains being closed. Sometimes male relatives would hold watch over the coffin throughout the night preceding the funeral.

On the day of the funeral residents of the street would close their curtains as a mark of respect. The cortege would leave the house for the church service and if the funeral was conducted on olden lines, the ladies would travel in motorised transport and the men would walk behind, both to the church and again to the churchyard if this was a distance away. All mourners, men and women, would be in black and black ties and bowler hats would be worn or carried by the men. On the route of the procession villagers would stop and turn to the cortege with the men removing their hats.

By the end of the 1940s cremation was becoming more acceptable and crematoria were being planned, erected and opened in towns to serve the needs of the surrounding area.

A decade after the Second World War it was deemed necessary to provide a new cemetery for Langley Park for those who still wanted internment. Various locations were considered and after a great deal of discussion the new site was on land beyond Stringer Terrace. A short time after the new burial ground had been consecrated and interments begun it was discovered that coffins were being placed the wrong way round. On discovering the error this was corrected but visitors to the cemetery will notice that the earlier graves are a different way round to the rest.

In recent times villagers will remember the funeral of the late Jack Munsey. It was Mr. Munsey's wish to be carried to the church and cemetery in a horse driven hearse. The occasion brought a feeling of the way funerals would have been carried out in days gone by.

> ***Undertakers*** Well known in the village as a joiner Mr. J. Iveson was also known as an undertaker as was Frederick Teasdale who had a business near the Hippodrome Cinema not far from the establishment of Mr. Iveson. Mr. Teasdale was also described as a carpenter and wheelwright. He served the community for 30 years and retired at the age of 65. Born at Carter's Cottages he moved to Elm Street in 1912. During the First World War he served in the Royal Engineers. Mr. Teasdale died in January 1979 aged 90. His wife, Lily, pre-deceased him in 1965. By the time the 1960s arrived The Co-operative Funeral Service was providing a service, as were R.W. Alderson and Sons of Ushaw Moor and Durham based John Smurthwaite.

37/2

The title funeral director has now become fashionable although even today villagers still refer to this service as 'The undertakers'. In 1992 Stuart Wright Funeral Service opened in the premises next to the newsagents in Front Street. Mr. Wright had been an apprentice with John Smurthwaite's firm and following Mr. Smurthwaite's retirement worked for three years with the Co-operative Funeral Service. Serving not only Langley Park but also the surrounding area Mr. Wright in April 1997 also opened a second Chapel of Rest in Marshall Terrace, Gilesgate Moor, Durham. As a church organist he could provide an additional service by advising on planning the music for a funeral service The City of Durham has honoured Mr. Wright by making him a Freeman of the City of Durham.

38

THE LYNMOUTH DISASTER
MR. AND MRS. BENJAMIN COULT

In the summer of 1952 disaster hit the picturesque holiday resort of Lynmouth in Devon. Two Langley Park people, Mr. Benjamin Coult (then aged 56) and his wife Mrs. Emma Coult (52) were on holiday in the area with friends from Langley Park and staying in Lynmouth on the night the East and West Lyn Rivers overflowed following torrential rain. Water cascaded down from the higher resort of Lynton bringing with it death and destruction.

The Coults were two of a number of people who lost their lives in the disaster. Their friends, who were staying at a different address, were unharmed.

Langley Park was shocked by the news of the deaths of a very popular couple. Following an inquest Mr. and Mrs. Coult were brought back to the village for a funeral service at the Baptist Church. The day before the funeral hundreds of people visited the flower filled church where they lay to pay a final tribute. On the day of the funeral the cortege stretched for a quarter of a mile and the church was packed to capacity for the funeral service. Hundreds of people stood outside in the street and the proceedings were relayed to them by loud speakers. The Rev. C. E. Swift a Gateshead Minister conducted the service and the underbearers were Mr. A. Munsey Senior, Mr. A. Munsey Junior, Mr. M. Watson, Mr. W. Raper, Mr. W.E. Lane, Mr. D. L. Lane, Mr. P. Wyatt and Mr. M. James. Following the burial villagers were seen making their way to the churchyard until late in the evening to pay their last respects.

Mr. and Mrs. Coult had been the first couple to be married in the Langley Park Baptist Church after it was licensed for weddings. They had three sons, Sidney, Stanley and Robert.

A memorial to the disaster, which includes the names of Mr. and Mrs. Coult, can be seen in Lynton Church in Devon.

MURDER OF A KITCHEN MAID

On Monday 6th May 1935 Langley Park was celebrating the Golden Jubilee of King George V and all had had a happy day. Then at around midnight murder was committed.

Amanda Sharp was brutally attacked and died almost immediately. She was aged 20 and was employed as a kitchen maid at the Isolation Hospital in Langley Park and was a resident of that establishment. The matron at the time, Miss Brench had given the staff extended leave until midnight in order they could attend a bonfire at Ushaw College. The victim had left the hospital at about 5 p.m. to go to her mother's house in Garden Avenue for tea and then proceeded with female friends to Hill Top. The man with whom she had been "keeping company" was seen in the vicinity.

With the festivities over Miss Sharp and friends began making their way back to the village at around 11 p.m. The Isolation Hospital was situated some 200 yards from the main thoroughfare and was surrounded by trees and green fields.

While walking along the lonely road with her friends she suddenly met her "boyfriend". The friends moved on but were soon shocked to hear screams and shouts which were also to awaken the residents of Carter's Cottages and Finings Street nearby. Quickly returning they found Miss Sharp lying on the ground with stab wounds. One ran to the hospital to seek help while the other hurried into Quebec Street to find a telephone.

The call to the police was answered swiftly and soon Superintendent Kirkup of Consett and Inspector Holmes of Lanchester were on the scene but by now Miss Sharp was dead.

Amanda Sharp

A little while later there was a knock on the door of Cross Fell House in the village and 28-year-old George Hague was arrested. Until a short time ago he had lived with his mother at this address but she had gone to live with a married daughter at Hill Top. Mr. Hague was described as an unemployed 'bus conductor who did summer relief on services to Scarborough. He and Miss Sharp appear to have had a "misunderstanding" because he had been to see Mrs. Sharp on the Sunday evening to ask her to speak to Amanda regarding getting them together again. Mrs. Sharp indicated it was not her place to do so as it was up to her daughter to decide if she wanted to see him again.

Following the tragedy an inquest was held in the Reading Room of the Langley Park Institute and Mr. Hague, who had appeared before the local magistrates, was now remanded in custody.

39/2

After the euphoria of the Jubilee Celebrations the village was in a state of shock. Amanda Sharp's funeral was held on Saturday 17th May 1935 in the Methodist Church. Leading the cortege were three of her closest friends Mary Craggs, Elena Ritson and Connie Jopling. A tall, well-built girl with fair hair she had been a leader of the Methodist Church Sunday School and was held in high esteem in the village.

On leaving school she had worked for Mrs. W. Heppell, wife of the Langley Park postman and then obtained a post as kitchen maid for the domestic staff at the Deanery, Durham. About two years before she died she joined the staff of the Isolation Hospital.

Mr. Hague, described as medium build and with a tousled head, stood trial at Durham Assizes. There had been cases of mental instability in his family but a suggestion that he was insane was quickly ruled out.

The jury returned a verdict of 'Guilty' and Mr. Hague was sentenced to death.

40/1

ROYAL CELEBRATIONS

THE CORONATION OF KING EDWARD VII

On Coronation Day 9th August 1902 the Esh, Hill Top and Ushaw Flower Show was held and it was reported that the weather conditions were better than they had been for the previous year's event. This year the show along with children's sports also honoured the Coronation of the King. Mr. H. J. Morin (?) the secretary and assistant secretary Mr. George Caley made arrangements.

THE CORONATION OF KING GEORGE V

The Coronation of King George V took place on 22nd June 1911. Langley Park is now mentioned in the celebrations along with Esh, Hill Top and Ushaw. The day started cloudy but everybody was cheerful and looking forward to the procession that took place through the village starting at two o'clock in the afternoon. Flags were flying from many windows and it was indeed a remarkable procession being ½ -¾ of a mile long. The leading ladies and gentlemen of the district turned out, District and Parish Councillors, leading officials of the colliery and the miners' union and leading tradesmen of the district. The Salvation Army Band from Sacriston provided rousing music and following them were the Vicar of Esh, The Rev. D.D. Firth who was chairman for the organisers of the event, The Rev. Father Harris of Esh Laude, The Rev R. Ireland, curate and treasurer, the Salvation Army Captain and Mr. William Hall a non-conformist who was also secretary. J. Pickering one of the 'darkie mimics' marched in costume and led the children who were accompanied by the school staffs. The Boys and Girls from Langley Park Council School, Esh Church of England and Esh Laude and Langley Park Infants all waving flags. There were about 1,300 of them and they marched four abreast.

The march terminated at a field loaned by Annfield Co-operative Society. Here the children formed a square and conducted by schoolmaster Mr. Hollingworth they sang. Afterwards they sat down to tea and were presented with Coronation mugs and sweets. Many prizes were on offer for the children's sports and Mrs. Firth was on hand to present the prizes. The caterers were Mrs. Halkier James of Langley Park and Mr. Jones of Hill Top. A vote of thanks to the organisers was proposed by Mr Stephenson and seconded by Mr. Brown. It had indeed been a remarkable day.

THE SILVER JUBILEE OF KING GEORGE V

Early in 1935 a Committee was set up following a meeting in The Co-operative Hall to organise events to celebrate 25 years of the King's reign. Councillor Mrs. R. Rutherford was Chairman and Mr. T. Miller was elected secretary with Mr. W. D. Hall as treasurer. It was eventually decided that mugs be given to all children of school age. On the day, the 6th May 1935, the school children met at Langley Park Council School and, led by the Langley Park Band, marched to the cricket field. Sports were organised for the 3 – 14 year olds and they were given a tea. Residents of the village over 65 years of age later sat down to a Jubilee tea.

CORONATION OF KING GEORGE VI AND QUEEN ELIZABETH

Langley Park British Legion members were invited to attend a Coronation Royal Review for Ex Servicemen held in Hyde Park, London on 27th June 1937. Those chosen were Captain P. A. Ross (President), Mr G. Jameson, H. Morgan (Chairman) and Mr. C. Smith.

On the day of the Coronation, 14th May 1937 there was a cinema show for children at the Hippodrome. Each received a souvenir mug and a bag of sweets. The Langley Park Band led a parade and in the grounds of the Church Hall the colliery manager, Mr. J. Rogers, planted a commemorative tree on behalf of the local Gardeners' Guild. A tea for the old people of the village was laid on and each was given a souvenir cup and saucer. For an evening concert The Halle Concert Party were engaged.

On the following Monday there was a musical evening organised by Mr. W. E. Cooper, Secretary of the All Saints Church Council. Entertainers included J. Eccleston, J. Abbs, W. Rose and R. Rutter. Also R. Abbs and Misses D. Wilkinson, E. Eccleston, B. Dawson and N. Carpenter. The Girls Friendly Society appeared in a sketch. Taking part were A. Hoggart, L. Hoggart, F. Broughton, E. Henderson and N. Kirkup.

THE CORONATION 1953

Queen Elizabeth II succeeded to the throne in February 1952 and nationally arrangements were soon proceeding for the Coronation in June 1953. This was to be the most spectacular event seen in the country since before the Second World War.

In the autumn of 1952 Langley Park people had formed a Coronation Committee. Mr. W. Beavis was Chairman and Mrs. M. Johnson Vice Chairman.

On Coronation Day a Fancy Dress Parade was organised. Led by Langley Park Colliery Band there was a procession from the Parochial Hall to Langley Park Modern School for competitors to be judged by local Sub-Postmaster Mr. S. Hoggart. Some 250 children, up to three years of age, received glass tankards and there were 900 bags of refreshments for the four to fifteen year olds.

On Saturday 6th June 1953 there was a special Aged Peoples' Tea for older residents to celebrate the event. The Jolly Boys providing the entertainment.

A children's sports evening was held at the school on Friday 12th June 1953 when ballpoint pens, still a relatively new invention, and blue beakers were given as prizes. Mrs Groves and Mr. Stan Lewis were two of those involved in the planning.

The Coronation service itself was televised live in black and white. To see this event in the home television sets arrived in the living rooms of houses for the very first time. Anyone in the village who possessed a set had a houseful of people, all in party mood, to witness the ceremony. About a week after the live transmission the proceedings could be seen at local cinemas but this time processed in colour. This version proving very popular.

Lance Corporal Bernard Harrison of Langley Park was outside Westminster Abbey on Coronation Day 1953 escorting The Queen's personal friends. On the eve of the event he was at a reception at Westminster Hospital and met The Lord Mayor of London and The Queen's Physician. Son of Mrs. and the late C. E. Harrison he was 22 years of age and his civilian employment was as a dispenser at Consett.

A village celebration: Could this be the Coronation 1911, an Armistice Celebration 1918 or a local Carnival? A photograph from the opposite direction appeared in the March 2006 edition of 'Esh Leaves'.

41/1

THE FIRE BRIGADE

Probably originated as the Auxillary Fire Service with volunteers from the Colliery and the cokeworks, during the 1939-1945 war years it became The National Fire Service (N.F.S.). Prior to the Second World War it would appear that Crook Fire and Rescue Services were attending to incidents in the village although there had been attempts to obtain a service locally. The lack of finance seems to have prevented this happening. After the war ended in 1945 the village continued to have an emergency service supplied by the Durham County Council. This came into effect on 1st April 1948.

In October 1956 R. Groves of Crossfell House was appointed foreman electrician at the Langley Park Coke works. He had attended courses at Rutherford College, Newcastle. His new promotion led him to resign his position as retained leading fireman in the County Fire Brigade.

Then for many years Bob Walker was Sub Officer of the Langley Park team. He and all the other volunteers carried out their duties as well as carrying out their normal working day employment. After 25 years service he retired in January 1965. Two years earlier Clarence Birbeck, who had 20 years service, received the Fire Service Medal for long service and good conduct. Divisional Officer J. W. Smith presented it to him. Other long serving members of the Langley Park team included Messrs. Cartmell, Hutton and Bunn.

Villagers were always aware of a call-out. The old air raid siren would be sounded and could be heard all over the village. The crew largely made up of colliery and coke-works personnel would make full haste to the fire station from wherever they were in the village at the time either by foot or by bicycle. First at the station would find the location of the incident while the rest of the crew made ready to depart in double quick time. Boarding the distinctive red vehicle they hurried off of to render assistance with bells loudly clanging.

In October 1950 Langley Park entered a fire brigade competition at Felling and won the major trailer competition with a time of 2 minutes forty-two seconds. The runners-up were Ferryhill. The Langley Park team was R. Walker, C. Birbeck, R Groves, G. Benton and J. Cooper. This was one of the many events in which the fire brigade participated.

In February 1956 Langley Park received a new fire engine, which was one of the most advanced models in the country. There were many new features in the vehicle. Not only did the tender carry 400 gallons of water but it was also fitted with electric and hand operated bells! and, of course, it had many modern additions.

An interesting event occurred on Saturday 3 March 1956. There was, for what was believed to be the first time in Durham County, a Fire Service ceremonial wedding. The event took place at Washington Village Lane Methodist Church. Fireman William Ernest Bunn from Langley Park married Leading Firewoman Olive Marriner. The bride had been a full time switchboard and wireless operator with the brigade. At the ceremony eight Langley Park firemen with shining fire axes mounted a guard of honour as the newly weds left the church. The new Mrs. Bunn was to continue in the volunteer fire brigade at Langley Park alongside her husband. Divisional Officer Stonehouse who had presented Langley Park Fire Brigade with the new vehicle was also on hand to present Mr. and Mrs. Bunn with a dinner set as a wedding present.

Recalling incidents in which the local brigade had been involved Mr. Bunn was later to quote the most memorable were the disastrous fire at the King's Cinema in 1953 and being called to assist at a blaze on Forestry Commission land at Hamsterley.

In August 1957 Langley Park fire fighters won three out of five team awards in a competition.

In October 1957 the new Fire Brigade Headquarters at Framwellgate Moor opened.

In the summer of 1958 C.V. Hall, Chief of the Durham County Fire Brigade paid a visit to Langley Park and made a presentation of a traveling clock to Mr. D. Cartmell who was leaving the Brigade after 18 years service. Daniel Cartmell was born in Leadgate but lived in Langley Park for over 70 years. He worked at Langley Park Coke Works, was for a short time a steeplejack and later worked for the National Coal Board Property Department. He died in January 1982.

The former Langley Park Fire Station situated behind Church Street Community Centre.

In April 1922 there was a violent explosion at Langley Park Cokeworks where there were large stocks of Tar, Benzal and other bye-products. Every man in the district turned out to fight the fire that resulted, working in unbearable heat. Eventually Fire Brigades from Northumberland and Durham Rescue Station, Elswick and from Houghton-le-Spring arrived to attend to and eventually extinguish the blaze.

Originally the fire engine was garaged on a site between the rear of the Co-op Buildings in Front Street and the end of Brown's Terrace. Later it moved to a specially built site behind the Church Street Community Centre where it remained until the local Fire Service was disbanded. The building was for a time then used by Derwentside College and in 2006 houses Langley Park Community Transport. Part of the building is the temporary home of a branch of the Durham County Library.

By arrangement with the proprietors of the Langley Park Hotel ('The Blue Star') an alarm bell was installed on the premises to alert any firemen who were frequenting the establishment at the time of a call-out.

THE WOMEN'S INSTITUTE

The Women's Institute began life in 1915. There are 215,000 members in England, Wales and The Islands. (Scotland has a similar organisation, which has a separate identity).

The organisation was founded to promote the ideals of truth, justice, tolerance and fellowship, these ideals being as strong today as they were in the dark days of World War I. It also exists to educate women to enable them to provide an effective role in the community, to expand their horizons and to develop and pass on important skills. In 1948 it was claimed there were 199 branches of the Women's Institute in Durham County with a membership totalling 20,000.

The Women's Institute is well known for its homemade produce and handicrafts. At one time markets were held in a number of towns selling their wares for local funds. Many institutes had their own choirs and a drama festival always attracted a large number of entries.

In today's world the old image of the W.I. is greatly out of date. Today's members are certainly not the blue rinsed, blue suited, middle-aged jam making matrons. Recently the Institute attracted a great deal of media attention through a group in North Yorkshire who produced a somewhat sensational calendar. 'Calendar Girls' a film based on their exploit also attracted a great deal of attention.

The first Women's Institutes in Durham County were formed in 1917. Witton-le-Wear and Cockerton were the first in the Durham County Federation.

Without sensation but creating a great deal of interest in the village a group of women met and on 4th December 1932 a branch of the Women's Institute was formed in Langley Park. In December of that year Mrs. W.E. Goodenough, wife of the Colliery manager, presided at a meeting of the newly formed group held in the Church Hall. Early members named include Mrs. Mulcaster, Mrs. J. Hepburn, Mrs. C. Burn, Mrs. C. Harrison, Mrs. Howe, Mrs. Teasdale, Mrs. J. Leeming Mrs. G. Hanson and Mrs. Helmsley who was a pianist. The first Secretary was Margaret Johnson, The Vice President was Laura Hepburn and the Treasurer was Mrs. P. A. Ross, wife of the Colliery under-manager. Langley Park was firstly in the Deerness Group but later they were unwillingly transferred to the Lanchester Group but soon made new friends. Over the years the membership was as high as 210 and the lowest 90. In 1961 the Langley Park branch had 90 members.

In February 1933 100 members closed a meeting by taking the floor for a progressive barn dance. Mrs. J. Hepburn was President in 1936 and in the summer of the following year she staged a pageant play 'Britain Awake' celebrating 21 years of the founding of the Women's Institute. 1938 was the 21st year of the Women's Institute in Durham County and by January 1939 Langley Park officials were President; Mrs J. Hepburn, Vice Presidents J. Hutchinson and Mrs Hansom. Mrs N. Holmes was treasurer and Mrs. M. Johnson was secretary. The assistant Secretary was Mrs. Stothart.

In July 1942 The Women's Institute had a picnic in the Welfare Grounds. Singing and games were popular. Mrs. Calvert won a golf competition and Mrs. Maguire showed a great deal of skill going away the happy winner of the egg and spoon race.

At the tenth annual party, held in the Labour Hall in January 1943, entertainment was provided by the branch choir and the official's table was decorated with red, white and blue candles. In February 1943 members were asked for ideas on how to brighten their wartime homes. Any member who failed to contribute an idea had to donate one penny to the local Red Cross Fund. Later in the year the competitions included 'the six most useful things to pack in the event of a blitz', 'a celebrity I would most like to meet' 'a musical kit-bag' and, at one meeting, there was a prize for the best whistler.

During the war years the local Institute also had a knitting secretary. The local ladies were making a considerable contribution with donations of items to the Langley Park Comforts Fund.

Nationally the Langley Park branch was represented at the 25th Annual General Meeting held in the Albert Hall, London in April 1944.

Ninety members were present for the 14th birthday in December 1946. Mrs. Clayton cut a cake that had been made by Mrs. Teasdale. Mrs. Skelton and Mrs Groves had been Presidents, Mrs. Meek was Secretary and Mrs. Agar, Treasurer.

In the years following the Second World War the officials who held office in the Langley Park branch included <u>Presidents</u>: Mrs. Skelton, Mrs. Graham, Mrs. Groves, Mrs. Helmsley, Mrs. Haswell, Mrs. Allison, Mrs. Anderson, Mrs Johnson and Mrs. Hill. <u>Secretaries:</u> Mrs. Meek, Mrs B. Pearson, Mrs. Cousins, Mrs. Reay and Mrs. Pickering. <u>Treasurers:</u> Mrs. Atkinson, Mrs. Angus, J. Watson, Mrs. Howe and Mrs. Histin.

In 1949 there was also a tea secretary, a home and country secretary, Handicraft secretary, sick visitors, a produce and guild secretary, a pianist. They were also making efforts to reform a choir.

At the time of Langley Park's 21st Birthday the office of President was held by Mrs. Graham, The Vice President was Mrs Harrison, Mrs. H. Cousins was Secretary, Mrs Howe, Treasurer. At the party the Vice President Mrs. Birbeck cut the cake.

The 25th. Birthday of Langley Park Women's Institute was celebrated in December 1957. At a special party held in the Church Hall 100 attended. Among the huge throng were the County Organiser Miss Haworth and past presidents of the local branch, Mrs. Inman, Mrs. Skelton, Mrs. L. Hepburn (who was chosen to cut the cake), Mrs. Groves, Mrs. Graham and Mrs. Anderson.

By the mid 1960s Mrs. Hill held the post of President and the Secretary was Mrs. Birbeck. In later years Mrs. Birbeck was President and Mrs. M. Groves and Mrs. Penny carried out secretarial and treasurer duties. In the early 1980s Mrs. A. Whitfield was President.

Over the years the pattern of meetings has remained basically the same. Proceedings open with the singing of 'Jerusalem'. Official, informal and mundane correspondence is dealt with, a member gives The Golden Thread and a competition is judged. There is also, usually, a speaker. Many topics are chosen reflecting the interests of the older and the younger generations. If time allows the evening ends with some entertainment usually a quiz. And, finally, time must be allowed for that much needed cup of tea.

Mrs. Groves cutting the cake at a birthday party held in the Church Hall (later The Youth Centre) in the 1950s.

Group meetings are held at regular intervals bringing together members from other branches in the area. Delegates are nominated to attend and report back on conferences including a national gathering, which is often staged at the Royal Albert Hall, London.

After the war the W.I. met in the now extinct Labour Hall but soon became resident in the Co-Operative Hall. For a time they met in the Modern School and in the Church Street Community Centre but now they meet once a month (every second Tuesday) in the Wood View Community Centre. New members are always welcome. In 2006 Audrey Whitfield is President, Eileen Bowyer Secretary and Joan Metcalf Treasurer.

Note: In mid June 1959 a folk dance festival was held at Brancepeth. Many children attended the event, which attracted an attendance of 700 people. <u>AND, IT WAS REPORTED THAT NOT A SCRAP OF LITTER WAS LEFT BEHIND.</u>

Footnote: At Langley Park in May 1970 a competition was held for the smartest ankle. And the winner was Mrs. *******!!

LANGLEY PARK LITERARY INSTITUTE AND LIBRARY 43

A red brick building situated at the corner of Church Street had originally reading, recreation and science rooms. At one time the library had 1,300 members. The Institute opened in 1902 and was the first step in providing miners with their own facilities. Providing billiards, snooker, skittles and table tennis the building also had a reading room.

Around 1906 Herbert Brook was Secretary. In 1910 George Peel was in office and during World War 1 John Angus.

Walter Dawson held the post in the 1920s and in the 1930s John Wilson Hall.

In 1947 the Colliery Welfare Scheme came into being. Colliery Manager E. Young was Chairman of the organisation in 1967. B. Smith was Secretary and H. S. Guildford Treasurer. At this time financial matters were causing concern. The coke-works had been closed for a few years and there was also a reduction in the number of men employed at the colliery. The labour force had been reduced by 400. Levies had been 3d. per week for each man. This had to be raised to 5d a week and in 1967 in was 1/- (5p) a week. The scheme was still running at a loss.

The colliery closed in 1975 and since then the Institute has been run as The Church Street Community Centre.

From the 1980s a mobile library served the village for three days a week. This being parked on land near the Langley Park Hotel.

By early 2006 plans were well formulated for the Durham County Council to set up a permanent library in the village using the Church Street Site.

Left: **The Church Hall (The Parochial Hall) and later The Youth Centre.**

The venue for many village activities including weddings, whist drives, dances and the annual Old People's Treat.

See No. 33/3 and 33/4

THE WOMEN'S CO-OPERATIVE GUILD

History: The Co-operative Women's Guild was formed in 1883 following the first inclusion of a women's page in "Co-operative News". Its aim was to spread the knowledge of the benefits of co-operation and improve the conditions of women with the slogan co-operation in poor neighbourhoods".

In 1885 the organisation changed its name to the Women's Co-operative Guild. In 1889 Miss Margaret Llewelyn Davies became General Secretary on a voluntary basis and Miss Lilian Harris was appointed Cashier to the Guild. Under the direction of these two women the organisation expanded rapidly from 51 branches and a membership of 1700 in 1889 to a peak of 1500 branches and a membership of 72,000 in 1933. By this time the name of the organisation had again been changed to the Co-operative Women's Guild.

In October 1933 The Divisional Secretary of the Women's Guild, Mrs. Gibbons of Annfield Plain, addressed a meeting in the Co-operative Hall. Afterwards a branch of the Guild was formed. Mrs. R. Rutherford was elected President, Mrs. Laing was originally named as Vice President, later Mrs. Pickering seems to have replaced her, the Secretary was Mrs. S. Britton and the Treasurer Mrs. Hocking.

The Guild was to hold fortnightly meetings in the Co-operative Hall or The Guild Hall, as it was sometimes referred.

In February 1936 at the second birthday party Guilds from Annfield Plain, Sacriston, Lanchester and Chester-le-Street joined in the celebration. Mrs. Teasdale made the cake and the President of the Langley Park branch, Mrs. Rutherford, who had cut the cake at the first birthday party the previous year spoke of working hard week by week pushing forward the aims and benefits of the Co-operative movement. At the time Mrs. Pickering was Secretary.

Names associated with the Langley Park branch over the years include Mrs. Dowson, Mrs. E. Smith and Mrs. H. Oakley who after a long term in office retired as President at the end of 1958, Mrs. Benton and Mrs. Holden. Early in 1959 Mrs. Spence is shown as President and Mrs. Stephenson Vice-President.

For a period in the 1940s Mrs. Oakley was treasurer. Mrs. Bramfitt held the post in the 1950s as did Mrs. Holden who had also served as assistant treasurer. Secretarial duties had been carried out by Mrs. Coulson. Mrs. Bramfitt and Mrs. Spence took the Guild into the 1960s and Mrs. Dowson and Mrs Benton were actively involved.

The Langley Park Branch of the Women's Co-operative Guild had a good following up to and including The Second World War and continued for many years afterwards.

LANGLEY PARK AGED PEOPLE'S CHRISTMAS TREAT

Langley Park Aged People's Christmas Treat began in 1927 when 130 villagers accepted the invitation to a tea and concert. It was made possible through weekly contributions and funds raised from all sections of Langley Park Colliery.

In December 1933, 350 invitations were sent out and 300 residents responded. In the pre-war years J. Robertshaw was Chairman and T. Miller Secretary. Among those attending the event in December 1935 were W. Foster (then 88), Mrs. W. Foster (85), R. Howe (84), Mrs. Wood (83), Mrs. Tomes (82), R. Shorten (81), Miss M. Robson 80, Mrs. Webb (80), Mrs. Deborah Clark (78), Mr. J. Sudder (?) (78) and J. Cooper (78). Councillor J. Robertshaw was chairman, Mr. J.Peel (treasurer) and T. Miller (secretary). Langley Park Band was in attendance as was De Albert's Concert Party from Brandon.

In 1939 R. Robinson became secretary and continued for 11 years retiring in 1950. J. Peel was the original treasurer in 1927 and was still serving in that office in 1938. In December 1939 war time conditions and the blackout made it impossible to hold the event but the following year it was possible to entertain 200 villagers for tea and the usual concert.

Figures show that in December 1950 some 550 elderly people attended and were entertained by Langley Park Colliery Welfare Band conducted by George Dover and pianist/entertainer George Adamson. Among the guests were Dr. Rutherford and the Colliery Manager, Mr. Reay. Two years later Langley Park Colliery Band were continuing the long association with the event, Mrs. A. Oakley provided two solos and Chester-le-Street Male Voice Choir with Mrs. Van Gaver as pianist entertained. Lord Lawson of Beamish was a guest. In December 1953 The Workmen's Club Jolly Boys and the Band were present.

In December 1957 Mr. I. Smith was Secretary of the Fund and a tea and concert for 500 took place. Again the band played and the Women's Co-operative Guild entertained. Mr. Dover conducted the band in 1958. Again 500 attended Mr. I Smith was still secretary and the Chairman was Mr. S. Maitland. Denton's Dance Band was engaged in 1959 along with the Band. The chairman was Mr. T. Miller and there was special praise for Mrs. T. Proud who had organised and arranged the serving of the teas for thirty years. Two years later Mr. I. Smith was still Secretary and Mr. Coult was in charge of catering. There was no event in December 1963 as the Church Hall was being refurbished to become the Youth Centre.

The Colliery and the Cokeworks may have disappeared but in recent times a dedicated band of men and women have continued the work started over 50 years ago. Throughout the year raising funds and giving up their time and a lot of energy they have continued to put on a remarkable afternoon for the old people. Organising entertainment is not an easy task but the organisers have been fortunate in obtaining the services of artists such as Holly Wood who has proved to be popular with a Langley Park audience. A feature of the event is the free raffle with its amazing number of prizes On some occasions there were 140. The last Aged People Treat was in December 2004. By December 2005 the Church Hall the only suitable venue for the event, was closed.

LANGLEY PARK OVER 60's CLUB

In June 1952 Councillor J. Robertshaw opened the first meeting of the newly formed Langley Park over 60s Club. With over 100 people attending the club got off to an encouraging start. The first Officials were <u>Chairman</u>: Mr A Scott, <u>Secretary:</u> Mrs. L. Charlton, <u>Treasurer</u>: Mr J Eccleston, <u>Committee:</u> Mesdames Carpenter, Birbeck, Emmerson, Penny and Messrs. Robertshaw, Hall, A. Shorten, Leeming, J Penny and A. Bolam (the committee made up from two members from each organisation in the village. In 1953 the Vice Chairmen were J. Davison and Mr. Hutton. W. Robson was assistant secretary.

Nearly every community in the area had an Over 60 Club and most of them managed to assemble a concert party – Langley Park was no exception. These parties travelled around the various Clubs and provided the evening's entertainment that was obviously much enjoyed. Various other concert parties or choirs from other organisations made regular appearances.

Eventually about 200 elderly people were regularly attending fortnightly gatherings. The Club was so popular that for some considerable time there was a waiting list of people wishing to join.

The fourth birthday party in June 1956 saw 200 members being entertained by Langley Park Women's Institute and in August 1957 70 members undertook a mystery trip which took them to Hexham and then to Whitley Bay.

In May 1957 the Vice Chairman of the Club Harold Bell left the village to take a part time job at a country house near Malton, Yorkshire. Aged 77 he had served in the South African War and also in India. He came to Langley Park in 1913. At the beginning of the 1914-1918 war he was in the army again. Captured in France he was a Prisoner of War for three years. He earned The Queen Victoria and King Edward Medals for the African War and he was always known to be soldierly smart.

One of the men instrumental in forming the Langley Park Club and its treasurer from the outset Mr. J. Eccleston died in the summer of 1958.

As well as their normal meetings mentioned above the club usually took members on an outing during the summer months. Around five coaches were hired for these occasions and during the Christmas season a special party was organised. In August 1957 70 members went on a mystery trip which took them to Hexham and then to Whitley Bay. The birthday in 1958 was celebrated with high tea being served to 200 members. Mr. E. Leeming (piano) and Crook Social Centre Concert Party provided the entertainment. Again with Mr. Leeming at the piano and also with Esh Winning Women's Institute providing the entertainment 150 members sat down to high tea in 1959. Also in the summer of 1959 five coaches carried the over 60s to South Shields for the day. Mr. Scott was Chairman until 1972 when he retired due to ill health. He died in July 1978 aged 76. Mr. Tom Burn also had a lengthy association with the club

The club was in existence for some thirty years.

SHOPPING LIST

INTRODUCTION

During the 1930s – 1950s one of the essential items for a housewife doing her daily or weekly shopping was a wicker basket or, for a trip into 'town.', a shopping bag. There were no 'throw away' bags given by local stores to carry groceries. If necessary, larger purchases would be neatly wrapped by skilful staff in brown paper and tied up with string. The rolls of paper being a normal feature of the shop counter. And for a lady going shopping a hat and coat were a necessary part of her dress. And trousers for women!!!!!. In shops an assistant served the customer. The arrival of the supermarket was still some years hence.

Right: T.A. Coates Family Butcher (see 53)

Advertisements

WILLIAM FORSTER

(Proprietor. JOHN FORSTER)
Head Office: Front Street, Sacriston. Branch: Quebec Street, Langley Park

Grocer, Flour & Provision Merchant Baker and Confectioner

A Large Selection of the Best Quality PROVISIONS Local and Foreign FRUITS AND VEGETABLES
TOBACCO and CIGARETTES SWEETS and CHOCOLATES

Home Baked Country Bread. Cakes and Confectionery

Delivery by our own Van

Telephone: LANGLEY PARK 218

B. NEWTON AND SON
(Proprietor: R. NEWTON)

Petrol, Oils, Greases, Tyres. etc. supplied

Repairs to any kind of Car. Motorcycle, Agricultural and Commercial Machinery. Regrinding. Reboring, Oxyacetylene Welding and Cutting

HIRE CAR SERVICE
Kaysburn Garage, Langley Park, Co. Durham

G.E.TATTERS
(Prop. B. G. & T. W. WATSON)

Provisions, Fresh Local and Foreign Fruits and Vegetables. Drapery
Tobacco, Cigarettes, Sweets, Minerals and Cordials. Toys, Games and Books.

Agent for The Northern Bus Co. Booking for Tours
42, Front Street, Langley Park

WATSONS' Drapery STORE
(Proprietress: E. ECCLESTON)
DRAPER and CLOTHIER

LADIES' and CHILDREN'S OUTFITTER and GENTLEMEN'S UNDERWEAR Boots and Shoes for Children, Ladies and Gentlemen
Agent for
SIRDAR   SECIL   BRENDA
& MAYTIME' WOOLS
39, FRONT STREET LANGLEY PARK, Co. DURHAM
Phone: LANGLEY PARK 342

SHORTEN BROS.
BUILDERS and CONTRACTORS

Building in All Branches. In Wood, Brick Concrete, Steel, etc.   Plumbing, etc.
Property Maintenance a Specialty. Farm Buildings to Order. Estimates Free. Registered No. IO2/45005/G.B.
21, FRONT ST., LANGLEY PARK DURHAM

Advertisements are from an unknown source probably circa 1945.

LANGLEY PARK POST OFFICE

Around the year 1879 Elizabeth Rapier is described as shopkeeper/receiver at Langley Park. From circa 1894 – 1897 George Ritchie who had been at The Co-op in the village was at the Post Office and also described as a shopkeeper. Leading up to the First World War letters arrived at the shop at 7.10 a.m. and 6.40 p.m. and dispatched three times a day at 7.15 a.m. 1.05 p.m. and 6.20 p.m.

Two names dominate the history of Langley Park Post Office. They are Davis and Hoggart.

Firstly Sub Postmaster Robert Davis. Alderman Davis, whose address was shown as London House, (i.e. The Post Office), Langley Park, died suddenly in the early hours of Wednesday 19th June 1935 aged 73 and his funeral took place on the following Saturday.

He had been a member of Durham County Council since 1919 and was a magistrate in Lanchester Petty Sessional Division. He had served 30 years on Lanchester Rural District Council and was on the local Parish Council. As Chairman he was associated with Langley Park Hospital Committee and was on the Lanchester Joint Hospital Board.

The day before his death he had been promoted from Vice Chairman to Chairman of the Durham County Water board following the death two days earlier of Peter Lee, well known in the area particularly as General Secretary of the Durham Miners' Association. The Water Board had lost two Chairmen in two days.

A Methodist (ex Primitive Methodist) Alderman Davis had lived all his life in Quebec and Langley Park. Married twice, his first wife died circa. 1907, he left a widow and one son Mr. Ernest Davis.

Until the time of his death Alderman Davis was well known in Langley Park as sub-postmaster Mrs. Davis continued to run the Port Office until the end of 1941. When she retired the Davis's had run the business for over 40 years. At the time Mrs. Davis said she was to continue living in the village.

Stephen Hoggart and his daughter Gladys (Hall)

In November 1936 Mrs. Davis's son Ernest was killed in a car accident at Bishop Monckton – Markington Crossroads near Ripon. He was driving home from a business trip to Harrogate when his car collided with a vehicle driven by a Markington farmer. He was 27.

On the 1st January 1942 Mr. Stephen G. Hoggart became sub-postmaster at Langley Park. When he retired his daughter Gladys (Mrs. Hall), took over. Between them they were to run the enterprise for a further 50 or more years and throughout it remained very much a family concern. The family not only serving behind the counter but also taking to the streets delivering mail.

Mr. Hoggart had been a farmer in Yorkshire for seven years. Coming to Langley Park in the early days of the twentieth century he spent seven years at Langley Park Colliery before joining Annfield Plain Co-operative Society in Langley Park. He served for 26 years and became manager of the greengrocery department. Mr. Hoggart retired in April 1961. Over the years he supported many organisations in the village. He served 21 years on Esh Church Council, was a sidesman at All Saints Church and President of the Cricket Club. He was associated with the Local Farmers and Tradesmen's Association and stood, unsuccessfully, as a candidate in local council elections. Off duty he enjoyed spending time working in his allotment. Until the 2nd World War the Post Office was located two doors away from the present site. A few years after Mr. Hoggart took over it was moved into the building that had housed Watson's Drapers, which also moved to a new position at 39, Front Street. Tom Elgey, a Gentlemen's Hairdresser, then occupied the old Post Office premises.

In the days when one needed an operator to connect a call The Post Office also housed the local telephone exchange.

Letters and cards posted in the letter box attached to the front of the building were collected up inside by the staff and each one was franked with the distinctive 'Langley Park' postmark – all franking down by hand with a stamp.

In the 'back room' of the premises incoming mail was sorted and prepared for delivery. Letters and cards arrived at villager's homes, in most cases, as they breakfasted. Parcels followed soon after. The yellow telegram, often the bearer of bad news, was commonplace and was delivered as quickly as possible.

Christmas put additional pressure on the resources of the staff. There was a vast increase in the number of packages coming in and going out. Outgoing mail continued to be franked by hand and the many 'local' items could be dealt with swiftly and delivery often achieved the same day. Nowadays all mail whether incoming or outgoing is dealt with at Darlington and carries a 'Darlington' postmark and the post box has been replaced with a pillar-box in the street. A high security screen has replaced the open counter of the past. The monopoly on the sale of postage stamps has gone and these can be obtained at various outlets. Post Office work has diversified to include such things as banking, road tax, foreign currency and travel insurance as well as the payment of Public Utility Bills. Like most businesses computerisation has brought many changes to the way the establishment is managed particularly regarding the payment of pensions and benefits.

In the hands of Stuart and Moira Harris, the Post Office continues to be a friendly, successful and indispensable part of Langley Park life.

William Heppell of The Haven, Langley Park died in March 1951 aged 76. He had been an insurance agent and a postman in the village.

Stuart Harris in the old post room.

THE CO-OPERATIVE WHOLESALE SOCIETY

In 1877 it was agreed to open a branch of the Co-operative Society in Langley Park. The decision was taken at a meeting of the Annfield Plain Industrial Co-operative Society Ltd. and Mr. George Ritchie was to be the first branch manager of the new amenity. A shop owned by a Mr. Foster was rented and the new store soon became very popular with local customers. Plans were drawn up for a new store. The result was the building that still exists today. It dates from 1884 and the design is typical of Co-operative Stores that grew up all around the area. In 1893 the local fire brigade were quickly on the scene when a blaze threatened to destroy the store but damage was limited. At the start of the 1900s William Short was manager – George Ritchie was then at the Post Office.

The Millinery Department. Located in the shop at the May Terrace end of the complex. Miss Ethel Mulcaster had 49 years service with the Annfield Plain Co-operative Society and was the well-known manageress. She retired in December 1957 and Mr. Scott, manager of the branch on behalf of the staff presented her with an easy chair. Having been manageress of this department for just a year Jean Heslop, who was planning to marry, died suddenly at the age of 23 in February 1959. She was a native of Esh Winning.

Butchers. Mr Frederick Cooper began with the Co-op as an apprentice butcher and eventually became manager at the Esh Winning branch. He returned to Langley Park as manager. In all he had 49 years service with the firm and on retirement was presented with a mirror. Mr Fred Wood was also employed in this department and was often seen around Langley Park with the butcher's van. A son of Mr. Wood was lost at sea in the early days of the Second World War when The Royal Oak was sunk at Scapa Flow.

Greengrocery. Mr. J. Wilson of Elm Street celebrated his 90th birthday in May 1961. Until circa. 1936 he had been manager of the greengrocery department. Not long after being appointed Manager and Buyer for the Society at the main store at Annfield Plain Mr. John Eccleston of Front Street died in August 1958 He had been 35 years with the Co-op and had been manager of the Langley Park Greengrocery and Bakery Department. He had a great interest in the local Over 60 Club that he helped to establish in 1952 and was treasurer. From 1957 Mr. George Hoggart was manager and others on the staff included Ken Cook, Ernie Coulson and Billy Layton.

Rule Book for Annfield Plain Co-operative Society 1928.

Hardware. In the early days of the Co-op Esther Peel was associated with this department. Her sister taught at the local infants school and another name from the past is Miss Cummings who came from Witton Gilbert. In more recent times Mr. Norman Paxton was a long time manager.

Drapery and Men's Wear. Thomas Hogg was a well-known manager of this section and employees included Mr. Jack Robinson, Alan Davison and Lena Wood, the daughter of Mrs. Ann Wood who for many years was Langley Park's oldest resident. Frank Richardson then came to the shop having been employed at the Medomsley Branch.

Miss Peel
In 1920 described as 'Furnishing and Boots'

The Chemists. In the years leading up to 1914 Harold Cheetham is named as a chemist and druggist in Front Street, Langley Park. For a great many years the pharmacy in the village (still known as 'The Chemists') has been in the hands of the Co-operative Wholesale Society.

Grocery. A long time manager of this department and overall manager of the complex was Mr. Wilfred Hocking. He was succeeded by Mr. Arthur Scott who was also well known for his connection with the Langley Park Over 60s Club. *(see No 46).* Well-known employees of the Grocery Department were Norman Holmes, Joe Hunter, Harry Maddison, Ernie Cox and Ted Edmundson known for his work on the bacon counter at the rear of the store. Edward Edmundson of Clifford Street died in February 1936 aged 61. Born in Alborough near Darlington he moved to Bridlington and was in business there at the age of 18. He came to Langley Park in 1909 and was well known at the Methodist Church in the village.

From a shopping list presented at the counter or given to one of the two order men who called at the house (Mr. Christopher Haswell who served for 45 years retiring in May 1952, and Mr. Tommy Wardle) a box of groceries would be packed and delivered to the customer's home. Protruding from the box would be a long slip of paper with each item and price individually listed by hand. No matter how large the order the amount owed, and sometimes the bills had a large number of items, would be totalled up without any mechanical means. Mr George Wilkinson who was Clerk for the Store performed arithmetical wonders in totalling up the bills George Wilkinson who lived in Quebec Street died in September 1937 having retired six months earlier. Aged 65 years he had worked for the Annfield Plain Co-operative Society for 42 years. For 30 years he was treasurer of the Workmen's Club and a long time member of the National Union of Distributive and Allied Workers from whom he had a certificate and a gold medal. He was born at Kyo and lived at Catchgate and Hare Law before moving to Langley Park. Mrs. Wilkinson died circa. 1926. They had two sons and three daughters. In September 1945 Amy Hogarth married Sergeant Thomas Brown of Witton Gilbert. At the time she was head clerk and comptometer operator at the Langley Park branch.

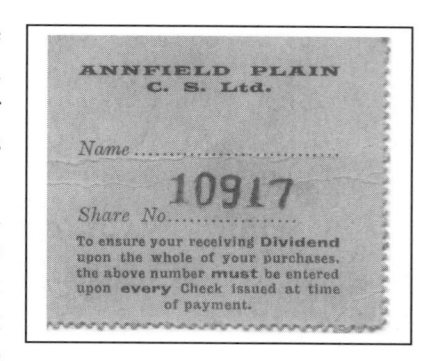

A great benefit of shopping at the Co-op was the payment of the 'divi' (dividend). Customers could be members of the Co-op and were given a number and a passbook. On each purchase a tiny receipt was given showing the number (e.g. 12345) and the amount spent. The shop copy went to the main branch and every three months a small percentage was worked out from the purchases and the amount of the discount was entered into the passbook that was handed in to the local branch at the appropriate time. The customer then had access to their divi. Many years after the system was abolished and even today some villagers can still recall their store number.

> *One Saturday morning in March 1929 a beast came hurtling through the window of the Co-op Butcher's Shop. The animal had been driven into the back of the shop and noticed an opening through into the front of the shop it dashed through leaped over the marble slab and through the window onto the pavement outside and ran down the village.*

One of the features of the Co-op was the door-to-door delivery – by horse and cart. This method was used until well after the Second World War. Residents can still remember purchasing their greengroceries from these carts and some of the horses got to know the route so well they would stop of their own accord at each point. Bearpark and Esh were also served. To get up the steep bank to the top of the hill leading to these villages two horses would have to be employed. Stables were to the rear of the Co-op Stores in Front Street and the animals had to be cared for 365 days a year by the horse keepers who were employed to look after them. The Grocery Department had 4 horses, The Hardware 2, Greengrocery 5 and the Butchers 4. There was also one for the Paraffin Cart. It was on this that Mr. George Hoggart began his long career with the Co-op. Mr. Jack Howard was known as a horse-keeper.

It took a week to serve all Langley Park with paraffin. In the days before electricity came commonly into use in the village paraffin lamps were the only means of providing illumination and, of course, with no street lamps, lanterns were essential for anyone setting out on dark nights.

There was a warehouse at the back of the store where Mr. Joe Wilkinson was employed putting up flour and meal. He lived in Crossways and retired in November 1956 after 47 years service with the organisation.

In 1970 Annfield Plain Co-operative Society merged with other society's in the area to become The North Eastern Co-operative Society. Following the reorganisation all the departments closed leaving only the Grocery Department that remains in business today.

> *In October 1956 Anne Mary Hocking then 78 was on her way to a Mothers Union whist drive from her home at 7, Laurel Terrace, Langley Park when she was knocked down and killed by a car. The coroner returned a verdict of accidental death. Her husband was Mr. Hocking who was then retired from his position as Manager of the Langley Park branch. They had two sons, one a schoolteacher and the other, William a store manager.*

Langley Park Co-op Building, Front Street 1920.

Photos: 'Jubilee History of Annfield Plain Co-operative Society Ltd 1870 – 1920 –(Ross and Stoddart.)

The Annfield Plain Co-operative Society had a shop at the other end of the village. Serving Stringer Terrace area and the council houses nearby it provided a service for many years. This shop was converted into a private house some time ago.

NEWSAGENTS
NICHOLAS ANDERSON

In September 1939 Nicholas Anderson of Front Street died at the age of 64. Mr. Anderson had opened a newsagents business in the village some twelve years earlier following a road accident in which he lost a leg. The accident appears to have happened in July 1924 when a motorcycle on which he was riding as a pillion passenger swerved to avoid a collision with a pony and trap at White Bridge. In January 1925 a whist drive and dance was held in the Church Hall for his benefit. 100 villagers attended. At the time he as living in May Terrace. Previously he had been a deputy overman at Langley Park Colliery. He was a member of the National Newsagents Federation. His widow Mrs. Alice Anderson died in January 1952 aged 79. She was a keen member of the Langley Park Women's Institute and the Mothers Union.

In the years leading up to World War One George E. Johnson was a newsagent/shopkeeper in Langley Park.

William Withers Eggleston(e) was a newsagent in the mid 1920s. He died in September 1928 after being in poor health for some time.

Their son Nicholas took over the Langley Park business in 1939 and they had two other sons who were newsagents E. H. Anderson at Middlesbrough and George T. at Billingham.

In August 1938 their daughter Alice married Andrew Marr of Consett who later became manager of Eden Colliery. Alice had been on the staff of Langley Park Girl's School and had also taught at Ushaw Moor Council School. Another daughter was the Headmistress at Malton Colliery and also became Mrs. Clark, the wife of a Swalwell farmer. Three other daughters were Mrs. Reay wife of a newsagent at Teesville, Mrs. Maloney whose husband was a schoolmaster at Houghton-le-Spring and Mrs. E.E. Maggett who married an engineer who worked at Washington Colliery.

Nicholas, at Langley Park, married Jenny Haswell in July 1940. Miss Haswell, in June 1938, had just gained her final State Midwifery Examination at Leeds. She began nursing in 1930 and trained for three years at Langley Park Isolation Hospital. She then spent four years at Sunderland Royal Infirmary before going to Leeds.

From the 29th March 1992 Mr and Mrs Keith Reay began running the newsagents shop in Front Street. They succeeded A. J. J. Calvert who had taken over the business in May 1972 from relatives of theirs, Tommy and Joan Winter.

Nicholas Anderson

J.W. COUSINS

Born circa 1869 Mr. Cousins came to Langley Park from Alston at the age of nine years. Two years later he took his first job at brickworks and then he worked at the pit. Later he was employed at a farm and then it was back to the pit.

He took premises at 47½ Front Street opening a newsagent's shop, which he ran for 45 years and at the rear of the building, set up a printing business. He claimed to be the only printer between Durham and Consett and Stanley and Crook He regularly worked an 18-hour day being up at 6 o'clock in the morning. On a Sunday he regularly walked five miles delivering newspapers. Mr. Cousins met his wife Ann Elizabeth when she was visiting Langley Park from her home in Dudley. She came back to the village the following year and this time when she returned home it was to prepare for her wedding. Mr. and Mrs. Cousins were to have four sons, Albert, Joseph William, John James and Harry and a daughter Mabel who in 1951 was managing the business. 1951 was the year Mr. and Mrs. Cousins were celebrating their diamond wedding.

Away from business Mr. Cousins had been a founder member of Witton Gilbert and Langley Park Workmen's Clubs.

At the age of 82 he had an ambition to travel in an air balloon. He wanted to look down on Durham County from the basket of a balloon. He considered this to be the only safe form of air travel. He had no love for aeroplanes, considering them to be too dangerous, too fast, too heavy and they had engines. Living above the shop Mr. Cousins had printed the following on a card which he placed on the door of his business giving a gentle reminder to customers:-

'Customers came and I did trust them
I lost my money and I lost my custom.
To loose them both it grieved me sore
So I was resolved to trust no more.'

Mr. Cousins died in April 1954 aged 85.

From the mid 1950s Mr. and Mrs. E. James ran the newspaper shop continuing until May 1972 when Mr. Joe Moralee took over the business.

Next-door Annie Lizzie James had set up a bakery and confectionery business in the late 1890s. From circa 1933 Ernie and Sid James ran the firm. By 1972 when he ceased trading Ernie James had been running the establishment on his own.

For 28 years Ernie James was a partner in the bakery business and then, with Mrs. James, was for 19 years, a newsagent. He retired in 1972 and died in January 1979. He was organist at the Baptist Chapel for 43 years and church secretary for 22 years. As a deacon he served the Baptist's for 27 years. During the 1939-1945 war he was a driver for the National Fire Service.

THOMAS RIPPON WATSON

Born in Willington circa 1871 he came to Langley Park around 1913 and opened a draper's shop in Quebec Street.

He also took a lively interest in local affairs. Keenly interested in youngsters, he annually at New Year, entertained children from Lanchester Cottages Homes to a tea held either in the Trinity Methodist School Hall or The Church Hall in the village, and a cinema show. The latter was held in the Hippodrome Cinema and The Gypsy Queen Bus Company provided transport for the children.

This he did for some 17 years until the war curtailed his activities.

A member of All Saints Church in Langley Park he held the post of vicar's warden for many years and served as Secretary for the Church Council. He was President of Langley Park Bowls Club and was also Treasurer of the Church Lads Brigade. At Christmas time Mr. and Mrs. Watson gave a parcel of groceries to each inhabitant of the Langley Park Miner's Homes.

Thomas Rippon Watson died in 1944 at the age of 73.

ENID ECCLESTON

Daughter of Edward Eccleston, who came to Langley Park as a boy and spent all his working life at Langley Park Colliery, retiring in 1933. He held a diploma for fifty years membership of Durham Miners Association and for 38 years had been financial secretary of Langley Park Miners Lodge. He was on the management committee of Durham Hospital having been a member for many years. He was well known in the village for his fund raising activities for the Hospital. Mr. Eccleston died in January, 1941 aged 72

and Sarah Jane Eccleston who died in February 1944 aged 72 who was also an ardent worker for Durham County Hospital. Born in Witton Gilbert she had lived in Langley Park for most of her life being a staunch member of All Saints Church and the Mothers Union. As Chairman of a local committee of Friends of the Hospital she along with Miss Dawson was known for her Easter Collection, which raised large sums of money and collected thousands of eggs for wartime hospital patients.

Miss Enid Eccleston was well known in Langley Park for her association with Watson's Drapery Store.

Born c 1911 Enid worked for Mr. and Mrs. Watson in their drapers shop in Quebec Street. Her first wage was 7/6d (37½p) per week. In those days the business was

On her retirement Miss Eccleston re-called her memories of knitting etc:

"Knitting was a necessity, darning a regular occupation and knit two purl two for pit stockings could hardly be described as a hobby. Yarn was sold in cuts and it took five cuts to make a pair of stockings. There were ways of dealing with the turning of the heels on socks for all members of the family – 'Dutch' heels differed from 'French heels and I'm not sure where 'auto' heels came in.

Babies were cocooned in petticoats and pilches. Women wore knitted sleeping vests and even men's underpants were cast on at the left leg and knitted to back shapings with buttonholes in strategic places.

Even crochet work was functional, nothing too frivolous. Mercer cotton was eleven old pennies a ball and a book of patterns for knitting or crochet 1/- (5p). At December 1981 cotton was 85p a ball.
Iron and kettle holders were crocheted or knitted, pillows, table cloths, best sheets, bedspreads etc. were all products of deftly plied needles. Embroidery silks and cottons in an assortment of colours were in regular demand. But then along came nylon!".

Two ladies on a park bench knitting for relaxation and necessity

situated in the building that is now Langley Park Post Office. In 1943 Mr. Watson retired from the business and Enid took over the running of the shop. She was responsible for the transfer to Front Street (Fothergills Pie Shop until recently occupied the site). Throughout her long career Enid kept the name of Watson's Drapery alive. To villagers, however, it was Enid Eccleston's. With the untiring help of her sister-in-law Jenny the shop always provided a warm welcome to customers and to visitors calling on matters associated with her work for local organisations.

She keenly supported the local branch of the British Legion and in November each year made a shop window available to display wreaths and crosses as a prelude to the annual Remembrance Sunday Service.

For over forty years she was head of All Saints Church Sunday School and served many years on the Parish Church Council and was long time treasurer of the Church Magazine Accounts.

Enid could recall the time some 200 children were attending Sunday School and, in a day when there were few cars, organised some sixteen coaches to take pupils and accompanying adults on a summer trip to a seaside resort.

In January 1937 Enid Eccleston appeared in a one-act play 'Pandora's Box' one of four one act plays marking the public debut of the Langley Park Drama Class which was formed under the direction of Miss E.M. Westhorp. In an All Saints Church nativity play at Christmas 1938 Enid stepped into the role of the Virgin Mary at eighteen hours notice. Mrs. Barnett, the wife of the curate, had to withdraw at this late stage because of a family bereavement.

Like her parents she was very active in the work of The Friends of Durham Hospitals being a founder member of the Langley Park branch and served on the Management Committee of Durham Ladies Lecture Club.

After she gave up the business in Front Street in December 1981, Enid enjoyed a happy retirement and continued with her varied interests until failing health curtailed her activities.

Described as an 'institution' in Langley Park and sometimes referred to as 'Miss. Langley Park', Enid Eccleston died on 12th July 2002 aged 91.

JAMES ECCLESTON

A brother of Enid, James married Renee Lumley who was a teacher at Staindrop Church of England School. Mr. and Mrs. Eccleston had two children. Having obtained a M.A. (B.A. Durham University) James taught at various schools in County Durham between 1936 and 1941 doing supply work.

World War 2 saw him serving in the R.A.F. in North Africa. He was a pilot for six years and was awarded the A.F.C. On leaving the R.A.F. in 1946 Mr. Eccleston taught at Darlington Grammar School. In September 1957 he was appointed Headmaster to the British Army Children's School in Tripoli where he served for three years. He then moved to West Germany and finally to Berlin.

In his younger days James Eccleston was a keen cricketer and played in the village team. He was also well known locally as an amateur actor. He played Bede in an open air production in the grounds of Durham Cathedral and in Langley Park at Easter 1938 appeared in a passion play 'Good Friday' at All Saints Church. His brother John was also in the cast. In December 1939 he appeared with the Youth Fellowship of Players in the village in 'Man On The Edge and also wrote a burlesque which was performed in the same programme of one act plays.

James Eccleston retired from teaching in 1974 and moved to Eggleston, near Barnard Castle where he still lives in happy retirement.

JOHN ECCLESTON

Enid's brother John married Jenny and they had two children. During World War 2 John served in the R.A.F. He was employed for 35 years with Annfield Plain Co-operative Society becoming manager of the greengrocery and bacon department. He had just been appointed buyer for the greengrocery department when he died in August 1958 aged 49.

Mr. Eccleston was instrumental in forming the Langley Park Over 60s Club and was the treasurer.

For 31 years he sang in All Saints Church choir and served on Esh Parochial Church Council as vice chairman and treasurer.

THOMAS A COATES AND SONS
FAMILY BUTCHERS

The Coates family enjoyed over 100 years of trading in Langley Park being a household name from the beginning of the village's life. Recent memories are of Ray and Frank Coates the sons of T. A. Coates but it was in 1890 that Joseph and Thomas Coates bought a butchery business in Cornsay Colliery from John Kipling Coates, a brother, and somewhere about 1909 opened another shop in Langley Park.

Their nephew, Thomas Atkinson Coates was born in 1899 and began his working life as an apprentice with Hunters who had a butcher's shop in Front Street, Langley Park. He then joined his uncles in their shop up the road. He was to take over the running of the business on the deaths of his uncles Thomas who died in 1927 and Joseph who died six years later. He ran the Cornsay shop and the premises at 29, Quebec Street which had an off licence next door. At the time of his death in 1927 Mr. T. Coates was described as a 'man of a genial and bright disposition and highly esteemed by everyone'. By the beginning of 1952 Westoe Breweries had acquired the Langley Park shop and began negotiations to open what was to be The Ram's Head Hotel'. The Coates family moved to 31 and 32 Quebec Street and another move came about in 1983, the year T. A. Coates, died. The new address was 11, Quebec Street.

And so we come to Ray and Frank who carried on the family firm from then on until 1995 when Ray died. Frank and Ray's son Michael ran the shop until Frank retired in 1997 and the name of Coates disappeared from local business life.

In earlier days some five men were travelling around delivering meat, the original mode of transport being horse and cart. Frank himself was regularly seen around the village with the firm's distinctive van. At Christmas time extra pressure was on the family as they coped with the extra demand for meat and poultry and the extra home deliveries that were involved. But it was all carried off with the same efficiency and friendliness that made the business so popular.

Other Butchers. *In 1894 William Adamson Holmes had a shop and later along came James Robert Hunter, William Pearson and Nicholas Nattrass. Also George Crondance Douglas. Other shops remembered are The British Argentine Meat Co. (1923) Ltd and Arthur Thurkettle 'the smiling butcher'. Mr. Thurkettle came to Langley Park aged 15 to serve his time in his father's business. Thirty-six years as a butcher on his own account brought him many friends who were all his customers. For some time two little schoolgirls called at his premises every day on their way home to change the calendar in the shop He was a Past President of Durham Butchers Association. His wife Mary also worked for him in the shop and in the slaughterhouse. Mr. Thurkettle died in July 1962. During the 50 years of his business life he only took two holidays. There was also Arthur William Dobbin who took over from Hunters in Front Street and in the mid 1920s a pork butcher John T. Parker. In more recent times there was Tom Bell also in Front Street. (Co-op Butchers see 49/1).*

Despite the change in shopping habits it is pleasant to report that, today, Langley Park still has a butcher's shop, situated next to the Baptist Chapel in Front Street. 'Porkies' (Colin Johnson and Tracey) is a recent arrival having taken over the business from John Hanley. Originally it was a smaller shop but Mr. Hanley acquired the shop next door and made the two shops into one.

MORE VILLAGE SNAPSHOTS

Two postcard views of Walnook Mill. Below E. James collecting flour for his bakery,

Top left : G.E. Tatters Shop Front Street .Above: Mr and Mrs T.W. Watson on their wedding day 1937.

Below: Ernie James and Florrie with young Eric James.

Below: T.A. Coates with his son Raymond and prize- winning beast at Lanchester winter show. Below: Frank Coates, Raymond's brother

AROUND THE SHOPS

By 1879 the growing population in Langley Park was attracting tradesmen to set up shops to meet the needs of the community. Among those established by that year included Jonathan Willey and Thomas Robinson (butchers) Samuel Brown (a greengrocer). Robert Burton and Jonathan Wardle had shops as Boot and Shoemakers, Thomas Guest was an ale and spirit dealer and William Buxton was a tailor. George Welford (joiner), George Wherly (draper) and Richard Nelsom (a grocer and draper) are named alongside other shopkeepers Charles Brown, Thomas Irving (circa 1890 and later shown as a beer retailer), Nicholas Nattrass and George Soames. Thomas Burdon was a tailor in Quebec Street at this time and continued working into the 1900s By the 1920s his son had followed in his father's footsteps. In the late 1890s Mrs. Ada Waugh was a shopkeeper and a beer retailer and another lady Mrs. Eliza Sudder had opened a shop. In the years leading up to 1900 James Robert Hunter and Nicholas Nattrass were butchers in the village, the latter also sold beer. There was an earthenware dealer named Meshach Vaughan. Earlier Thomas Urwin was in the same business.

Established by the early days of World War One **The Meadow Dairy Co. Ltd** were trading in Front Street and continued to do so until well after the Second World War. Also in Front Street, **Walter Willson's** was another popular shop that began in the village in the early 1900s. Mr. Bellinger was manager of the Langley Park Branch and during the World War Two years his daughter, Edna Hill, succeeded him. In March 1972 at the firm's Team s Valley Headquarters The Hon. David De-Lancie Ritchieson presented her with an inscribed gold watch for thirty years service with the firm. Mrs. Hill was also well-known in the village for her association with the Women's Institute and other organisations. Her son Michael had joined the Merchant Navy at the age of 16 and by August 1956 had obtained his 2nd Officer's Certificate. In 1957 Michael represented the Merchant Navy at the Anzac Day Ceremony in Auckland, New Zealand, presenting Merchant Navy flags to the Governor General. He married Doreen Watson who in the late 1950s was appearing in productions staged by the Langley Park Players. Mr. Bellinger was something of a 'dandy' being known in the village for his wearing of spats, striped trousers and an 'Anthony Eden' hat. Pearl Wiseman, Hannah Burgess and Dora Maddison (later Mrs. Munsey) were well known as members of the staff of Walter Willsons.

R. and B. Robson took over the shop from Walter Willsons, moving from 33, Front Street where they had succeeded Mr. R. Harron who had traded there as a General Dealer for 3 years. Mr. Harron moved to Chester-le-Street. Originally Robsons ran the old Walter Willson's shop as a cash and carry business but later traded under the V.G. sign. From 1986 it became the Spar and the business was extended to take over the ex-butcher's shop next door.

Gertie Tatters was well-known in the village not only for her association with the Baptist Church but also for the fruit and vegetable business at 42, Front Street. She died in March 1957 and had lived in Langley Park for over 70 years. Mrs. Tatters had a daughter Bessie, who in October 1937 married Thomas W. Watson of New Brancepeth. Mr. and Mrs. Watson took over the business and continued to run the shop until 1977. The premises are now part of the newsagent's shop that was extended when the greengrocery shop was vacated. One of the services provided by Watsons was an agency for booking bus tours for the Northern General Transport. Mrs.Watson died in March 2004 and Mr. Watson in February 2006. Their daughter, Margaret, in 1977, began a business trading as Country Style and situated in Quebec Street.

In November 1960 Mr. W. Summerside, who had been connected with the grocery trade for 51 years, retired. Thirty-three of those years were with **Thompson's Red Stamp Stores** and twenty-seven were as manager of the Langley Park branch that was situated below the Co-operative Wholesale Society Buildings in Front Street. A keen member of Langley Park Bowling Club, Mr. Summerside was also a member of the Welfare Committee.

Fish And Chips Well remembered are the days when one could call at the fish and chip shop and buy a fish for 2d or 3d and chips for 1d. Fish cakes cost 1d or, if fried 1½d. Today Langley Fish Shop has premises in Quebec Street once occupied by Ardleys, always a popular shop due to their special batter! Later Gray's took over the business and Mary Gray became well known in the shop. In the years of the Second World War customers took their own old newspapers along to the fish and chip shop for wrapping up their purchases and the staff had to peel all the potatoes by hand and put them through the 'chip chopper'. Eventually Wilson's opened in competition higher up Quebec Street. In earlier years Emma Wilson had worked for Ardleys. A fish and ship shop at this location was in business until very recently. Other names associated with fish and chips are Kings and Peter Bunn. If you made the journey along the corridor next to Martin's Bank that was situated in Front Street, you came across Dodgsons run by Mrs. Dodgson.

From the early life of Langley Park the village has never been short of these businesses. Looking back over the years there has been John Grafton who moved to Blackpool, Annie Hanson at 47, Front Street and Walter and later Stanley Thompson in the years around the First World War and in the 1920s and 1930s the names of William Dodgson and Edward Johnson appear.

Drapers. Listed as Drapers from the early 1900s are William Crossman and Mrs. Martha Allan. Thomas Bell who was trading in the years leading up to 1939 was based in Quebec Street next to Aynsleys.

Tailors As well as Mr. Burdon and Mr. Buxton mentioned earlier there were circa 1890 William John Buckton, circa 1894-circa 1897) Thomas Johnson, circa 1890 John Thomas and circa 1914 Atkins and Watson.

Milliners Two names connected with millinery were Mrs Bertha Elliott around 1910 and in the late 1920s George Dawson.

Painters and Decorators George Caley and Sons were offering a service in the mid 1920s, as was Robert Bowden who was still in business shortly before the 1939-1945 war.

Hardware   In the 1920s there was a dealer, George Hammel in Front Street.

Hairdressers. By 1906 William Williamson had opened a shop as a hairdresser and on the outbreak of the First World War there was Thomas Williamson. From the 1920s through to the 1930s Edwin North and later Frederick George North had businesses in Front Street as did John R. Williamson who worked in a hut next to the Gypsy Queen garage.   Before the Second World War Walter Thompson occupied premises in Quebec Street.   After the war the familiar red and white pole was seen outside the shop run by Tom Elgey.
In the late 1930s we come across ladies hairdressers. Miss Clara Forster and Connie Keenlyside. The latter had opened a shop in Quebec Street and another lady associated with hairdressing was Lena North. Jean Richardson had a business for some time on premises near the Kingsway Nursing Home that at one time had been a cobbler's shop. In the early 1960s 'Denise' was at 3 Front Street   Women in the village were known to do their own hairdressing at home. Curling tongs heated by a coal fire were common. After the Second World War the Toni Home Perm became popular and 'The Marcello Wave' was fashionable.

Joiners   From the end of the 1890s through to the 1920s William Foster was a joiner in the village.

Banks   By 1906 North East Banking Co. Ltd had opened for business in Langley Park on a Tuesday and Saturday morning.   By 1925 The Bank of Liverpool and Martins Ltd (later Martins Bank Ltd.) were in the village for two mornings a week. Just before the Second World War Lloyds Bank and Martins were offering customers a service on Monday Wednesday and Friday mornings.   G. H. Grimwood was supervising business for Lloyds Bank in April 1957. He came from the Durham branch and attended on Tuesday and Fridays for two hours each morning. Both firms had offices in Front Street. The site of Lloyds Bank is now a funeral directors and Martins is now part of a butcher's shop.

'The Ice Cream Shop'. By the 1920s and 1930s Pasquale Tomassi was an ice cream vendor in Front Street. He died in Southend in January 1958 and the funeral service was held at St. Godric's Church in Durham. In 1938 Andrew Masserilli is described as a confectioner and following in the ice cream shop were Messrs. Petrie and Citrone.

Boots and Shoes.   For Boot and Shoe repairs or to buy these items the customer could go to Nicholas Pitt Patterson (circa 1890 – 1897), Robert Cousin around the time of the outbreak of World War 1, Thomas Goundry in the early 1920s, John Harrison in the 1920s and 1930s and John Johnson who was at 16, Quebec Street. George Cox was also a boot-maker in 1925. At one time the Co-op had a boot repairing shop and Mr. Bowes moved into No. 16 Quebec Street having started in a house in South View.

Builders. John Robinson was a builder and leading up to the First World War John Johnson was a builder. Edward Rutter, who in earlier years was described as a blacksmith, and Sons of Front Street were also well known in the village as builders and along came Edmund, later Edward, Shorten who were also based in Front Street. Robert Rutter was the last of the Rutter family and he died at the age of 89 in February 1959.

Prior to the 1914 – 1918 war **William Aynsley Ltd**. had opened a grocer's shop in a building that had been designed as an hotel in the early days of Langley Park life. The corner of Quebec Street opposite the War Memorial was to become known to villagers as Aynsley's Corner. **Glendinnings** had a high-class shop at 16 Quebec Street and Morland's located where **Hunters Wallpaper Stores Ltd/Billy Bell** was to open a shop was popular for the sale of Carrick's cakes. In January 1957 **Mr. T. Carpenter,** who lived in May Terrace at the time, died aged 81. Carpenter's had a greengrocery business in Quebec Street. Later **Jonty Smith** had the shop and **Halls** were well known occupiers of the premises. A charity shop is now situated in the building. In March 1934 **Annie Lizzie James** died at Holly House aged 69. For 35 years she had a bakery and confectionery business in Langley Park. Very involved in the British Women's Temperance Association and The Women's Own at the Baptist Chapel, she and her husband had three sons and two daughters who all survived her.

Arthur William Dobbin established a General Dealers business at No. 3 Quebec Street in 1939. He had at first been an apprentice butcher with Mr. Hunter in Front Street and had taken over that business. Mr. Dobbin died in April 1948 aged 63. Ruth Dobbin who lived in Langley Park for some 63 years ran the business until October 1951 when she retired and moved to Station Road, Ushaw Moor. She had been a shopkeeper for 20 years. Later **Crosby**'s ran the shop that had become known to customers as 'the off license'. Mrs. D. Crosby died in the Spring of 1961, eight months after she left the shop. **Jack Munsey** and others occupied the shop and today trades under the name of **Langley Park Village Shop.**

On Sunday 5th June 1938 there was a fire at Prospect Villa. Mr. and Mrs. Richard Alfred Twidal lived above **a bakers and confectioner's shop** owned by Mr. Twidal's sister. Using knotted sheets Mr. Twidal lowered his wife to the ground before escaping himself. The Crook Fire and Rescue Service were quickly on the scene but there was damage to furniture, the staircase and the shop amounting to about £100.

Sally Dickinson. In September 1942 Sally Dickinson married Dick Richardson of Quebec and she took over the running of a general dealer's shop that had been in the hands of her mother. The little shop at the corner of Laurel Terrace was generally known by Mrs. Richardson's maiden name and was popular with residents in the locality both in war-time and in the years of peace that followed. With her cheery personality she ran the business for many years. It was one of the last surviving 'corner shops' and although it was eventually taken over by new proprietors the business soon disappeared from the commercial world. Mrs. Richardson retired to live in Palm Street and eventually ended her days in a bungalow in Browney Court.

Living in Yew Terrace **Mrs. Stephenson** ran a small tuck shop. Located next to the infants school she used to sell sweets to the children at playtime through the railings that surrounded the school. **Clementina Burrell** ran a General Dealer's shop at the cricket field end of Quebec Street for 23 years. She died in May 1979 aged 82 and had lived in the village for 73 years.

In February 1960 **Mrs. Twidal** died aged 81 after a long illness. Known as 'The Lady Who Kept The Little Sweet Shop', situated opposite the Co-op Stores, in Front Street she had lived there for 54 years and had been unable to walk for 50 of those years.

The increasing popularity of the radio (or wireless!) and the gramophone enabled **David Jelley** to start a business and by the mid 1930s he was a dealer in both and also a wireless engineer.

The demand for television at the start of the 1950s saw **Jack Groves** dealing in Television and Radio. Registered with the Electrical and Radio Dealers he was also involved in haulage work in the village.

Dentists. In the mid 1920s H. Urwin L.D.S Glas. and Frederick Theodore Haycroft visited Langley Park and during the 1930s Messrs. Curry and Purdie, dentists came to the village on a Wednesday afternoon and held a surgery in the front room of No 4 Front Street, Langley Park. By the 1950s Mr. Searle of Durham was offering a similar service in a house in Quebec Street. Mr. Searle was later to marry Edith Bellinger a Schools Inspector and well known in Langley Park as an active member of the Women's Labour Party. Her sister was Edna Hill.

Haulage. At the beginning of the twentieth century **Matthew Simpson** was a cartman and in the 1920s and 1930s **Robert Randell** was in the same business and in the mid 1930s there was a haulage contractor **George Flynn**. Before the Second World War Samuel Groves, father of Jack, who lived in May Terrace was described as a cartage contractor. Samuel died circa. 1949. Later there was **Jack Groves** and at one time cattle carriers were **The Langley Park Carrying Company. Jack Munsey** was also involved in haulage work. One of the contracts he had was, in the days of earthen closets, to go round the houses emptying the 'middens'.

Smiths. Plying these necessary trades in the early part of the twentieth century were Alfred Munsey, Herbert James Brown and Mrs. Frances Munsey.

Millers (water and steam). It seems that from around 1873 there was milling in the village. In the 1890s William Robert Wiggen was a miller at Wallnook. On his father's death in October 1876 he had taken over the business. W. R. Wiggen was also author of 'Esh Leaves' (1914) and he died in 1918. By 1902 Robert Dodds. Later Dodds and Son are named.

<u>Joplings</u> were also well known until after the Second World War for their shop in Quebec Street that offered a delivery service to surrounding villages.

<u>**Door-to-Door** Services.</u> There were innumerable door-to-door trades people. Rington's Tea continues to provide a service delivering tea etc that the firm has done for many years. There was Wood and Watsons for mineral waters and Fentiman's who supplied ginger beer in returnable stone jars. It was not unusual to see a French onion man on the streets in the area and an important home caller was the yeast man. Essential for the housewife who, on a Friday, was confined to the kitchen baking including the weekly supply of bread.

The Milkman. Always an early morning caller. In earlier times the customer went out to meet the supplier with an empty jug and this was filled using a ladle and taking milk from a churn on the back of a wagon (probably a horse drawn vehicle). In bad winter weather the streets were often impassable due to snow and it was known for people to have to walk up the bank to Hill Top to collect a supply of milk from Wallace's farm. Farmers Moralee, Hedley and Graham also delivered milk. Later The Co-op offered a delivery service and other local businessmen have followed.

At the beginning of 1951 Mrs. S.E. Pearson having reached the age of 70 retired. She had been in business for many years at New Brancepeth and Langley Park. Her fish shop at 36, Front Street was taken over by Mr. George Thompson.

Having been in business at 3, Quebec Street, Langley Park, Ruth Dobbin retired in October 1951 and moved to Station Road, Ushaw Moor. She had lived in Langley Park for 63 years and had been involved in shop keeping for 20 years.

Ronald Newton of Kaysburn died in March 1968 at the age of 59. He owned Kaysburn Garage which had been established by his father in 1922 A member of the Vintage Motor Cycle Club he was also, for five years, Honorary Secretary of the Langley Park Farmers and Tradesmen's Association. He once sold a vintage car for £65 which, at the time of his death, as in an American museum and valued at over £3,000.

Over the years there were many tradesmen offering their services to the local community. Some in business premises and some operating from the front room of a house. A random selection shows the following people vending their wares with approximate dates.
In November 1923 Thomas Cumberledge (grocer) of Catchgate bought 11-12 Quebec Street for £730 and continued in business in the village for some years. In 1934 Misses J. and H. Hunter (bakers, confectioners and tobacconists) are shown.
1938 Thomas Burdon and Robert Graham of Quebec Street and John Burrell.
Also W. Forster, Grocer, Quebec Street, Mrs. Ethel Gerry, Jopling and Hepburn. Metcalfe's Stores and Wilkinson Hand (confectioner).

In earlier days there was William Williamson, General Dealer, William Dodgson (shopkeeper), Mrs Margaret Halkier (confectioner), Robert Tatters and Sons (Grocers), Mrs. Elizabeth Cowley (shopkeeper), Dimambro and Son (confectioners around 1914), Edward Hedley (grocer) and Mrs. Elizabeth Dick at 3 Front Street. In 1890 Stewart A. McIntyre is described as a Surgeon's Assistant.

What would mid twentieth century villagers have thought of betting shops, sun tanning, tattooing, carpet fitting, computer merchandise, Prime Pizzas, Chinese meals or hearing aid specialists. All are now to be seen in Langley Park.

An Industrial Estate has quietly taken the place of the mighty colliery. Here among business concerns is a pet crematorium and a recent attraction is Diggerland where the contractor's J.C.B. has been transformed into an entertainment for budding operators. This stands near where at one time Compass Caravans had a factory. Diggerland offers buckets of fun and is one of three locations in the country. The other two being at Strood in Kent and at Cullompton, Devon.

Football   LANGLEY PARK - LANGLEY PARK VILLA

Langley Park at the end of the 1919 – 1920 football season won the Durham Central League championship and many old supporters considered the team to be one of the best in their class of football. This season they had also won the Durham County Aged Miners Cup and the Durham County Amateur Cup. Playing the final on the old Garden House Ground at Durham they defeated Trimdon to win the Durham Hospital Cup for the first time. Despite poor weather 2000 spectators paid over £100 to watch the game. The side also reached the last eight of the F.A. Amateur Cup but were beaten by Bromley. At that time C. Shaw was secretary. In 1920 –1921 the club joined the Northern League and in the following seasons were playing teams such as Scarborough, Stockton, Redcar and Bishop Auckland.

By March 1926 Langley Park were experiencing financial difficulties and two years later the team was disbanded. The team re-emerged as Langley Park Villa (see note) during the 1929-1930 season with C. Shaw as Secretary and J. Ritchie as Chairman.
At the end of the 1933 - 1934 season Villa had beaten Quarrington Hill at Holiday Park, Durham to win the Durham Hospital Cup. In April 1934 the Villa side was J. Mordue (captain), Gleghorn, Jackson, Walters, Robertson, Bragg, Buddle, Carroll, Harker, Morris and Holden. The team were undefeated from 27 November 1933 until the end of the season and that season also carried off the Durham Central League Championship, the Brandon Aged Miners Cup, the Deerness Aged Miners Cup and the Durham Central League Cup.

Players in the 1934 – 1935 season included Liddle, Urwin, Walters, Davidson, Buddle, Bragg, Crowe, Pinkney, Mordue, Morris, Holden, Wilson and Jackson. The team finished fourth in the Central League Championship and reached the semi-final of the Durham Hospital Cup and the Deerness Aged Miners Cup. Mordue scored 46 goals during the season including nine in one match.

The side were very clear winners of the Central League at the end of the 1935-1936 season. The league itself was celebrating its 30th season and by January 1936 Langley Park was celebrating the fact that it was unbeaten in 25 league and cup games. In the last month or so of the season the success led the Villa having to play 23 games. They won the League Cup and the Sacriston Aged Miners Cup. For a tie in the Durham Challenge Cup 600 supporters travelled by special train to Jarrow. The list of players included Raybole, Walters, Jones, James, Pinkney, the brothers Raymond and Norman Buddle, Bragg, Dickenson, Mordue, Dunn, Plank, Holden, Scott, Walton, Steele, Jones and Brogan. Also Lee, Hanson, Russell, King, Banks, Turnbull and Brynne.

> *NOTE; In the early 1920s Langley Park Reserves are shown in League Tables for the Deerness and District League and from 1922-23 in the Central League Division One. The last mention of them appears to be in the 1933-1934 season.*
> A team called Langley Park Villa is shown in Division Two of the Central League from around the 1925-26 season and from 1928-1929 in the Durham and District League until 1932-1933 when they are back in the Central League.

In February 1936 Pinkney left the village having obtained a job in Bury St. Edmunds. Raymond Buddle, then 18, had been approached by Leeds United, Huddersfield and Northampton but he had not taken up the offer for trials. Manchester United had also shown an interest.

Langley Park A.F.C. circa 1914-15 with Durham Amateur Cup and Deerness Aged Miners Cup. Centre Iin uniform H. Clark who was later killed in action. See War Memorial and back First player J. Grafton (of Fish and Chip shop) see 54) and third from right G. Hemsley (see 65 cricket)

At the A.G.M. it was reported that Villa had played 63 games, won 48, lost 8 and drawn 6. There were 232 goals for and 23 against. J. Ritchie was chairman, T. Trotter secretary and J. W. Wadge treasurer.

A good start was made to the 1936-1937 season, a season that included among the players, Raybole, Jones, Walters, Dunn, Brayan, Bragg, Wilkinson, Hoult, Evans, King, Lee, Pearson, Turnbull, Gleghorn, Dailey, Lumley, Turnbull and Suddes. In March 1937 Pinkney was on the team list.

At the end of the 1937-1938 season Langley Park Villa were 5th in the league and in May 1938 lost to Shildon in the Crook Nursing Cup semi-final. They had reached the last qualifying round of the Durham Challenge Cup but lost 3 – 0 to Stanley United. On the field this year were Gleghorn, Wilson, Scott, N. Buddle, Peveller, Alderson, Morris, Barlow, Fisher, Holden, Walters, Evans Sillett. Bragg. Hubber, Gowland, Jackson and Johnson.

In January 1939 Villa lost to Tow Law in a Crook Nursing Cup tie by a goal scored five minutes from time. Nearing the end of the season they were second in the league.

In August 1939 Langley Park Villa were continuing in the Durham Central League with a semi-pro team. Ex Hull City and Ashington inside right or centre forward John George Hancock joined the side. Two players left. Goalkeeper John Elliott who lived at Consett was on a month's trial at Charlton Athletic and Matt Alexander left half from Leadgate was to have a trial at Southampton. In September, 1939 Norman Buddle, who had played for Langley Park Villa for seven seasons and was captain of the side married Verna Birbeck whose mother was secretary of the Langley Park branch of the Women's Section of the British Legion. Norman, in earlier days, had also played football for Shildon, Eden C.W. and Crookhall C.W.

In 1942 Langley Park Juniors were playing their first season in the Auckland Junior League and at the end of the season were heading the league and in the 1942 – 1943 season while Langley Park were having only moderate success in the Durham and District League.

FOOTBALL FOCUS

LANGLEY PARK C.W. 1960

Left: Back Row: G. Brown (capt), D. Lumsden, L. Towers, J. Morton, J. Wilson, J. Whitfield. Front Row: G. Tobin, S. Myers, E. Kirby, J. Mordue E. Peart.
Below Left: With ladies -including Mrs. Lumsden, Mrs. Aberdeen, Mrs. Morton, Mrs. Whitfield, Mrs. Myers, Mrs. Guildford and Mrs. Hardy. Below: With officials incl (seated H. S. Guildford and J. Ritchie. Standing A. Hardy (Treasurer) and committee members J. Aberdeen and W. Louth.

In season 1958-1959 Langley Park C.W. having won the Wearside League Championship were invited by Durham Football Association to enter the Durham Benevolent Bowl, previously an exclusive Northern League Competition. The village team won 4 – 3 in the final. How dare they!! Langley Park were never again invited to compete in this competiton

Langley Park Juniors 1948-1949. Team includes Bobby and Ronnie Robson

Langley Park Coke Works team 1953: Back left E. Bunn and back right C. Birbeck.

Football

LANGLEY PARK UNITED - LANGLEY PARK C.W.

In the 1943/1944 season Langley Park United was one of ten teams playing in the Durham and District League and during the autumn months had a 100% record in the league. Finnigan and Renwick were the scorers in a 2 – 1 win against Gilesgate Labour Party but later lost to Waterhouses Home Guard and again to Burnhope Home Guard. Ritchie was a promising young goalkeeper and Holden, Tench and McDonald were also in the side.

In November 1944 with a strong wind blowing Langley Park scored a victory over Cornsay United in a Durham and District League Challenge Cup. Players were Ritchie, C. Johnson, Rutter, F. Johnson, Jackson Aberdeen, Finnegan, Firth, Mulholland, who came from the Leadgate area, Davidson and Renwick. Mid November saw a 5 – 1 win playing Kimblesworth Youth Club in Brandon Aged Miners Cup, goal scorers were Wilson (2) Renwick (2) and Jackson.

By January 1946 United were heading the Durham and District League but were beaten 5 – 1 in round 2 of the Durham Challenge Cup. Hartlepool United Reserves being the winners. In the village team were Gregory, Morgan, Bonney, Gallagher and Renwick. Later in the month the team lost 3 – 1 against Bowburn in the Durham and District League Cup. In March 1946 T. Nicholson was best man at a wedding in the village but dashed away to change into football kit and score two goals for United before returning to join in the wedding celebrations. At the end of March 1946 Langley Park beat Chester Moor 7 – 4 in a match (Agar 3, Catton, Nicholson, Cave and Davidson being the scorers. In the Brandon Aged Miners Cup there was a 3 –0 win over Bearpark Welfare. Renwick scoring all three goals.

Langley Park United won their first cup of the season, Sacriston Aged Miners Cup, beating Langley Park St. Josephs 3- 2 before one of the best gates of the season. C. Shaw of Edmondsley, secretary of the competition presented the cup.

At the end of the 1945/1946 season Langley Park United had won the Durham and District League, Sacriston Aged Miners Cup and reached the final of the Brandon Aged Miners Cup. It was announced that for the 1946/1947 season they would be joining the Durham Central League being one of 16 teams. Dr. R. Rutherford was elected president of the Club, J. Ritchie Chairman, R.T. Gauden Secretary J. Burnell treasurer and H. Guildford assistant secretary. The committee was D. Renwick, W. Gleghorn, H Carr, J. Gregory, T. Richardson, N. Wiseman, H Guildford and C. Firbank. At a "do" in the Parochial Hall Dr. Rutherford presented Savings Certificates to the players.

1946 – 1947 season. In September United lost to Evenwood by two clear goals in a preliminary round of the F.A. Cup. The following month the team included, Barker, J. Fletcher, McHugh, Huddle, Wilson, Embleton, Thorburn, F. Fletcher, Agar, Holden, Simons, T. Fletcher, J. Bonney, Gregory, Foreman and Cave. There was a 9 – 1 victory in a Sacriston Aged Miners Cup match with Sigmund Pumps Sports Club, Gateshead. before meeting Langley Park St. Josephs in the Durham Hospitals Cup and beating Bearpark 4 – 2 in another game. Just before Christmas United drew with Ferryhill Athletic in the Durham County Challenge Cup but were later beaten 3 – 2.

For years the team had been unable to attract really useful players but in April they won the Durham Central League Cup defeating Cornsay United 5 – 2. (Finch 2) McHugh, Agar, Hurst. Agar had been a North West Durham player and Simpson also in the side had been a partner with Wheatman at Horden. Gregory had played for Willington and Brandon Colliery and Fletcher left back at Easington. In April 1947 United were in the semi final of the Durham Central League Cup Agar scoring all three goals in the 3 – 1 win over Craghead. At the end of the season they defeated Cornsay 4 – 1.

At the Annual General Meeting in July 1947 Dr. R. Rutherford was to continue as President, R. Gauden chairman, T. Bailey succeeded J. Burrell as treasurer, H. Guildford, assistant treasurer. In the next season they were to play in the Durham Central League, Sacriston and Kimblesworth Aged Miners Cup, Brandon Hospital Cup, Durham Hospital Cup and the League Cup. From 1947 Langley Park C.W. became the name of the team.

The first round of the Brandon Aged Miners Cup Langley Park played Whitworth Park Rangers. The team this season was showing as players F. Steel, F. Fletcher, T. Renwick, H. Gregory, D. McHugh, Hird, Dixon, T. Nicholson (captain) G. McDonald, E. McDonald, Mayne, T. Rutter, W. Rutter, W. Agar, F. Agar, Snowball and Carr.

1948 started with an 8 - 4 win over New Brancepeth and later the local side beat Winterton Hospital 4 – 3 in the sixth round of the Durham Amateur Cup but lost 1 – 0 to New Brancepeth in the next round. In the third round of the Sacriston Aged Miners Cup Langley Park C.W. beat Blackhouse. Mackays Sports Club lost 3 – 1 (three goals for Nicholson) in another fixture.

Bill Agar was the only member of the team who was not a miner. He played for Gateshead during the war. In 1944 –1945 season Ted McDonald had been an amateur with Bolton Wanderers. His brother George, a boxer for the N.C.B., is outside left. At this time the chairman of the Supporters Club was W. Rose with A. Preston, Secretary and J. Burrell treasurer. There were 77 members.

In August 1948 practice was under way for the new season. In an early game Steel, Renwick, McPherson, Wilson, Gibbons, E. McDonald, Agar, Snowball, Davison, Ovation, Finch and Calland are named. In September Langley Park were knocked out of the F. A. Cup beaten in a preliminary round by Eppleton and at the end of the month the team was continuing to disappoint and to come there was an 8 – 2 loss to Quarrington Hill. In addition to players named above those playing were Stewart, Young, Laidler, Joe Wilson, centre half, G. McDonald, Dyson, Carr, Huddle, Raynor, Preston and Randle. After another defeat at the hands of Ushaw Moor the poor displays led to new signings. Into the team came Storey, Kilkenny, Cave. Centre forward Snowball signed for South Shields and also added to the squad were Whaley, Shakarian, Allen, R.J. Whaley, Lowther, Cobbin and Smith.

The 1948 – 1949 season saw in the side players Storey, Renwick, Oyston, Stewart, Whaley, Agar, Wilson, Whaley, Snowball, Langton, Cave, Smith and Shakarian. They lost to Craghead (5 – 1) drew with Bank Head and beat Witton Wanderers 4 – 0 (Smith 3, Shakarian) in a replayed Sacriston Cup. The side won the Sacriston Aged Miners Cup. Indeed in the immediate post-war years Langley Park won this cup three times in four years.

Into the 1949 – 1950 season Langley Park C.W. were fielding H. Elliott, J. Lumley, J. Simpson, R. Whaley, H. Gregory, H. Wilson, R. Wilkinson, Emmerson, T. Nicholson, W. Agar, J. Kilkenny, G. Sanderson, J. Robson, G. McDonald, Renwick, Trotter, Sherwood, Patterson, Ainsley, McEleavey, Forster, Hunt, G. Sanderson and E. Whaley. Langley Park C.W. continued playing in the Durham Central League. By October the village side had a new leader Hope who scored on his debut and Nicholson and Patterson were in good form. However the attendance at matches was poor and the team were appealing for support. At the end of the year there was a win against Craghead thanks to a penalty scored by Tommy Wilkinson. Jackson was a new signing and Albert Calland was catching the eye of scouts. Around this time Dr. Rutherford was President with F. Fletcher Chairman, H. Collinson Secretary/Trainer and G. Yates Treasurer.

In January 1950 the team had played 18 games in the league, won 12, lost 3 and drawn 3. Calland, Nicholson and McEleavey were scorers in a 3 – 2 win over Brandon and in the semi final of the Durham Amateur Cup beat Bearpark 2 – 1. By April they were third in the league, six points behind the first and second teams who had 42 points each.

The start of the 1950/1951 season there was a league game with Wolsingham, Langley Park scored 3 (Calland, Toward, Moss) but Wolsingham netted 4. This was played after a Durham Amateur Cup Final replay with Hamsterley at Annfield Plain. This had been held over from the previous season as two games had ended in draws. In August 1950 the C.W. team included Sherwood, Whaley, Rutter, Whaley Gregory, Jackson, Wilson, Patterson, Nicholson, Renwick, Aynsley and McEleavey.

As the season progressed there was a 3 – 3 draw with Cornsay. For the village side Calland scored 2 and McDonald 1. Calland had been in junior football the previous season. His brother was a professional at Torquay. Versus Deaf Hill in a Durham Central League Cup Langley Park had been leading by 5 goals to 2 but at full time the score was 5-5. The final result, after extra time, was 9 – 5. Away to Chilton Langley Park had a 4 – 2 victory (Morrow 2, Calland and Reid) but later lost to Cockfield 1-0. Support for the team at this time was described as disappointing. In December there was a game with Hedley Hill S.C. in the first round of the Ushaw Moor Aged Miners Cup and Langley Park were half way up the Durham Central League table. At the end of the year team members included, Hill, Renwick, Rutter, Whaley, Gregory, Wilkinson, Toward, McDonald, Ofield, Reid, Calland and Gilligan. In February 1951 Hope, Day and Pope were among the players.

In April 1951 the village side played Wheatley Hill in the final of the Durham Hospital Cup at Spennymoor. At the end of the season Langley Park had won the Sacriston Aged Miners Cup and were runners-up in the Durham Central League.

And so into the 1951-52 season. Defeated by Wolsingham 5 –3 (Walton, Rice, Millar) Langley Park then won against Cornsay 2- 0 and Langley Park Hotspurs 2 –1 (Millar and then Nicholson who scored a disputed penalty). In October 1951 there was a 1 – 1 draw with Bishop Auckland Reserves and a 4 – 2 defeat in a game with Cornsay Albion although the score did not reflect the match. Players this season were Hill (goal) Harrison, Weston, Walton, Curry, Millar, Turnbull, Hall, Robinson, Nicholson, Grayson, Randle, McEleavey. In November Langley Park beat Chilton 4 – 2 but by the end of the year they had not many wins to their credit but there was a good standard of play.

In October 1952 Langley Park recorded their first win of the season and before Christmas there was a goalless draw with Wolsingham and a 3 – 3 draw with Brandon C.W. The players: Westgarth, Hunt, Rutter, Whaley, R. Gregory, Bowater, Anderson, Nicholson, Kirby, Whaley, E. Cooke, Wilson, Hope, Hall. In February 1953 the village side beat Deaf Hill in a gale. Robson who had been in the Langley Park side before joining the forces was now back in the side. There had been a 3 – 0 win against Thornley St. Godrics and a defeat 6 –2 to Shildon Reserves in the first round of the Durham Amateur Cup. Earlier in the season Shildon Reserves had been beaten 9 – 2 and gained the village team the Durham County Press Football for most meritous performance of the year.

Continuing in the Durham Central League, Langley Park managed to lose the first seven games of the 1953 – 1954 season. In December players named include Wood, Moran, Weston, Bob Whaley, Wilson, Lumley, Anderson, Armstrong, Eric (brother of Bob) Whaley, Kirby, Holden, Williams, Wilson and Weston. Also Carr, Wilkinson and Kirby. Early in 1954 there was a 5 – 2 win over Spennymoor and they went into their first cup final of the season with a 4 – 1 win over Lumley Rovers (Armstrong, E. Whaley 2 and Anderson being the scorers).

At the end of the season Langley Park C.W. had won three trophies. The Sacriston Aged Miners Cup having beaten Sacriston in a replay of the Durham City A.F.C. Coronation Shield beating Mackays S.C. In the final of the Chester-le-Street Aged Miners Cup with twenty minutes to go Langley Park were losing 2 – 0 but managed to turn the tables and won 4 – 2.

Early in the 1954 – 1955 season the team included Wood, Hardy, Harrison, Weston, R. Whaley, Wilkinson, Lumley, J. Anderson, B. Lumley, Armstrong, E. Whaley, Draffin, Rees Holden and Ward. Results included a 3 – 3 draw with Craghead and a double victory against Sacriston. In January 1955 the average age of the team was 21 and included, Blythe, Harrison, Weston, Kirby, Wilkinson, Reed. Anderson, Armstrong, Lumley H, Lumley J, Robinson Edwards and Holden. A series of draws in February and March and a win against Thornley managed to put them in the running for the championship.

In 1955 Langley Park C.W. joined the Wearside League. Two of the biggest league gates for many years brought in the 1955–56 season. Playing in the side were Blythe, Harrison, Nattrass, Kirby, Gregory, Reed, Marshall, Smithson, Rice, J. Robson and B. Robson. In November they beat Eppleton in a replay of Sunderland Shipowners Cup and in a game with Wingate Langley Park were ahead 3 – 1 at the interval but Wingate ran up seven goals without reply. Over the Christmas period they managed only one point from two matches, losing to Silksworth and drawing with Ushaw Moor.

Further draws with Eppleton and again with Ushaw Moor in January 1956. Jefferson on leave from the forces was in the side. Axwell Park ended any hope of progressing in the Durham Amateur Cup winning 7 – 5.

Playing in an inch of snow in February Langley Park won 3 – 1 in a game with Boldon. Blythe, Harrison, Barker, Stoker, Nattrass, Reed, Marshall, Kirby, Robson, Lumley Malone, Milligan, Ertwhistle were in the side at this time.

Too many changes in the team was quoted as a reason the team was losing at the start of the 1956 – 1957 season and by October named in the side are Turnbull, Tooke, Renwick, Bell, Donnelly, Blackburn, Turnbull, Harland, Hodgson, Dimambro and Lumsden. There was a fixture with Barnard Castle in the League Challenge Cup Late in 1956 Barry Bell played his last game for the club.

From September – November 1957 players in the Langley Park side included Plummer, Franklin Hodgson, E.R. Lambert, Rattray, Turner, Turnbull, Lumsdon, Stott, Chapman, Gish, Dimambro, Small, Rice, Ward, Mordue and Mountain who had previous experience with Willington and Easington. Eric Franklin spent five weeks in hospital and late in the year Alf Kirby on leave from the forces was a spectator giving vocal support.

In April 1958 in the N.C.B. Carbonisation Cup Final at Belle View, Consett Langley Park eventually lost 4 – 2 against Derwenthaugh in a replay. The first game had ended in a draw and there was a dispute over whether extra time should have been played. At this time seven of the Langley Park players had previously played in the Northern League and included George Brown who was ex Willington and Durham. In October 1958 Gallagher, D. Brown, Hoggart and Donnelly are named. In December there was an 11 – 6 win for Langley versus Chilton. At the end of the season Langley Park had won the Wearside League Championship, Mordue had scored 46 goals, John Tobin 21 and Eric Peart 20.

The spring of 1959 saw in the side Towers, Lumsden, Wilson, Brown, Bell, Dimambro, Mountain, Myers, Tobin, Mordue and Peart. The Sacriston Aged Miners Cup and the Monkwearmouth Cup came their way. Runners up in the League the Langley Park players set out for a tour of Belgium in the summer of 1959.

There was a shaky start to the 1959 - 1960 season but games were soon being won. On the field were Towers, Lumsden, Wilson, Morton, John Whitfield, Davison, Myers, K. Wilson, Mordue, O'Connor, Peart, Petrie, Crabtree, Goodridge, David Elgey, Tobin, Harrison, Mountain. Peart, Kirby, G. Brown (captain) and T. Brown. Until February 1960 they were top in the Wearside League eventually ending the season as runners-up. The side had won The Sacriston Aged Miners Cup and The Monkwearmouth Cup. Don Lumsden and Steve Myers received County recognition and Jack Mordue was again top scorer for the team with 42 goals. The previous season he had scored 46 goals. The President of Langley Park C. W. was Dr. R. Rutherford, The Secretary H. S. Guildford (first appointed 1955) and The Treasurer was A. Hardy. Team captain George Brown was highly praised. After 40 years in local football J. K. Ritchie announced his retirement from active participation in the club's affairs. Later the team won a delayed 1958-1959 fixture with Willington by four goals to three giving them the Durham Benevolent Bowl.

The list of players during the 1960 – 1961 season included six under nineteen years of age. That list included, Towers, Lumsden, Wilson, Brown, Morton, Whitfield, Tobin, Myers, Kirby, Mordue, Peart, Robinson, Mason, Berryman, Oughton, Juniper, Sheekey, Quinn. Davies, Ross, Bolam, Redfern, R.V. Reddy. Crabtree, Ramton, Thompson, Pratt and Holden.

An early win over South Shields Reserves started the 1961 – 1962 season when players seen on the field included, Burdess, Lumsden, Berryman, Brankston, Brown, Morton, Whitfield, Pratt, Oughton, Readman, Kirby, Mordue, Billy Quinn, Croft, Mason, Juniper, and Laverick. After 290 mintues play Langley Park defeated Eppleton in the semi-final of the Sunderland Shipowners Cup but lost to Ryhope 1 –0 in the final.

Players in the C.W. side during the 1963-1964 season included Ramsey, D. Lumsden, G. Austin, Stewart, Myers, Brown, Oughton, Smith, J. Mordue, Smith, Turner, C. Morton, A. Bonney, Gray, Dunn, E. Atkinson, Liddle, Nicholson, and Donnelly. In January 1964 the side was unbeaten and the following month scored a 13 – 1 win over Eppleton in the Wearside League. However, they lost in the finals of the Shipowners Cup and the Monkwearmouth Cup. At the end of the season George Neal was top scorer with 37 goals including seven in one game all 'headers'.

Ex Hotspurs players Jack Ward, Alan Gregory and Bill Lockey were in the C.W. side for the 1964-1965 season.

Around this time support for the game faded and when only four people turned up for the Annual General Meeting it was decided to wind up the club.

In the autumn of 1963 William Louth was presented with a writing desk set mounted with the figure of a footballer for services to Langley Park football teams over 40 years. He had been referee, linesman and trainer and in 1962 – 1963 was Vice Chairman of Langley Park C.W.

In January 1967 Mr. J. Ritchie had devoted more than 50 years of his life to football. He formed and ran many leagues and charity cups and was very popular throughout the county. At this date he was Chairman of the Langley Park Aged Miners Cup Committee, President of Sacriston Aged Miners Cup, and on the Durham Hospital Cup and the Durham Central League Committees. He also held the post of Vice-Chairman of Pelton Juniors.

57

LANGLEY PARK ST. JOSEPHS

In March 1946 Langley Park St. Josephs were playing in the Durham and District League. They had reached the semi-final of the Sacriston Aged Miners Cup defeating Deaf Hill 5 – 3 (Coates 3, Rutter 2) and other members of the team were Steele, Glennon, R. Young, Johnson, Wilson, T. Young, Welsh, W. Rutter, Preston and T. Rutter. Before one of the best gates of the season a month later Langley Park United 3 – 2, beat them in the final. St. Joseph's scorers were Young and Coates.

During the season the players included Steele, Rutter, Young, Sherwood, Wilson, Laidler,

Starting the 1946 – 1947 season the team won two of their first four games in the Durham and District League and in October beat Ushaw Moor F.C. 5 – 4 in a Durham Challenge Cup match. In October they had a win in the Sacriston Aged Miners Cup and a month later faced Langley Park United in the Durham Hospitals Cup. Finnigan, Bland, Coates, Quinn, J. Cave, Rowntree, Johnson, Elliott, J. Bonney and Foreman were in the side. By January 1947 the team were struggling in the Durham and District League having gained only five points from nine games.

58/1

LANGLEY PARK HOTSPURS.

Coming into existence before Langley Park St. Josephs, Langley Park Hotspurs began playing friendly matches before embarking upon league football.

In September 1949 Langley Park Hotspurs scored a 4 - 3 victory over Chester Moor. Park scorers were Hunt 3 and Snowball. There were 4 penalties during the match and a visiting player was sent off. The team then played a came with Deaf Hill in the Durham Hospital Cup.

Playing in the Durham and District League they drew 2 - 2 with Durham St. Giles (Two goals by Snowball) and had a 4 - 0 win in a game with Gilesgate United. Before Christmas they had two wins in their fixtures with Witton Wanderers. Firstly 4 - 1 (Arthur Snowball 2, Philip Hall 2) and then 4 - 2 (Snowball 3 and Moss 1, his first goal of the season) For the Hotspurs Ralph Calland saved a penalty.

Players in the side during the spring of 1950 were Kirtley, Agar, Bunn, Calland, Gibbons, F. Hall, Thompson, Moss, P. Hall, Snowball and Richardson.

In December 1950 they drew 2 - 2 in a Sacriston Aged Miners cup tie and went on to win the replay 5 - 3 (Snowball 3, Hunter and Agar). Opponents were Shotley Bridge Hospital.

Hotspurs suffered a 2 - 1 defeat at the hands of Langley Park C.W. in October 1951.

Players in the side during the 1953 - 1954 season included Clark, Bunn, Maitland, Smith, Penny, Gregory, Hunt, Moss, Snowball, Hutton, Rose, C. Finch, Saville, Wilson, Preston, Finnigan, C. Welsh, Bunn, Renwick and Birbeck.

Familiar names feature in the 1954 - 1955 side along with others. Minnis, French, Trotter, Gregory, Penny, Parkin, Patterson, Welsh, Snowball, Emerson, Rose, Boyle, Hall, Sewell and Maitland.

Langley Park Hotspurs could only use the Welfare Ground when Langley Park C.W. were playing away. Up to the spring of 1957 they had only won one cup. The secretary of the club was N. Wiseman and the players were described as 'a team of local lads'. They paid all their own expenses and had few regular supporters. That support coming mainly from their wives. Hotspurs players in March 1957 were Fishwick, Cuthbert, Sinclair, L. Gray, Penny, Laidler, Foster, Maitland, Sewell, G. Gray, Ramsay. One disappointing result that season was a 4 - 1 defeat by South Moor in a Durham. Minor Cup-tie played at Cornsay.

At the end of the 1958 - 1959 season Langley Park Hotspurs were Durham and District League Champions.

In two of the opening games of the 1959 - 1960 season the side firstly beat Esh St.Michaels 9 - 1 (W. Calland 3, W. Canavan 2, B. Smart 2, T. Slater, J. Ward) and then had a 3 - 1 win playing Thorn's S.C. (Slater, Jones and an own goal). By the end of September, 1959 Hotspurs were third in the Durham and District League. They went on to win 4 - 3 against East Howle and at that time were fielding a team that included Turnbull, W. Cuthbert, Nattrass, E. Robson, R. Gregory, T. Welsh, Thompson, E. McDonald, F. Tulip, E. Suddes, J. Ward, Laidler, Atkinson, M. Tonner, Henderson and Canavan.

An October fixture saw Hotspurs defeat Allendale Rangers 2 - 0, Tonner netting both goals. Tonner and Suddes were the scorers when the team completed the double with East Howle. Soon afterwards Hotspurs were knocked out of the Durham Hospitals Cup. Beating Burhopefield 5 – 2 (Ward 3, Welsh, H. Willis) they were soon on top of the league having also scored six without reply in a game with Craghead Mechanics. Before Christmas they completed the double with another win playing Allendale Rangers. This time the score was 5 - 4. (Tonner 2, Ward, T. Welsh and Suddes).

Holding their position as league leaders the Langley Park club completed another double, this time against Durham St. Giles and followed this with a 5 - 1 win over Langley Moor St. Patrick's. Tonner 2 and Ward scored the goals in a 3 - 1 victory over Burhopefield in the semi-final of the League Cup.

The last three months of the season led to an exciting race for the League

Championship and Langley Park Hotspurs were just 'pipped at the post' by Thorn's Social Club, Spennymoor who were playing their first season in the Durham and District League.

During the latter half of the season the Langley Park players included W. Cuthbert, F. Tulip, B. Robson, H. Gregory, B. Suddes, R. Willis, Tonner, T. Welsh, J. Ward, McDonald, Sewell, Laidler, Henderson, Gauden and Pearson.

In January, 1960 a group of women had got together and started a Hotspurs Supporters Club. Mrs. B. Hall was appointed Chairman with Mrs. J. Gregory secretary, and Mrs. J. Snowball treasurer. As a result of their fund raising efforts they were able to buy new strips for the team.

This was going to be Harry Gregory's last season as a player. He had played competitive football for 25 years from schoolboy to Northern League but was disappointed he was never in a team that won the Durham Minor Cup.

At the end of the 1959 - 1960 season Langley Park Hotspurs travelled to Scotland to play Lorwood Amateurs. They had won the Edinburgh District League in the 1958 - 1959 season.

In the Hotspur's side during the 1960 – 1961 Durham and District League season were Gauden, Tulip, G. Gray, Gregory, Welsh, Suddes, Willis, Donnelly, Tonner, Wadge, who was just out of the Forces, Morris, Sewell, Robson, Sinclair, J. Gray, Smithson and Laidler. By October 1960 they had achieved eleven wins but then lost 2 –1 to East Howle in the Durham Hospital Cup. At the end of the season they had won the League Challenge Cup and had held, by a large margin, the top of the league position for most of the season.

The 1961 – 1962 season saw 15 teams in the Durham and District League. New clubs competing during this period were Framwellgate Moor Workmen's Club, Brandon C.W. and Dunelm Club. Langley Park players were Gauden, R. Smith, Geoff Gray, T. Welsh, H. Gregory (then aged 41), B. Suddes, J. McGuffle, J. Ward, W. Donnelly, D. Slater, Smart, James, Coulson, Kilkenny and L. Gray. A most successful season saw the club take the Kimblesworrth and Sacriston Aged Miners Cup, Durham County Minor Cup, Durham Hospital Cup and the Durham and District League Challenge Cup. They were also Durham and District League Champions.

The Hotspurs were in the Central League for the 1963-1964 season and were hovering near the bottom of the league table. Some of the above players and T. Fishwick, Laidler, R. Clish and T. Sewell are named. The first season in the league was described as 'favourable'. After the 1963-64 season the team is not included in reports of Langley Park football games.

Clarence William Birbeck died in March 1968 aged 57. Interested in all sports he was well known as a Northern League football referee. He worked at various collieries in the area and for 35 years was a blacksmiths welder at Langley Park Colliery and Coke Works.

Football

LANGLEY PARK JUNIORS

In the decade following the Second World War there was a great deal of interest in junior football in Langley Park The village was supporting not only keen but talented players who were attracting scouts from a number of distinguished clubs.

In the 1948/1949 season those playing in the side were Gauden, Slater, Kilkenny, Lyons, Liddle, Jobling, R. Robson, Cook R.W. Robson, Johnson, Wellesby, Harrison, Farrie, Cassidy, Vickers and Shovels.

In December 1948 the game between Langley Park and Sacriston ended in a 2 – 2 draw. Sacriston becoming the first team that season to return home undefeated. In a hard fought and rousing match in the Lady Eden Cup played in January, 1949 Shildon Works Juniors beat the village side by 5 goals to 3. Playing in a league game in April 1949 Langley Park defeated Stanley Boys Club 6 – 4. Scorers for the winning team were Lyons (2) Liddle (2), Peart and Cook. A couple of weeks later on a windy day. Birtley St. Josephs lost by 5 goals to nil. Peart scored three in the first thirty minutes of play. A record crowd attended another match with Sacriston this time in the league. Scorers for the winning side were Peart (5), Robson (3) and Jobling. Langley Park Juniors had gone 15 games without defeat Peart had scored 15 goals in 8 games and in one of those games he had played in goal. He had also been chosen to play in a game for the league. A few days after the Sacriston meeting a total of £47 was taken for a match with Kimblesworth – a record.

Opposing goalkeepers were spending a lot of time collecting the ball from the back of the net during the 1949/1950 season. In the autumn of 1949 results included Langley Park 13 Kibblesworth 1, Langley Park 4 (Dale (3) Robson), Chester Moor 0. Langley Park 7 (Brankston 3, Kilkenny, Dale, Johnson, Robson) West Stanley 0. By October 45 goals had been scored with 7 against. Gate receipts were totalling £11. In the Langley Park Aged Miners Cup in November another win against N.W. Durham Boys Brigade this time by 9 goals to 1. (Bobby Robson 5, Brankston 2, Eltringham and Johnson) Those playing in the side at this time also included Finley, Slater, Welsh, Darwin, Renwick, Kilkenny and Moss.

Twelve goals were scored by Langley Park without reply in a County Junior Cup game with Hamsteels Choir Boys (Robson 5, Dale 4 and Moss 3) Richard Brankston who had scored 25 goals this season so far failed to add to his total. However over the Christmas period he netted 6 goals in an 11 – 2 win over Ouston. Other scorers being Robson 2, Moss 2 and Dale.

At the end of the year 1950 Langley Park Juniors were again showing an unbeaten record but in February 1951 they suffered their first defeat of the season going down 3 – 1 to Lumley Juniors but they were soon back in the goal scoring business with a 10 – 0 victory over Holmside (Boyle 5, Hill 4, Rose) and 11 – 0 against Billingham Synthonia (Hill 4, Boyle 2, Finnigan 2, Johnson, Brankston and Dale). In the Spring of 1951 the Langley Park team included Allen, Gregg, Glasgow, Cook, Renwick, Brankston, Dale, Boyle, Hill, Johnson and Mordue.

In May, at the end of the 1950/51 season Langley Park Juniors had had a record year. In one two week period they had played ten games and appeared in three finals Langley Park Aged Miners Cup, the League Challenge Cup at Murray Park, Stanley beating Lumley Juniors by 7 goals to 2 and the Hare and Pelton Association Cup. They had also won the league title. During the season 238 goals had been scored with 47 against and they had played 42 fixtures. Chief goal scorers were Hill 60, Boyle 4 and Johnston 44. Many prominent teams were anxious to sign Boyle, Dale, Johnson and Cook.

The start of the 1951/1952 season again began well. Langley Park Juniors scored 17 goals in the first two matches of the season.and in September the winning run continued 8 – 5 (v. Lumley Juniors), 5 – 0 (v. Kimblesworth) and going on to to keep their 100% record with a 8 – 3 win (Brankston 3, Dale 2, Mordue 2 and Hanson). Dale and Fulwell were chosen to appear in a Durham F.A. Trial Match. The team now included new Member Murray in goal, R. Bell, Fulwell, Atkinson, Renwick, Biggs, Dale, Hanson, Brankston, Mordue, Williams and W. Bell and Parnaby were also named.

'Goals Galore' was the name being used to describe Langley Park Juniors as the year 1952 approached. There had been 8 – 1 and 8 – 2 wins at mid-season.

Three players were on the move Johnson, Brankston who went to Lincoln City and Raynor who left for Grimsby. Clubs were interested in other players and Fulwell was considering an offer from Bishop Auckland when he finished with junior football. In the Spring of 1952 we find in the team Hayton, R. Bell, Fulwell, Atkinson, Renwick, W. Bell, Saville, Ferguson, Parnaby, Boal, Trotter and J. Mordue who is a nephew of a former Sunderland player. Also mentioned are Hanson, Williams, J. Steel and James.

By the end of the season in April 1952, the winning form continued and they became champions of the Chester-le-Street Junior League and defeated Lumley Juniors in the Chester-le-Street Junior League Challenge Cup played at N.G.T., Chester-le-Street.

Players with Langley Park Juniors in March 1953 included Fishwick (an ex Chester-le-Street goalkeeper) Ferguson, Fulwell, Bent, Trotter, W. Bell, Welsh Hall, Williams, Hazell, Forrester, Hunter, Boyle Rovie and Bailes. Raymond Bell had signed as a professional with Luton Town.

A year later we find in the team Fishwick, Hanson, Weighill, Watson, Trotter Cuthbert, Wright, Nattrass and Robson .

At the beginning of October 1954 the list of players included T. Fishwick, S. Hunter, W. Johnson, J. Nattrass, W. Cuthbert, S Iveson, R. Thompson, B. Hunt K. Bradley, J. Beecham, M. Donnelly, Hodgson, N. Wadge, Hoggart and Ritson.

In December 1955 in a team hit by injury Blythe, Renwick, Parker, Stoker, Gregory, Reed, Marshall, Kirby, Rice, J. Robson and B. Robson are named.

60

THE METHODIST YOUTH CLUB

In the season 1951 – 1952 The Methodist Youth Club were fielding a football team. Among the players in the side were R. Hunter, G. Hammel, R. Coult, G. Dixon, N. Bates, R. Maddison, D. Catton, A.E. Smith, W.H. Foster, G. Dent, T.W. Morrell, R.F. Smith, Saville, M. Ward, K. Dawson, J. Coates, G.R. Laine E. Wharton, Lane, N. Wright, J.W. Morrell and Heron.

61

ALLEN FERGUSON

During the Durham Central Area Schools Athletics meeting at Langley Park in June 1953, Mr. H.W. Clear, Headmaster of Brandon Modern School and Chairman of The Durham County Athletics Association presented Allen Ferguson with the Durham County Athletics Association Badge. He had been competing in the All England Inter County Athletic Championships meeting in Southampton in July 1951. He gained 4th place in the final of the Junior Long Jump with a distance of 18 ft 5¾ inches. Mr. Ferguson left Langley Park County School in December 1951 and started work at Langley Park Coke Works, first as an office boy then as an apprentice joiner. He did not continue with athletics but enjoyed playing football in the local villages. He married and later took up teaching in Durham City and Houghton-le-Spring. Now a widower he lives in Durham City, has two sons and three sisters – Brenda lives in Newton Hall and Hazel and Marie live in Langley Park.

62

SCHOOLBOYS

Despite the lack of sporting facilities at school premises most classes in the boy's school enjoyed football playing teams from other villages in league matches and competitions.

In November 1946 Langley Park schoolboys had won every game of the season and were fielding a team that included Clark, Parnaby, Welsh, Anderson, Renwick, C. Coult, H. Coult, Firbank, Saville, Johnson and Rose. In December 1946 they won 5 0 in a County Cup match (H. Coult 3, Ross and Saville were the scorers. In January 1947 Nattrass was in the side in place of Saville. At the end of that month they beat Ushaw Moor 8 – 0 in a Londonderry Cup. The Langley Park boys hadn't had a goal scored against them all season.

In June 1947 Langley Park County School played Ryhope Grammar School in a cup game. The tie attracted 2,500 spectators and 300 supporters went with the team in ten buses to Ryhope. Johnson, aged 14 was outstanding. He was to go to Sunderland A.F.C. and had acquired an apprenticeship in joinery. Goalkeeper Cuthbert and W. Bell, aged 11 were also praised. The result was a 1 – 1 draw.
(See also 16 'School').

WILLIAM T. SURTEES

Mr. William T. Surtees came to Langley Park circa 1953 from Dean Bank and worked as a coal hewer at Langley Park Colliery.

On the 8th January 1944 he passed his football referees examination and as soon refereeing his first game - Broom Home Guard v Fishburn in the Ferryhill and District League.

He was soon refereeing in Bishop Auckland, Ferryhill and Durham Districts and in 1945 became a linesman in the old North Eastern League.

In the season 1954 – 1955 he was a linesman in the Football League 1957 saw him at the Hartlepool's v Bishop Auckland game in the Durham Challenge Cup and 1958 at the Sunderland v Darlington fixture for the Durham Senior Professional Cup

In 1958 he became a Football League referee and in 1961 was officiating at games including Manchester United v Tottenham Hotspur. He had also been in charge of an amateur international – Scotland v Ireland at Hampden Park, Glasgow and his ambition was to take charge of a F.A. Cup Final. Football League matches did not come his way every week. It as usually one a month and often two. However, he was in demand for Northern League games.

In April 1960 his engagements included Leeds v Preston, Barnsley v Accrington and the international mentioned above. In the Durham Football Association Handbook he was described as a Class 1 Referee with an asterisk against his name that denoted he had reached the top as far as the County Association classification was concerned.

In younger days he played football himself but not to a very high standard. Following an injury to his knee he was persuaded to take up refereeing.

In the Football League he was called upon to be a linesman at Newcastle and Sunderland games but because of his close association with the region could not referee. On the field he found a handful of spectators could be more aggressive than a 65,000 crowd as a stadium such as Old Trafford. Up to 1961 he had been in charge of 455 matches in 17 years and 25 cup finals and 19 semi finals in Durham County Cup matches.

In the world of cricket Mr. Surtees played 19 seasons at Dean and Chapter and 3 for Langley Park.

He trained for football each week on the Langley Park Colliery Welfare ground.

Surprisingly Mr. Surtees, who was highly respected as a referee, lost his place on the football league list for the 1961 – 1962 season. H. G. Wilson of Norton replaced him. Apparently Mr. Surtees name was omitted due to a controversial decision he made on the field during an important match. It is said he never refereed another game.

SIR BOBBY ROBSON

Robert William Robson was born in Sacriston in February 1933. From 1938 to 1945 he attended Langley Park Council School before proceeding to Waterhouses Modern School. In June 1955 he married Elsie at Esh Laude. Around the year 1950 he was playing football for Langley Park Juniors and played cricket for the village side. He then took up football professionally at Fulham and a well-recorded international career followed.

OSWALD LEE

Well known in Langley Park as a cricketer Mr. Lee began playing at the age of 17. During his playing career he had been seen as a member of the Durham City side that won the Durham Senior League Championship. As an opening batsman he had many successful seasons with the Langley Park club. During the 1947 season he scored 1,107 runs.

In younger days he had been a talented footballer gaining a county cap as a schoolboy and was an amateur cup medal winner while with Kimblesworth F.C. At tennis he also won a cup in an open tournament.

Eventually ill health had forced him to retire from active sport but he kept his interest in cricket alive by becoming an umpire. He was due to umpire a game at Durham on Saturday 2nd June 1951 but he collapsed and died earlier in the day

D. G. HARRON

Mr D.G. Harron signed a two-year contract at the beginning of 1950 to play for Leicester County Cricket Club.

Born in Langley Park he showed batting promise while still a boy playing for the local club in the North West Durham League.

During his service in the R.A.F. in wartime he had little time for cricket but did manage to appear in a number of services representative matches.

In 1946 he was opening the batting for Langley Park scoring over 500 runs during the season. On three occasions opening the batting was either not out at the end of the innings or last man dismissed. The following year he was among the runs for Durham City and played for Durham County.

He left the area in 1948 to work in Coventry.

CRICKET

Few of today's residents of Langley Park can remember the names of Bill Spiller, captain and fast bowler and Jack Ardley, wicket-keeper in the days when the village team was described as 'outstanding'.

At the beginning of the 1920s those playing for Langley Park included the afore-named along with H.A. Penny, F. Hall, P. Nichol, Joe Penny, M. Shaw, W. Gibson, G. Hemsley, J.J. Penny, W. Cooper, Stewart Hall, N. Rutter, J Lowes, G. Britton and J. Watson.

The local side were to appear in the North West Durham League for many years and in 1922 won the League Championship for the first time in their history. That season Spiller took 74 wickets in league fixtures and J.J. Penny took 88 wickets.

During this period Spiller was scoring great success as a bowler with figures like 7 for 28 and 7 for 13. Langley Park and South Moor were involved in an exciting game during the 1923 season when the final result was a tie. By the middle of the 1920s J. Mitchell, W. Heron, J. Tobin, T. Penny, W. Harron and T. Gale were playing. Mr. G. Hemsley being Secretary of the club. In 1925 Langley Park won the Durham Aged Miners Cup beating Horden in the final by one run. Over the years the side has had its ups and downs and has produced seasons of excellent cricket and has turned out some talented players.

14th June 1919 *George Hemsley playing for Langley Park in a North West Durham League game scored a record 198 not out. Team photograph shows Mr. Hemsley with bat and pads and on his right Jack Ardley.*

By the end of the 1920s and into the 1930s players named include J. Ardley, A. Elsdon, J. W. Sherrington, M. Shaw, J.F. Cook, G. Graham, R. Calvert, J. Penny, J. W. Ardley, B. Dodgson, H. Penny, R. Stockdale, W. Louth, J.J. Read, H. Elsdon, G. W. Sheridan, M. Sharp, D. Graham, J. Penny, M. Kindred, E. Herron, W. Harron, R. Stokoe, E. Newall, J. Mitchell, L. Staff, J. Tobin and D. McCready. By 1931 J. Jackson was in the side. In the 1933 season North West Durham League players included T. Penny, J. Mordue, J. Jackson, H. Penny, R. Stoker, D. McCready, E. Newall, M. Shaw, J. Mitchell, H. Ardley and L. Staff.

The 1935 North West Durham League side included T. Penny, E. Newall, J.W. Jackson, H. Penny, H. Barker, J. Green, J. N. Brighton, J. Mitchell, M. Shaw, L. Staff, and W. Raper.

Ossie Lee who was to become a firm favourite at Langley Park was playing for Durham City in the mid thirties.

In August 1935 there was a Ladies versus Gentlemen cricket match played in the village. The Ladies scored 166, the Men 127. Leaving the Ladies triumphant winners by 43 runs. The teams: LADIES: Miss K .J., Burn, Miss L. Ardley, P. Turner, F. Metcalf, M. Sullivan, L. Burdon, L. Watson, J. Emmerson, B. Emmerson, R. Sproats and E. Coulthard. The GENTLEMEN: (J. W. Hepburn's X1) W. Cummings, C. Shaw, J. A. Proud, G. E. Hemsley, W. Moore, R. Campbell, G. Greenwell, W. Potter, T. Weighill, W. Milner and J. W. Hepburn. After the game the teams and umpires were entertained to tea by Mr. and Mrs. Hepburn.

Miss L. Ardley, who came from a well-known local cricketing family scored six runs and took two wickets.

At the end of the 1936 season Langley Park finished third in the North West Durham League. A large number of players are listed. A. Stockdale, E. Newall, J. Jackson, H. Barker, J. N. Brighton, J. Mitchell, M. Shaw, W. Gleghorn, L. Staff, T. Penny, J. Waters, E. Mawson, Rev. E. Barnett, W. Lough, H. Hunter, J. Ardley, R. Stoker, C. Birbeck, T. Gardner, J. Eccleston, A. Wadge, J. Harper and J. Fletcher. The second X1 finished level at the top of their league with Sacriston but lost a decider.

> George Edward Hemsley was born in Nottinghamshire in February 1880. He was employed for 36 years at Langley Park Coke works 31 as head clerk. For 31 years he was Secretary of Langley Park Cricket Club and 20 years of the local football club during the Northern and Durham Central League days. He had succeeded John Best as Secretary of the North West Durham Cricket League and was an umpire. He was also Secretary of Langley Park Literary Institute. Mr. Hemsley died in May 1954.

In 1937 Mr. G. E. Hemsley was celebrating 25 years as secretary of the Cricket Club. At the end of the season the first X1 had finished fourth in the league and won the Durham Aged Miners Cup. O. Lee topped the batting averages and L. Staff the bowling averages. He also took most wickets. J. W. Jackson was top scorer. The second X1 were top of their division (they hadn't lost a match since May 1936). D. Harron topped the batting averages and C. Birbeck the bowling averages. At the A.G.M, in addition to Mr. Hemsley, the Chairman was Mr. J. Hepburn and the treasurer Mr. G. H. Greenwell. J. N. Brighton was elected captain of the first team for the 1938 season with H. Barker as vice captain and H. Ardley (captain) and Norman Paxton (vice captain) were chosen for the second team.

One of the highlights of the 1938 season was an opening stand by J. W. Jackson and Ossie Lee. They put on 158 runs for the first wicket in a North West Durham League game with Tanfield Lea. The close of the season saw J.W. Jackson topping the batting averages followed by O. Lee and H. Barker. G. E. Hemsley was continuing as secretary and J. Rogers was chairman. For 1939 J.N. Brighton and H. Barker were to be captain and vice captain for the first team and W. Gleghorn and G. Davison for the second team.

In the summer of 1939 the prospect of war was not dampening the enthusiasm of Langley Park cricketers. Having started the season in cracking form winning the first four league games (then they were beaten by Mainsforth) on the eve of the declaration of war the village side were scoring 201 for three wickets. Ossie Lee hitting 109 not out. During the year the team consisted of O. Lee, D. Harron, J.W. Jackson, M. Fletcher, A. Stockdale, H. Barker, A. Ward, G. Davidson, M. Shaw, W. Dixon L. Staff and J.N. Brighton.

In 1940 because of the war the league was only able to muster eight teams.

At the wicket during the 1941 summer were J. N. Brighton, J. W. Jackson, O. Lee, J. Mitchell, H. Barker, M. Shaw, J. Fairbank, T. Hunter, M. Fletcher, L. Staff A. Elsdon and T. Nicholson. In a high scoring game in aid of the Children's Sports Committee Langley Park Cricket Club beat the Consett Divisional Police by 26 runs. In August 1941 a presentation was made to Mr. Hemsley who was retiring as Secretary of the League. The Langley Park cricketers were top of the league in the final table of the season.

Most of the names mentioned above played during the 1942 season in the North West Durham League. Only 6 teams were competing – Burnhopfield, Sacriston, Kimblesworth, East Stanley Welfare, Leadgate and Langley Park. The secretary for the league was J. W. Jackson.

Eight teams were in the league during 1944 East Stanley Welfare is not listed but also named are Birtley Sports Club, The Royal Ordnance Factory and Craghead. In a game with Kimblesworth, Langley Park lost five wickets for 8 runs (6 were extras) but Jackson (50 not out) and Mitchell took the score to 104. The innings ended at 115 for 7 wickets. Kimblesworth made a brisk start but Langley Park won in the last over by 7 runs. They were runners up in the North West Durham League and at the end of the season Mr. G. Greenwell retired as treasurer after 17 years in the post.

Throughout this period getting teams together and travelling were proving major problems in fulfilling fixtures.

September 1945 saw Langley Park finishing third in the league. Again only eight teams. East Tanfield C.W. and Annfield Plain are named. O. Lee topped the batting averages and J. Stephenson received the J. N. Brighton Cup.

The following year a win against Crook in the opening fixture in the North West Durham League started the season well and re-introduced some ex-servicemen back to their old haunts. A renewed interest in the game led the club attracting larger crowds particularly in a Matthew Oswald Cup Tie when Langley Park unexpectedly beat Horden C. W. by 19 runs with only five balls left. At the end of the season they were runners up in the league and had appeared in the final of the Matthew Oswald Cup. The Second 11 were league champions. At the Annual General Meeting Johnnie Ritchie was presented with the J.N. Brighton Cup as the most promising young player,

J.N. Brighton, who had been captain of the team, had been appointed manager of Langley Park Colliery earlier in the year after fourteen years as under-manager.

Going into the 1947 season J. W. Jackson was Captain of the first X1 and W. Agar Vice Captain and for the Second X1 W. H. Gleghorn was Captain and G. Harron Vice Captain. The Club Secretary was R. Shaw, The President J.N. Brighton, The Chairman J.W. Hepburn and Treasurer J. E. Newell.

Friday 15th August 1947 was a great day for Langley Park Cricket Club and sporting enthusiasts were surprised and amazed at the team who beat Seaham Harbour, a Durham Senior League side in the John Saunders Cup Final. The village side had bowled out their opponents for 11 (eleven) runs! Even though they lost to Burnmoor three days later in the Durham Aged Miners Cup the win over Seaham dominated conversations and is still remembered by cricketers today. At the end of the season they had won the North West Durham Knockout Cup and during the season Ossie Lee had scored 1,107 runs in 37 innings, W. Agar 757, J. Maughan took 148 wickets and W.T. Minchell 122.

The side won the Richard Murray Cup and the Walton Bowl and were runners up in the Matthew Oswald Cup and the North West Durham League. Minchell who had been professional with the club then left Langley Park to join Eppleton Cricket Club as professional for the 1948 season leaving J. Maughan who came from Sacriston to fill the vacancy.

In 1948 Langley Park fielded two teams in the newly formed Durham County League. In the opening fixture of the season both sides achieved victories against Hetton Lyons. The First X1 players for this new chapter in the club's history included J. W. Jackson, W. Agar, J. Stephenson, O. Lee, J. Ritchie, Martin Fletcher, W. Canavan, H. Barker, E. Newell, newcomer Ron Bradley and Joe Maughan who took four wickets for 29 runs in the opening game. In the Second 11 we find W.H. Gleghorn, W. Clark, S. Blackett, H. Emery, C. Firbank, J. Moralee, J. Mitchell, S. Randall, A. Hunter, L. Gray, L. Gardner and J. Gleghorn.

About a month into the season Johnnie Ritchie batted throughout the innings and hit 116 not out in a fixture with Sunderland Police. An innings that included 17 fours and 2 sixes. At the end of July, Ritchie hit 103 in a high scoring game which his side lost to Peases West. Losing in a cup game Langley Park's all ten wickets were taken by South Moor bowler W. Roxby. An interesting year but by September the club secretary was glad to see the season over. Holidays and absences for other reasons had made team selection difficult. At the last home game about 20 supporters turned up and it seems spent most of the game standing on forms watching a football match on the other side of the fence.

For the 1949 season Joe Maughan, a County bowler and professional at Langley Park for two years returned. This season great things were expected from Ron Laidler.

Players in the 1950 side included J. Ritchie, C. Firbank, T. Renwick, R. Robson, W. Agar, H. Barker, G. R. Willis, S. Randall, L. Gardner, M. Fletcher and A. Johnson.

Joe Maughan was injured for some of the games but the side reached the semi final of the John Saunders Cup then narrowly lost to Philadelphia.

Sadly Martin Fletcher collapsed during a game during the 1952 season. By September Langley Park had won the Durham County League Championship. T. Gardner was Chairman of the Club S. G. Hoggart President, and Dr. R. Rutherford and J. Reay were Patrons. W. Calland was awarded the J. N. Brighton Cup given to the young player showing the most improvement. The first team captain was J. W. Jackson and H. Barker was to be the Vice Captain for the 1953 season.

> **WESLEYAN CRICKET**
>
> In the late 1920s and throughout the 1930s Langley Park Wesleyans supported a cricket team in the Coxhoe and District League and for some seasons in the Deerness League.
>
> Players at the start of this period included J. Watson, J. Swinbank, F. Proud, W. Ward, F. Swinbank, J. Dodgson, T. Preston, S. Williams, J. Coult, L. Booker and J. T. Raper and D. Cartmell. Later others named were W. Sharp, N. Foster, P. Dodgson, S. Williams, R. Booker and S. Coult. Teams in the Coxhoe and District League in 1929 were Binchester, Coxhoe, Mount Pleasant, Tursdale, Davy Lamp, Cornforth R.C., Fishburn Welfare, Durham Prison Officers and Langley Park.
>
> During the 1933 season Langley Park met Davy Lamp and the game ended in a tie 52 – 52. In the same year R. Clark achieved a hat-trick in a fixture with Fishburn.
>
> The team in the Deerness League in 1935 consisted of R. Keenleyside, D. Cartmell, F. Wilson, J. R. Watson, P. Dodgson, W. Wood, R. Mace, T. Preston, J. Ashworth, L. Dover, T. Craggs. Teams in the league were Stanley, Broompark, Browney, Southill, Esh Winning, Oakenshaw, Quebec, Waterhouses and Wooley.
>
> The following year Deerness League players are named as F. Wilson, B. Wilson, J. R. Watson, J. Ashworth, P. Dodgson, W. Wood, T. Preston, L. Dover, W. Brown, E. Milner, W. Hodgson, J. Wilson and A. Askew.
>
> In 1938 there is still mention of a team in the Deerness League

Players in 1953 were J. W. Jackson, H. Barker, J. H. Ritchie, A. Johnson, C. Firbank, T. Nicholson, A. Gillespie, G. Carr, Ian Gray, W. Calland, Bobby Mole, W. Surtees, J. Dumighan, R. Willis and J. Maughan. In the second team were D. Ritchie, E. Newall, R. Laidler, S. Randall, A. Firbank, T. Fishwick, D. Rose, H. Gregory, Laurie Gray, E. Hutchinson who was just out of the army, W. Gleghorn, E. Bunn, T. Hunter, W. Welsh, D. Fletcher, E. Callan, S. Blackett and R. Hunter. In July Bobby Robson returned to the village to play some matches for the club. At the end of the season T. Gardner was Chairman and S. G. Hoggart was President. The first team had won the N.C.B. Cup and the second team had had success in the County League. The Brighton Cup went to J. Dumighan. E. Hutchinson in his first season had taken 94 wickets. J. Maughan was elected first team captain with A. Johnson as vice captain.

All matches had to be played away in 1955 due to problems with the home ground. Nevertheless the village side had a good season. Most of the players already named were in the side but others included A. Agar, J. Nattrass, R. Walker, R. Soulsby, D. Ritchie, R. Hurst, J. Stephenson, K. Robson, M. Ritchie, T. Robinson, A. Hunter and L. Teasdale. At the A.G.M. in December 1955 Patrons of the Club were named As Dr. R. Rutherford and J. Stoker, the Chairman and President were re-elected,

L.Teasdale was appointed Secretary, J. Ritchie assistant secretary, E. Newall Treasurer with C. M. Fletcher as assistant.

During 1956 new names in the team included J. Ridley, J. Cook, W. Brass and K. Armstrong and a fairly successful year was reported. For 1957 C. Firbank was appointed captain of the first X1 with J. Ridley vice captain. Second team captain was D. Ritchie.

After the 1958 season the S.G. Hoggart Cup for the most improved young player went to G. Wilkinson and during the season K. Armstrong and E. Hutchinson took over 100 wickets each.

Familiar names in the 1958 squad were T. Renwick, A. Firbank, J. Dumighan, R. Hurst, C. Firbank,, Arthur Johnson, G. Winn. R. Winn, P. Teah, J. Maughan, E. Clark J. Jones, J. Hall, E. Hutchinson, R. Soulsby, A. Henderson, B. Wilkinson, J. Hall and W. Calland. In November 1958 Mr. H. Ardley, Mr. M. King and Mr. R. Rutter were made life members of Langley Park Cricket Club.

Langley Park 1st X1 circa 1959: Back row- Messrs. Wilkinson, Calland, Teah, Henderson, Laidler, Fishwick.: Front row- Messrs. Maughan, Dumighan, J. Ritchie, Welsh, Hurst.

Among those stepping out in the summer of 1959 were T. Fishwick, B. Wilkinson, J. Dumighan, J. Ritchie, Hall, W. Calland, R. Laidler, P. Teah, J. Maughan, Hammell, Hutchinson, T. Welsh, T. Renwick, R. Soulsby and J. Hurst.

Hopeful of a League Championship win in 1960 the Langley Park side found their hopes fading by mid August following a defeat at the hands of Seaham Park. Early in the season bowler S. Stoker was in fine form taking seven wickets for 21 runs in a game with Tudhoe.

Players in 1961 First Team: J. W. Jackson, W. Calland, J. Hall, D. Catton, J. Dumighan, C. Firbank, T. Renwick, L. Firbank, T. Welsh, E. Clark, E. Hutchinson, D. Henderson, P. Teah and R. Laidler. Second Team: R. Walker, J. T. Fletcher, A. Ferris, D. Ritchie, M. Greenwood, W. Gleghorn, R. Hunter, R. Soulsby, V. Taylor, V. Jupp and R. Stoker.

At the end of the 1961 season it was feared that the club may have to be disbanded through lack of support both in fund raising and attendances at matches. At the A.G.M. in November it was reported that the first team had finished joint third in the Durham County League and were runners up in the Walton Bowl. Stan Stoker received the President's Cup for the most improved player. For the 1962 season Mr. S. Hoggart was President, Mr. E. Dennison, (Chairman), L. Teasdale (Vice Chairman) and Harry Nelson (treasurer). The meeting had not decided on first team captaincy but D. Ritchie and W. Gleghorn were appointed captain and vice captain of the second eleven.

J.H. Ritchie

Players in the 1962 season included J. Ritchie (captain), J.W. Jackson (vice- captain), P. Teah, E. Hutchinson, T. Fishwick, T. Welsh, C. Firbank, R. Laidler, D. Catton, J. Hall, R. Bradley, D. Henderson, L. Firbank, W. Calland, R. Hunter and J. Dumighan. Second X1 members are named as D. E. Ritchie (captain), W. Gleghorn (vice captain) R. Walker, R. Hancock, J. Jupp, H. Dent, G. Walton, L. Teasdale, C. Firbank, G.T. Clark and V. Jupp. In 1963 J. W. Jackson and J.H Ritchie were leading the side and also included were B. Wilkinson, D. Catton, G. Walton, W. Calland, C. Firbank, D. Henderson, P. Teah, R. Soulsby and B. Thompson. In the Second X11 D. E. Ritchie, C. Firbank who was Vice captain, R. Hancock, J. Turnbull, J. Jones, E. Birbeck, A. Firbank, W. Gleghorn, S. Randall, L. Teasdale, J. Calland, T. Greener, J. Turnbull, W. Walsh,, T. Bulmer and D. Richardson were players. Turning out for the club in 1964 were J.W. Jackson, J. Ritchie, B. Wilkinson, A. Gregory, T. Fishwich P. Teach, D. Catton, D. Northey, E. Birbeck, M. Greenwood, T. Taylor, A. Firbank, G. Donnelly, R. Hancock, L. Birbeck, J.G. Calland, B. Robson, W. Welch, D. Richardson, W.Penny, L. Teasdale, B. Howell, T. Bulmer, J. Ward and P. Howe.
And so the history of the club continued. Into 1965 J. Ritchie led the first team and C. Firbank was captain of the second eleven.

Thirty years later in 1995 the players in the Langley Park cricket team were J. Cruddas, K. Smith, M. Horn, K. Donnelly, T. Jones, D. Gladstone, T. Hudson, M. Shelton, F. Daugherty and K. Riley and in 2005, J. Lee, D. Crocker, D. Wilkinson, P. Clish, S. Gray, A. Dinsdale, G. Coates, S. Huscroft, J. Sales, D. Gladstone, D. Jones, N. Ellison, P. Daughtry, R. Moralee and J. Winn.

In April 1963 Mark Shaw died at Morecambe aged 65. Before the 1914-1918 War he played cricket in Langley Park Second XI. Wounded in 1917 he spent some time in a military hospital He became a long serving member of the village cricket team he moved to Morecambe in 1948 and continued his interest in the sport becoming coach to the Trimpell Works Cricket Team.

Testimonial to R. Robson June 1961. Langley Park players in 'celebrity' side'. Back Row (left R. Laidler, 2nd from right J. Dumighan. Front Row: centre: R. Robson and J.H. Ritchie.

The participants in sport are named earlier or later in these memories.. Behind the scenes mention must be made of the remarkable teams of ladies who over the years have supported the clubs in various ways. They have provided valuable service to the players by providing tea and refreshments. No names but they know that their help has been and is greatly appreciated.

LANGLEY PARK BOXING CLUB

At the end of the 1939–1945 war amateur boxing was in a low way in Durham County but the Amateur Boxing Association and the National Coal Board brought about a revival.

George White was running a gymnasium on the premises of the Seven Oaks Inn at Quebec. Mr White was well known in the area. He had a good record as a boxer and as a trainer turned out four pitman's champions.

At Quebec tables and chair had to be removed to give space for training to start. Conditions were not much better when he moved to an old N.C.B. winding house in Langley Park. The Langley Park Club came into existence in 1950. There were no mod. cons, no hot and cold running water, just an old stove in the corner to keep one warm in the cold winter nights. Also a shower after a hard work out administered by George White or the Secretary of the club, George Maddison, was a mouthful of water and a spray. It certainly revived the lads and brought tears to the eyes. Norman Wadge who lived close by supplied the water. Norman himself was quite a character. Despite all the problems the venue was home to many a champion in its day, A.B.A.-N.C.B.-Boys clubs etc. Early members of the Langley Park Club were George Macdonald, well known in the area, the late Bart James and David Ogilvie. Ogilvie boxed as a professional under the name Dave Brandon

It was from here Johnny Cuthbert set out on his successful career in the hard world of amateur boxing. In the early 1950s boxers would have to box up to five times a day when competing in championships.

Alan Blakey was another very able pupil of Mr. White. He was having some considerable success in boxing tournaments. He held County and Northern Counties light welter weight titles but he was dogged by ill health and had to retire from the ring. Later Terry Halpin also had success with the club as did Eddie Ginty.

Members of Langley Park Boxing Club Left: Alan Gardiner and Johnny Cuthbert. Centre (sitting) George White. Right of picture standing Richard Brankston, Alan Blakey and George Maddison

By this time Johnny Cuthbert had been conscripted into the army for National Service and other hopefuls had problems. Mr. White was suffering from ill health and in August 1956 the Langley Park Boxing club closed.

On his return to Langley Park it was revived successfully by Johnny Cuthbert.

A finalist in the North East Divisional Competition in 1966 was a newcomer Harry Hope. Vincent Halpin was a Yorkshire A.B.A. champion and an all England finalist in 1961 and 1962. He also held the Durham Boys' Club and North-Eastern Counties junior titles, Derek Spoors was another junior doing well with the club. Terry Coulson, who was twice North-Eastern Divisional Champion, once fought Alan Rudkin who eventually became the British bantamweight champion. Following the closure of the Langley Park Colliery Mr Cuthbert went to Consett Sports Centre working for the local authority as a sports supervisor and assistant manager. Retiring in 1992 he was then manager.

JOHNNY CUTHBERT

or as he is known to his friends in the village Jackie.

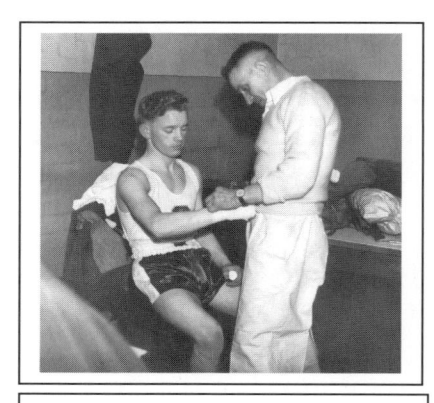

Gloving up for a fight at St. James's Hall, Newcastle with George White attending.

Johnny was born in Langley Park in 1934 and went to school in the village. His full time employment was as a painter and decorator working for many years for the local authority but it is in the field of amateur boxing that Johnny became a national star.

As a schoolboy he was introduced to boxing by his Uncle Edward and was soon attending the Seven Oaks Gym at Quebec under George White, himself a successful local boxer. It was Mr. White who was his trainer and the man who took him to national success.

From Quebec they came to Langley Park It was from the primitive surroundings of the Langley Park Boxing Club based in an N.C.B. winder house that Johnny set off for most of his boxing tournaments all over the country and further afield.

By 1953 he had a string of successes to his name and the impact he was making in the boxing world was becoming apparent.

Following an impressive performance at the Empire Pool, Wembley at the A.B.A. Championships he was chosen to represent the A.B.A. for Great Britain against a Golden Gloves team of America. In connection with this notable event both teams found themselves being presented on the stage of The London Palladium.

From 1955 to 1957 Johnny was conscripted into the army for National Service. He became a Physical Training Instructor to recruits and regular soldiers, his ability in the ring was a major asset and the facilities available were top class, far removed from those at Langley Park.

Originally a bantamweight Corporal Cuthbert moved up into the featherweight division and by the end of 1955 and six months of service he had won all his fights in the army and had the benefit of being trained by first class army instructors.
He was also representing Great Britain against teams from other countries and was experiencing a life style unknown to a lad brought up in a colliery village

Early in 1956 Langley Park C.W. had opened a testimonial scheme for him gaining international status and Langley Park Sub Postmaster Mr. Stephen Hoggart made a presentation on behalf of the scheme. The people of the village were saying well-done Johnny.

The following are just some of Johnny Cuthbert's achievements in a remarkable career
4 years North Eastern Champion
2 years Northern Counties Champion
4 years Northern Counties finalist
Fought for England against Norway (twice), Germany, Wales (4 times), Scotland (twice) and Ireland.

Appeared in A.B.A. semi-finals and finals and many more.

Johnny with Glenn McCrory after McCrory's British Empire and World Cruiserweight Championship win.

During his time in the Army he represented Two T.R. Royal Signals, his regiment, Northern Command and was in The British Army Team.

In the 1950s he was rated by The Ring Magazine as the number one amateur bantamweight in Great Britain and would also go on to be number two at featherweight .

On retirement from the ring in 1958 Johnny became an A.B.A. Advanced Coach and re-started Langley Park Boxing Club, which had closed on the departure of George White. He was A.B.A. Coach there for some time but with the closing of Langley Park Colliery he moved in a similar position to Consett Sports Centre.

As a result of his involvement in boxing Johnny met many of the famous boxing personalities and trained an eleven-year-old local boy Glenn McCrory who became a junior A.B.A., Champion and later in his career won a version of the World Cruiserweight Championship.

During his career Johnny had many offers to turn professional but declined them all. He always acknowledges that a lot of his success was due to the hardworking George White and his chief second George Maddison and also to another local boxer, Alan Blakey who was often his sparring partner. Unfortunately Mr. Blakey had to give up boxing for health reasons.

In the 1950s Johnny was described as always level headed and the enormous success he had made had not gone to his head. Today in happy retirement Granddad Cuthbert is still the same modest and quiet person. In company with friends he is more likely to talk about the achievements of others rather than his own. With his wife and family (a son David, daughter Dawn and grandchildren Claire and Martin) he stills lives in the village in which he was born.

Way back in 1956 Langley Park said 'well done Johnny' and, in 2006, the people of the village will happily endorse that remark.
(A version of this article appeared in Esh Leaves July 2005 edition)

LANGLEY PARK CHESS CLUB

For many years Langley Park had a Chess Club that played matches in the North West Durham Chess League.

In the autumn of 1944 those playing included T. C. Dobbin, Dr. W.M.N. Melrose, J Hayton, J. Lowdon, J.T. Lowdon, H. Palmer, J. Goundry, M. Bergna, Mrs. Bell, H. Cooper, W. Joynes, J. Bell and Mrs. R. Fenwick.

In the 1944 – 1945 season Langley Park had won both divisions of the North West Durham Chess League. Dr. H.C. Rollin made a presentation at a meeting of the league in Esh Winning. In the afternoon Mrs. J. Bell won the Red Cross Handicap Tournament (Division 2). In February 1945 team members included M. Bergna, W. Joynes, W. Mole, J. Dunn, C. Lowther, H. Cooper, J. Nicholson, J. Bell and Mrs. R. Fenwick.

For one match in April 1947 they were only able to muster five players in a league game that resulted in a 10 – 2 defeat against Craghead. The Club later drew 5 – 5 with Chester-le-Street. Members included T.C. Dobbin, J. H. Hayton, H. Palmer, J. Palmer, Rev. M. Ferguson, Mrs. M. Bell, and R. Atkinson.

In February 1948 the team was reported as being in strict training for a friendly with Rowlands Gill which they won 5 –2. The team consisted of some of the members named above together with F. Rushford and W. Agar. The training put them into good form and at the end of the season finished third in the league.

After a summer rest they made ready for the 1948- 1949 season and in October they were preparing for their first fixture of the season with players T. C. Dobbin. J. Palmer, H. Palmer, J.H. Hayton, Mrs. M. Bell and Rev. M. Ferguson.

LANGLEY PARK BOWLING CLUB

Langley Park Bowling Club was formed in 1910. From 1910 to 1921 the team played in the North West Durham League then in 1922 joined the newly formed Durham and District League alongside Malton Colliery, Dunelm, Ushaw Moor and Waterhouses. For the first five years of this league's existence Langley Park were league champions and up to 1966 had won the title ten times. In 1921 President of Langley Park Bowling Club was Mr. W. E. Goodenough, John Crossman was Chairman, Mr. William Pickering Treasurer and the Secretary was Mr. W. Crabb.

Teams in the league in the mid-1920s were Esh Winning, Ushaw Moor, Waterhouses, Belmont, Malton Colliery, Dunelm and Langley Park. During the 1920s members of the club included G. Raynor, H. Perry, J. Crossman, W. Brown, R. Campbell, W. Cooper, W. Perry, W. Crabb, R. Wilkinson, J. M. Hunter, W. Pickering, W. Gregory, T. Turnbull, J. Gibson and M. Ritchie.

R. Campbell was awarded a gold medal by the Durham and District League in 1924.

In the Spring of 1927 Mr. W. Crabb who had been Secretary of the Durham and District League since its formation had to relinquish the position due to ill health.

In 1929 they were runners-up (Dean and Chapter won the league by two points) but in 1930 Langley Park were again champions. Members of the team in the seasons 1929 included J. Scott, W. Gregory, M. Ritchie J. Campbell, A. Smith, W. Cooper, A. Stokoe, M. Willis, J.T. Gibson, J.T. Scott, W. Gregory, W. Brown and Joseph Turnbull. J. Crossman was Chairman, T. Thompson Secretary and H. Perry Treasurer.

Teams in the league in 1934 were Langley Park, Bearpark, Ushaw Moor, Brancepeth, Dunelm, Waterhouses, Peases West, Browney and Sacriston.

The summer of 1935 shows some of the members to be J. Blankley, T. Thompson, R. Campbell, H. Perry, R. Raper, M. Ryan, T. Harris, J. T. Scott, A. Smith, W. Cooper, J. Gibson and D. Birbeck In September 1938 Langley Park are shown holding fourth position in the league.

Always enthusiastic and keenly interested in the welfare of the club Mr. E. Shorten was appointed Secretary in 1938. He was to hold that position for many years.

Just before the start of the Second World War a Women's Section was formed and hoped to attract a good membership. At the start of the 1939 season Mrs. Skelton bowled the first wood for the ladies and Mr. Watson for the men. Later there followed a tea and whist drive. At the time W. Simpson was Secretary of the Club. In March 1939 following the club's first annual whist drive and dance it was revealed that £8 4s 1d. had been raised for club funds.
At the end of the 1939 League season they had played 20 won 7 and lost 13. J. Crossman and partner were pair's champions and T. Thompson and partner were rink champions. In 1939 twelve teams competed in the league – Bearpark, Spennymoor,

69/2

Brancepeth, Kimblesworth, Bowburn, Dean Park, Langley Park, Peases West, Browney, Brandon, Waterhouses and New Brancepeth.

Bowling continued uninterrupted during the war years. 1940 saw 12 teams in the league. The 1942 season concluded with teams finishing in the following order. Ushaw Moor, Bearpark, Waterhouses, Langley Park, Kimblesworth, Peases West, New Brancepeth and Brandon. Only eight teams competed during the 1944 season Brandon, Ushaw Moor, Sacriston, Bearpark, Waterhouses, Addison Park and Langley Park… The Brandon side were league champions having finished bottom the previous year. In the Langley Park team were Messrs. Gregory, Reeve, Fordham, Penny, Swinbank, Shorten, Raper, Blankney, Hunter, Penbro, Indian and Cowley. Along with Mr. Ardley, T. Thompson and Messrs. Hutton, Skelton, Humphreys, Williams and Brenkley.

In the season 1945 members of the club playing for the team in the Durham and District League included F. Humphrey, R. Raper, R. Walker, T. Thompson, E. Shorten, T. Fordham, T. Penny, J. Penny W. Cowley, T. Harris, J. Brenkley, J. M. Hunter and O. Birbeck. At the beginning of August they were topping the league but hopes of league honours were dashed when they failed in their last two matches and finished third.

By August 1946 the Club had gained 11 points from 11 games and we find named T. Harris. S. Skelton, F. Humphrey, O. Birbeck, R. Walker, S. Williams and N. Rynn. Also named were R. Raper, T. Thompson, E. Shorten, T. Penny, J. Penny, J. Brenkley and J. M. Hunter.

A year later they had won 4 out of 9 games played in the Durham Bowls League and some members had represented Durham and District in a match with the Durham County Association.

August 1949 saw the Langley Park Club top of the bowling league. Ushaw Moor, Waterhouses, Addison Park, Peases West, Sacriston, Brandon, Bearpark were other participating teams in the league.

Among the team members playing in the 1950 season were Messrs. Indian, Thompson, Fordham, Walker, Shorten, Rowe, Cowley. Humphrey, Lightfoot, Summerside. Mr. Humphrey is named as skipper for the 1952 season. W. Summerside and T. Penny Junior are also mentioned.

The season 1954 proved to be their most successful season to that date having broken all records including winning the County Rink Championship while R. Walker, O. Birbeck and T. Penny carried off the Charlton Bell Bowl. T. W. Penny was also included in the success of the above. Membership at that time numbered 22. The club had also won the North East Builders Cup (E. Shorten, R. Walker, E. Richardson and W. Summerside. The Carbonisation Shield (R. Walker, O. Birbeck, J. Cooper, A. Richardson, F. Humphrey and A. Bell) and the Durham Hospitals Cup (E. Shorten, T. Fordham, W. Cowley). Langley Park were holders of the Durham and District All England Championships.

During 1955 the Bowling Green at Langley Park was re-laid.

There were ten teams in the Durham and District League for the 1960 season. Bowburn, Leasingthorne, Vane Tempest, Sacriston, Brancepeth, Spennymoor, Mackays Sports Club, Addison Park and Waterhouses.

Players in 1961 included Messrs. Maddox, Christian, T. W. Penny, Williams, Dixon, Walker, Morland, Bullows, Sykes, Milner, Summerside and Kirk. The order the clubs finished in the A section of the league that year was Bowburn, Waterhouses, Mackays S. C., Langley Park, Leasingthorne and Spennymoor.

In the 1960s the team was also competing in the N.C.B. No 4 Area League and four years later E. Shorten, W. Summerside, G. Christian, E. Stoker, R. Cassidy, T.W. Penny were in The Durham and District League side.

During the 1980s Carpet Bowls was proving to be a popular sport and in the Spring of 1987 Langley Park finished third in the North West Durham Carpet Bowls League with 52 points from 16 games. Moorside were top of the league with Swalwell A runners up.

Indoor Bowls during the winter months was a popular recreation. In January 1964 the elderly Langley Park players were anxious to improve their position in the league of which the club was members so they decided to 'run up and down the 'silly steps' to improve their wind!!!' J. Bolton and S. Tighe were first and second in a local competition and others named were J. Ritchie, T. Cook. H. Carr, W. Wood and R. Milner.

Langley Park Bowling Club 1950s
Back row: T.A. Coates, H.Sherrington, N. Anderson, M. Indian, W. Summerside. Front row: E. Shorten, ?, T. Penny Jnr, R. Walker, T. Penny Snr and F. Humphreys

In 2006 Langley Park Bowling Club continues to flourish and has an active membership. In September of 2005 Langley Park were second in the Durham and District League. Other teams in the league being Shotton, Bowburn, Murton, Brandon, Vane Tempest, The King George V, Newton Hall and Witton Gilbert.

THE LANGLEY PARK ANGLING ASSOCIATION

The Langley Park Angling Club was formed in 1951 and in 1952 G. White was Chairman and T.B. Fishwick Secretary. In those early days T. W. Calland was Treasurer. In July 1953 Joe White Junior was presented with the Coronation Cup awarded to a junior member. In September 1953 the club had been in competition at Piercebridge. The President's Trophy went to T. Morland, Jack Anderson received the trophy for a junior member and Mr. J. Hayton had caught the biggest fish.

At Wooler on the River Till Langley Park beat Cornsay in the Langley Park and Cornsay Challenge Shield during the 1954 season. In December of that year a Presentation Dinner was given at the Co-operative Hall. Mr. E. Hall was President and the President's Cup, named The Hall Cup, was given to Mr. O. Morland Junior who also won the Coronation Cup for the biggest fish caught in 1953. The Coronation Cup for juniors went to B. Murray. Other trophy winners were G. White, W. Penny and J. Richardson. A special award was made to J. White Junior for the largest catch. T. Morland received a miniature trophy for a 1953 win. Meetings were held in the Army Cadet Hut and Mr. Fishwick was given a special award.

A successful season had been had in 1955. Alan Ives, aged six, won the Coronation Cup for juniors, George Morton won the President's Cup, The A.C.A. Cup went to Joe White and the largest fish caught prize was presented to Chris Morton. In August 1955 anglers named included J. White, M. Hayton, G., Morton and J. Hayton who had competed in the Langley Park and Cornsay Challenge Cup. Members named in 1956 included T. Moreland, W. Joynes, H. Hayden, G. Morton, F. Murton and G. White.

The year 1957 saw difficulties due to polluted waters in the district nevertheless various competitions between clubs were keenly contested.

Formed in 1959 by ten clubs the North East Angling Association was formed. G. Maddison received a tankard at the first presentation.

In December 1960, 45 members and friends attended the Annual Dinner of the Langley Park Angling Club. The President was E. Hall and Mr. Fishwick announced his retirement as Secretary. Award Winners were President's Trophy – R. Morton, H. Samuel Trophy – Mr. Morton, T. Moreland Trophy – F. Harrison, The Coronation Cup – G. Morton and the prize for the heaviest fish caught went to A. Curry. Among the junior members at the time were M. Anderson, C. Murray and C. Curry.

At the end of 1962 The Garden House Hotel, Durham was the venue of the Annual Presentation Dinner at which The President's Cup was awarded to R. Morton. In late 1966 A. Curry is shown as Chairman of the Club and W. Penny, Joe Hall and John Wharton are also mentioned. Forty years on the sport is still supported in the village with Mr. W. Merrigan of Sacriston being Treasurer and membership open for junior and senior members.

With William Merrigan as Secretary/Treasurer and Richard Davison, Junior Match Secretary the Langley Park Angling Association is still in existence.

SPORT MISCELLANEOUS

DARTS

In 1938 a darts league was formed in Langley Park and District with fourteen teams competing from Public Houses in the area. The Chairman was J. K. Briggs of Langley Park, T. Ather of Esh was Secretary the Treasurer was J. Wood of Esh. Participating establishments were The Robin Hood, Stag's Head, Cross Keys, Fir Tree, King's Head, The New Inn, Glendinning Arms, The Royal Oak, The Colliery Inn, Quebec, The Colliery Inn, Sacriston, The Station Hotel, Jaw Blades, The Black Bull and The Blue Bell.

PIGEONS

The keeping and racing of pigeons has always been a popular pastime among local men. Three generations of the Rose family have been actively involved. Alan Rose is still 'flying' (2005). Johnny Iveson and 'Tucker' Stokoe were also very early members of the pigeon fraternity in Langley Park. The names of Messrs. Crossman, Elliott, Appleton and Fletcher are mentioned as being connected with the pigeon world in 1927. Members of the local Homing Society in 1948 included Messrs. Fletcher, Todd, Laidler, Gibbons, Forster and Sons, Clayton, Slater, Raine, Oakley and Reynolds and Bunn. Mr. N. Anderson is reported as winning a silver cup. Mr. J. Wade was President of the Society in November 1951, Mr. A. Smith, Chairman with W. Chapman as vice Chairman and R. S. Bradley as Secretary. Among the members at this time were Messrs. Ross, Wiggham and Moralee. In 1962 Mr. Wade is still shown as President with J. Fletcher as Chairman and the Secretary was J. C. Ewan. John Rose scored a success in the Thrapston (Peterborough) Pigeon Race in May 1963. In 1964 Jim Fletcher of Irene Terrace one of the village's most successful racers, won first and second place in a competition. He should have been presented with a cup at Lanchester Agricultural Show but only the money prize was received. The cup arrived at a neighbour's house some months later, his name had not been inscribed and there was no replica.

> **GAMBLING**
> Until gambling became legal and betting shops became part of the village scene 'bookies' collected bets from punters who had chosen their hopeful winning horse, either be 'casual' meetings in the streets or at houses which were probably visited under some other pretext.

QUOITS

Quoits was a popular outdoor activity on various sites in Langley Park and at the Board Inn at Hill Top.

Using a pitch in the Recreation Ground Langley Park Workmen's Club in the late 1960s played matches in the Kimblesworth and District C.I.U. League with considerable success winning the league. Players included Bob Cuthbert (captain), Tom Greener, Jeff Turnbull, H. Welsh, J. Spence, Arthur Cuthbert, David Burgess, R. Wilkinson and R. Maddison.

GREYHOUNDS AND WHIPPETS

Greyhounds and whippets had their place in the lives of men who were enthusiastic supporters of racing.

GARDENS GUILD

Langley Park Gardens Guild was formed in 1935 with the membership fee set at one shilling (five new pence) per year. The Rev. C. R. Ninham was chairman and also involved were Miss Dawson, Miss M. A. Dover, Mr. and Mrs. P. Ross and Mrs. Hepburn. Mr. Ross was chosen as President. In 1938 J. Rogers was President, Miss Hunter, Treasurer and Mrs. S. Howe, Secretary. By the following March C. E. Harrison was President, C. Thompson, Secretary and W. Clegg, Treasurer and the Guild was reporting a good membership and every effort was being made to brighten up and create a garden atmosphere in the village streets and surrounding areas.

In May 1946 with J. R. Brighton as President enthusiasts were keen to revive the Guild after the war intervened. The Vice President was the Rev M. Ferguson with Mrs. Benton as Secretary and Mrs M. A. Howe assistant secretary. Other interested villagers included Miss. M. Hunter, appointed Treasurer, G. Egglestone, A. Buchan, Miss H. W. Dawson, Councillor, J. Robertshaw, Mrs. M. Groves and Miss Mulcaster.

GARDENING ASSOCIATION

There was also a Gardening Association in the village. In 1947 George Harrison was President, George Thompson (Secretary) and Wilf Clegg (Treasurer). There was also a poultry secretary and a storekeeper. Mr Clegg who was an Air Raid Warden during the 1939 – 1945 war, he was Treasurer for the Gardening Association for well over 30 years.

In a competition organised by The Gardens Association in September 1930 Messrs. Thompson, Dover and Graham were winners of prizes.

In the mid 1920s G. Thompson was organising an annual flower show in the village and in mid 1924 a competition for Aged Miners showed John Harris, William Sharp, Thomas Parker and Mrs. E.W. Harrison having success.

For some years Lanchester Rural District Council organised a competition for the best kept council house garden and there was keen participation among tenants for the top awards. In September 1963 the list of prizewinners included L. Gardner, R. Ather and T. Dover. 1965 winners included L. Gardner, W.C. Firbank, R. Ather, T. Dover, R.W. Milner and J. Metcalfe. Two years later W. .C. Firbank, R. Ather, W. Lane, J. A. Spence, H. Nelson ,R. Smith, F. Jackson and Mrs. M.E. Coulthard are named. Three times in four years Bob Ather won the area prize. An ex Brandon and Byshottles painter in later life he suffered from arthritis in his back and neck. His council house plot was described as 'a miniature Kew Gardens'.

THE VILLAGE POLICEMAN

The village policeman was a well-known figure on the streets and had a permanent residence in the village. In the early life of the village the police station was situated in one of the Cross Streets. In the late 1940s, on the new council housing estate, a new police station was built in Park Drive. From here the local police operated and got to know the local population very well and were a welcome and reassuring presence.

A name from 1935 is P. C. Armstrong and later P. C. Wood was known in the village. At this time the mention of the police constable's name was enough to deter prospective 'mischief makers' from causing trouble. A villager standing waiting for a friend in the evening would be politely warned that loitering was forbidden.

In April 1948 Sergeant Andrews left Langley Park for Boldon. Born in Darlington he began in the Durham Constabulary at Jarrow before serving at Tudhoe, Houghton-le-Spring, Cockfield, Boldon Colliery, Langley Park, Consett and again at Langley Park. As a footballer he played for the County team.

Around 1950 P. C. Shaw was stationed in Langley Park. Later P.C. Chambers was well known in the village.

> *On a Monday evening the Headmaster of the local school would often attend a performance at the Kings Cinema. Sitting in the front row of the circle he could look down on children watching the show in the stalls. Should there be any mischief the offending child would be reprimanded at school the next morning. Later in the day that child, on arriving home from school, would be further reprimanded by the parents.*

In the days when there were very few vehicles on the roads the control of traffic was no problem. If residents owned cars they were securely locked away in garages. The local 'bobby' had occasionally to take a resident to court for a minor offence.

Sledging. With the roads being relatively free from danger the winter months gave young villagers the opportunity for additional sport – sledging. A heavy snowstorm left the roads in ideal condition, as gritting did not take place. Anywhere there was a sloping piece of road would see sledging taking place. A favourite pastime was to walk up the road to Hill Top, set off and sledge all the way down to the 'Blue Star' (Langley Park Hotel) without confronting traffic on the way. If one had the energy one could go back and do it all over again.

I want to be locked up", said a man who threw a stone through the plate glass window of a shop in the main street of a small town near Langley Park. The police duly obliged. (April 1941).

> **Settling a Dispute:** It was not unknown for two men who had a disagreement to participate in a fight to settle the argument. A contest was arranged and took place either at the Kop or behind the Langley Park Hotel (Blue Star). This attracted many onlookers. After the fight the winner and loser shook hands parted and went about their normal business - and that was the end of the matter.

74

LANGLEY PARK WOMEN'S LABOUR PARTY.

In June 1946 the Durham County Labour Women's Gala was revived after seven years. 2,000 attended the Wharton Park gathering and heard speeches from Jennie Lee and the Minister of Education, Ellen Wilkinson.

The Women's Labour Party had a strong influence in village life. In late July 1926 they received a new banner which was unveiled by J. Batey M.P.

Among those associated were Mrs. R. Crossman, Mrs. Firbank and Mrs. Snowball. Towards the end of the 1950s Mrs. L. Smith, Miss Bellinger are named. Mrs Cheek was Secretary and Mrs. M. Williamson is shown as Treasurer.

75

REBECCA RUTHERFORD

In March 1946 Councillor Rebecca Rutherford resigned from Esh Parish Council having served for 21 years and during that time was Chairman seven times. She had been the only woman on Lanchester Rural District Council. She was for 12 years with that authority and had been Vice Chairman for a term. Mrs. Rutherford was also associated with the Garden's Guild and helped found the Langley Park and Witton Gilbert Nursing Association being Chairman for eleven years. As one of the founder members of the Langley Park Women's Labour Party she held office as Secretary and President. She was also Divisional Secretary for the Labour Party and at Langley Park Council School was a School Manager. Her name was also linked with the Langley Park Branch of the Co-operative Women's Guild. During the 1939 – 1945 war she was Vice Chairman of the Langley Park Comforts Fund and undertook much of the organisation of the VE/VJ treats in the parish. Mrs Rutherford died in March 1959.

76

JOSEPH ROBERTSHAW

Councillor Joseph Robertshaw died in June 1954 aged 64. A very active participant in the work of the local branch of the Labour Party, Mr. Robertshaw used to live in Ushaw Moor. He was a resident of Langley Park for thirty years. As a member of the Lanchester Rural District Council from 1935 he served on various committees and held the office of Chairman on more than one occasion. In Durham, Mr. Robertshaw was on the Area Planning Committee, a representative on the Durham County Rural District Council's Association and served on other organisations. Locally he was involved with numerous groups in the village including the war time Comforts Fund, The Old People's Treat and was on the board of the Lanchester Joint Hospital. From 1925 he was a long serving official and chairman of the Miner's Lodge at Langley Park Colliery where he worked as a check weighman. A member of Trinity Methodist Church he was also known as a local preacher particularly in the New Kyo area.

(In November 1927 J. Gilliland of Durham opened Langley Park Labour Hall. At the ceremony there were speeches by Mr. J. Swan and Mr. T. Sexton).

SNIPPETS

On 3rd July 1954 housewives tore up ration books in Trafalgar Square, London to mark the end of rationing after fourteen years.

In the years before the Second World War Langley Park had its own Musical Appreciation Society and there was a Choral Society in the village.

A made to measure suit bought a Burtons in the spring of 1936 cost 45/- (£2.25). Raincoats were 25/- (£1.25) each.

The salary of a senior assistant in the Accounts Department at Shire Hall, Durham was between £325 and £375 a year.

In June 1937 Councillor J. Robertshaw opened new sewage works at Kaysburn. Built by Lanchester Rural District Council at a cost of £12,864 they replaced an old irrigation system.

In January 1939 Mr. T. Firbank claimed he had climbed the 'Silly Steps' every day for thirty-eight years.

Advertised in May 1937 a five-day coach tour to North Wales cost £7 as did a similar tour to The Trossachs. A mystery tour with tea was 7/- (35p) and a longer tour with lunch and tea cost 10/- (50p)

In 1960 a Langley Park man was fined £3 for using a County Council danger lamp as a parking light for his car.

There has not been a troop of boy scouts in Langley Park for many years. Scout Masters in the late 1920s/1930s included Messrs. Carter, Wright and Holiday. Former young scouts, now elder citizens, will recall Frank Agar as Scout Master.

When the working day was over two men became known as entertainers at social events in Langley Park. The late Bobby Rynn was a noted trumpet player as was the late Eddie Leeming, a talented musician. Mr. Leeming was featured at dances and other events in the village for many years.

Those serving on Esh Parish Council in September 1949 were J. Lyons, J. K. Ritchie, W.P. Beavis and Councillor Mrs. R. Crossman. In May 1957 the Chairman was Mrs. W. Snowball. Miss. E. Bellinger, Mrs. Cheek, Mrs. R. Crossman and Mrs. C. Smith were on the Council. In later years Wilf Cave was Clerk To The Parish Council a post he held for a long period.

In September 1960 Gladys Illingworth was appointed part time librarian at Langley Park Branch of the Durham County Library.

It was always an honour to be chosen to carry the banner on Durham Miners Gala Day. Those named in 1938 were T. E. Gardiner, A. Thompson, W. Ramm, F. Gardiner, G. L. Bell, A. Liddle, H. Smith, T. Elgy, W. Rose, J. T., Cairns, J. W. Preston, M. Ritchie. Reserves were named as H. Hutton and G. W. Steel.

David Kirby rescued a child from the River Browney. At the time, May 1969, he was in the 3rd Form at Greencroft Grammar Technical School.

77/2

In August 1924 an attempt was made to change the name of Witton Gilbert Station to Langley Park Station. The North Eastern Railway Company turned down the request because "there were several stations bearing names similar to Langley Park and confusion would thus be created". An earlier request 28 years earlier had been turned down for the same reason.

A fire at the premises of Eleanor Forster of Front Street, Langley Park described as a carting contractor destroyed a cow byre, a wood stable and killed one Jersey Cow. The damage was estimated to have totalled £300. The premises were insured.

Early in November 1923 it was announced that twelve new homes were to be built for Aged Miners.

A request for a Labour Exchange for Langley Park was turned down on the grounds of economy in January 1925.

When the village blacksmith found a smoothing plane of his missing he said to Mr. Robert Coult who was present in the smithy at the time "By gum, my plane's gone". "By gum", commented Coult, "there's some sharp 'uns about. In October, 1929 at Lanchester Court, Coult himself was fined one pound for having stolen the plane.

In October 1930 a General Bus swerved to avoid hitting a boy who ran into the road and crashed into the window of the shop belonging to Mr. T. Carpenter in Quebec Street.

In the late 1920s/1930s Mrs. Robson of Quebec Street organised a village carnival to raise funds for Durham County Hospital. There was a procession from the Aged Miners' Homes to land near the Isolation Hospital belonging to Mr. J. Swinhoe. The band was in attendance and there were ambulance displays and a baby show. In 1929 Watson's in Quebec Street won first prize in a window dressing competition with a display set up as a miniature hospital. In second place was Mr. Tomassi.

Well known in the village as an electrician Harry Cousin died in April 1964 aged 62. He worked at Langley Park Colliery and for Lanchester Rural District Council. He also helped in the family newspaper business. During the 1939 - 1945 war he served in Civil Defence. The previous summer (1963) his younger daughter Margaret had passed her final examination in domestic science and homecraft at a Sheffield College and had accepted a post at a Nottingham School.

During the 1960s Arthur Munsey and N. Lane were having success showing dogs at shows including Crufts.

The summer of 1917 saw the establishment of Langley Park Naturalist and Research Society under the leadership of the Rev. Arthur Watts, Rector of Witton Gilbert. The first visit members undertook was to the ruins of Langley Old Hall. There were also outings to Finchale Priory and to Lanchester. W.R. Wiggen of Wallnook Mill, who had compiled the book 'Esh Leaves' (1914) proved to be an interesting guide when the group visited Old Esh.

Edna Bellinger, daughter of Arthur Bellinger, who later became Mrs. Edna Hill, in July 1931 passed the final State Examination for Children's Nursing at the age of 21. She had trained for three years at Booth Hill, Manchester and was a silver medallist in the Booth Hall Examinations.

In the New Years Honours 1958 Mr. T. Miller was awarded the B.E.M. In 1975 Mr J. Stephenson was similarly honoured. Married in September 1945 Harry Guildford and his wife Nancy celebrated their Golden Wedding in 2005. Awarded the M.B.E. in 1998 Mr. Guildford has served for long periods on Lanchester Rural District Council, Derwentside District Council and Esh Parish Council.

In April 1928 Langley Park and District Motor Club was formed. Dr. T. A. Wilson was President. C. Crozier was elected Chairman, Hon Treasurer was B. Newton with F.C. Burn as Secretary. R. Newton was Assistant Secretary Mr. H. Hunter was appointed Captain and W. Scott Vice-Captain. Members were soon attending events at various venues including Croft Spa and Ripon. At a whist drive held in order to raise funds the first prize was a leg of pork and the second prize was two stones of flour.

As a member of the Langley Park Brownies in 1964, Margaret Ions was the first local girl for several years to gain a first class certificate in proficiency.

An unusual event took place in October 1964 when there was a double wedding. Langley Park sisters Shiela Gleghorn and Eileen Gleghorn married George Kelly and Brian Wilkinson at All Saints Church in the village. Thirty years earlier, in 1934, there was another double wedding. The two couples leaving the church were Mr. and Mrs. J. S. Dunn and Mr. and Mrs. W. Raine.

At the Miners Gala in July 1932 a huge patch of calico covered the face of Ramsay Macdonald that was featured on the Langley Park banner. The action created much controversy.

Having attended the Aged Peoples Treat a few days earlier Robert Stockdale died suddenly in December 1965 at the age of 57. He had been a member of Lanchester Rural District Council since 1949 and served on Durham County Council from 1954 holding the post of Chairman of the Education Committee and later the Museums and Libraries Committee. He held various other positions and was a magistrate and a churchwarden at All Saints Church in the village.

Mr. and Mrs. Sydney Lowdon were also well known in the village for the service on the local council and Mrs. Lowdon was very active in the Womens' Labour Party.

At the beginning of the 1900s a popular feature in Langley Park life was the annual Langley Park Floral, Industrial and Live Stock Society exhibition. The show was held in a field '5 minutes walk from Witton Gilbert Station'. The President was Mr. W. Logan and the Secretaries were W. Crabb and J. W. Cousin. 1902 was the sixth time the show was held and it was claimed to be one of the largest shows of its kind in the area.

ROBBIE IONS

Robbie Ions in his heyday

George Robson Ions was born at Allendale Cottages near Medomsley in 1921 the son of Thomas Ions, a miner, and his wife Margaret (known as 'Meggie').

Schooldays were spent at High Westwood, near Consett. At West Lane Methodist Church near his home he met a gentleman of Norwegian extraction, Aasmund Pattinson who taught his how to play the church organ. It was at West Lane Methodist Church young George first played in public.

Following service in the R.A.F. during the early days of the Second World War an enthusiastic Mr. Ions decided he would like to study the theatre organ. The distinguished organist Frank Matthew came to his aid and he was soon sitting at the consul of the famous 19 Rank WurliTzer organ in the Odeon Cinema, Newcastle. Then he went on to the Westgate Cinema, Newcastle, the Odeon South Shields and the Odeon in Gateshead. Robinson Cleaver, the well-known Granada organist and a popular broadcaster gave George (as he was known in those days) a lot of advice but he was never contracted to the Granada organisation.

George was inevitably becoming known as Geordie so he changed his professional name to Robson Ions. That, of course, led to Robbie and that name remained.

Robbie was a popular figure at the Casino, Sheringham and the Gaumont Oldham.

Cinema, theatre and ballroom tours followed necessitating long periods away from home. Engagements with Combined Services Entertainments took Suez, Nice, Malta, Tripoli, Egypt and the Holy Land.

Ken Dodd

Robbie headed for a quiet summer season at Will Parkin's luxury Holiday Camp and Hotel at Plemont, Jersey. The year was 1947 and little did he know at the time that a young man named Peter Sellers was the entertainment's manager. Mr. Ions 'gooned' his way through the season finding himself taking part in many of Mr. Sellers' crazy stunts but survived to be able to carry out his musical duties. Peter Sellers father was a brilliant pianist and Robbie got to know him quite well.

'Uncle' Will Parkin presented shows at the open air Coliseum Theatre on the promenade in Rhyl for well over 20 years. Robbie Ions was engaged for the 1952 season. In the company were Leslie Noyes and Freddie Dexter, who was the brother of Tommy Trinder. Here Robbie got to know boxer Randolph Turpin who was a frequent visitor to the show.

There was a long association with Macari. Macari and His Dutch Serenaders being one of the top-liners in variety and on the radio.

Peter Sellers

Robbie has happy memories of variety theatres and recalls many that are long forgotten - The Palace, Ramsgate, Opera House, Tunbridge Wells, The Granville, Walham Green, The Shakespeare, Liverpool, Wood Green Empire and The Empire West Hartlepool. Also some of the big theatres on the Stoll and Moss circuits such as Birmingham Hippodrome, Brighton Hippodrome, Finsbury Park Empire and the lovely Pavilion Theatre in Glasgow. In Scotland there were venues in such towns as Kilmarnock and Aberdeen.

During his career Robbie rubbed shoulders with many of the famous names of the day. He appeared on the same bill as Morecambe and Wise before they became nationally known, Ken Dodd before he had decided to become a full time professional and put Knotty Ash firmly on the map, Al Shaw of The Blue Hawaiians fame, Tommy Cooper, The Deep River Boys, David Whitfield, Jimmy Wheeler and Jon Pertwee – 'a very clever man'. Then there was Anne Shelton who Robbie describes as 'a wonderful lady'.

Blackpool is remembered for the fact that the three piers each had a full orchestra and that Reginald 'Mr. Blackpool' Dixon was at the organ of The Tower Ballroom. Ernest Broadbent who succeeded Dixon was a close friend of Robbie's and often stayed in Langley Park when he had engagements in the region.

It was while playing the organ at the Regal Cinema, Durham (later The Essoldo, later The Classic and later still the site of Robbin's Cinema) he met Eunice who was a cashier at the theatre and the couple married in 1947. They had two children. Gerald who had a career in the R.A.F. and lives in Langley Park and Margaret who has married and lives in Lanchester.

Anne Shelton

After a hectic career on the road Eunice and Robbie settled down in Langley Park and Robbie took a job with Durham County Council. By October 1957 he had retired from the entertainment business – or so he thought!

He formed a dance band locally and continued to practice on an electric organ at Satley.

In the 1960s club entertainment was growing in popularity and Robbie accepted an invitation to play the organ at West Cornforth United Social Club. This venue was chosen to house a Mighty WurliTzer Organ that had been purchased from the Gaumont Cinema, Bradford, the Cornforth Club having invested in new modern premises. At the opening concerts on 21st April 1974 and 5th May 1974 it is not surprising to find Robbie Ions on the bill alongside Ernest Broadbent, Melvyn Heslop, Con Doherty, Bill Thomas and Norman Green.

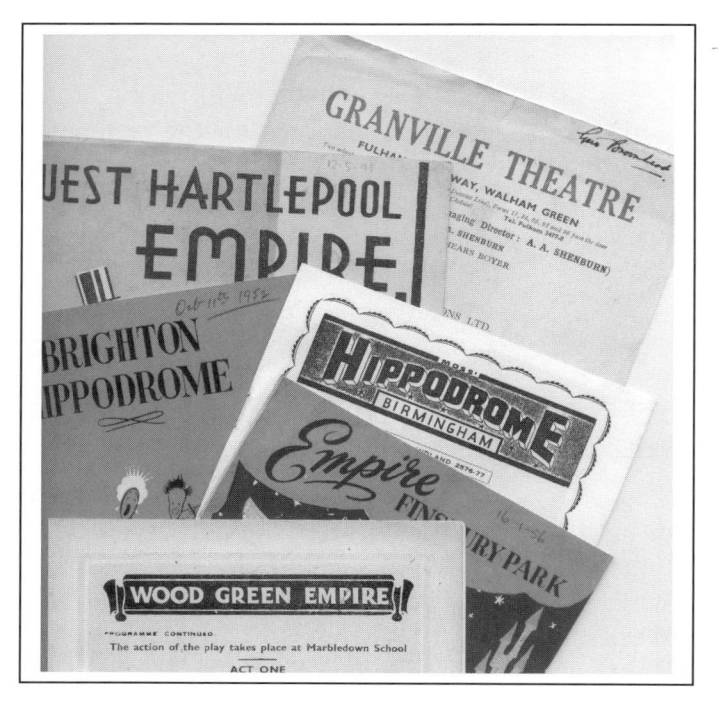

March 1986 saw another opening performance of the WurliTzer now at the New Victoria Centre, Howden-le-Wear. The North East Theatre Organ Association who were involved in the West Cornforth project and the one at Howden-le-Wear were delighted that the instrument had found a permanent home in view of the fact that many locations had been proposed and for various reasons had proved unsatisfactory.

Advancing years have made the 'dizzy fingers' of yesteryear less dexterous. But there are gramophone records. Over the years Robbie made many broadcasts for Radio Durham and Radio Newcastle. A request made to Frank Wappatt of Radio Newcastle could result in hearing music of those bygone days expertly played by the one and only

ROBBIE IONS AT THE WURLITZER ORGAN.

JOAN WADGE

It is a long way from a mining village in County Durham to the bright lights of London's West End. Performers are known for the top billing they receive but one girl from Langley Park has made a big success behind the scenes as a costume designer – her name is Joan Wadge.

Joan was born in and still visits Langley Park from time to time. Daughter of Angus and Elizabeth Wadge, she has a brother Peter. Her father worked in Langley Park and her mother had considerable artistic talents.

Joan began her education in the village attending Langley Park Modern School during the time Mr. Miller was headmaster. Already showing artistic talent herself she went on to study as Sunderland Art College.

Once qualified she embarked on a career in theatre by taking up a job at the prestigious Mercury Theatre, Colchester. After a spell in regional theatre she joined B.B.C. Television in 1979 where her costumes have greatly enhanced many top comedy shows and drama series.

She designed for 'The Lenny Henry Show' and programmes such as 'Ghost Story'. Then there was 'Ivanhoe', 'HenryV1' and 'The Adventures of Christopher Columbus'.

Outstanding were the brilliant costumes she designed for the highly successful series about a fashion house 'The House of Elliot' which gained her high praise from viewers and the profession and for which she was justly awarded a B.A.F.T.A. Award and an EMMY Award for Costume Design.

Joan has also been employed by some of the country's top theatre companies. For the Royal National Theatre in 2000 she worked on 'Albert Speer' by David Edgar. The following year she was at the Young Vic for a revival of David Rudkin's 'Afore Night Comes' and then moved on to design for the English Stage Company at the Royal Court Theatre and for the Pegasus Opera Company.

One of the major stage productions of 2004 was 'Festen' a production described as 'electrifying' and 'dramatic dynamite'. A huge success at the Almeida Theatre it transferred to the Lyric Theatre in the heart of London's West End. Designed by Ian MacNeil (settings) and Joan Wadge (costumes) full houses are still the norm and the production won The Evening Standard Award' for Design. So remember when you are sitting watching your favourite actor or actress on your television screen or in the theatre, the costume they are wearing may be designed by 'a lass from Langley Park'. Watch the credits!

(In August 1938 Angus Wadge, son of Mr. and Mrs. Wadge of Garden Avenue married Elizabeth Wardle, daughter of William and the late Mrs. Wardle of Ash Street, Langley Park. Given away by her brother in law Mr. W. Smith, Doris Weatherall was bridesmaid and Ronald Newton, a cousin of the bride, was best man. The Rev. E. S. Barnett conducted a typical Langley Park wedding sevice at All Saints Church next to the cricket field. Three hours after the ceremony the newly married Mr. Wadge was back at the cricket field to play for Langley Park 2nd X1 in a North West Durham League game with Mainsforth 2nd X1.

Part of this article and the article re Robbie Ions have appeared in 'Esh Leaves. .

JACK ARDLEY

Jack Ardley was one of three children born to John and Laura Ardley. The eldest daughter Hilda became a school teacher as did Jack. The third child was another daughter, Sybil, who married Jim Mitchell. Mr. Mitchell was for a long time associated with the Langley Park Cricket Club and Mrs. Mitchell was to become a popular teacher at Langley Park Girls' School.

Mr. Ardley senior came from Coggleshalll in Essex. Mrs. Ardley (nee Shorten) was born in Norfolk. The couple spent most of their lives in Langley Park and were the first couple to be married in the newly opened All Saints Church in the village. That was in 1888. However, some hours after the ceremony they were shocked to find they were not legally married. Due to an oversight the church had not been licensed for weddings. The matter was rectified the next day but they had been 'living in sin' for nearly twenty four hours.!!!

Mr. Ardley retired from his employment at Langley Park Colliery in April 1932. Mrs. Ardley died in January 1940 aged 75. Mr. Ardley died in 1944.

J. Ardley and Son were very popular in the village as Fried and Wet Fish Dealers. They had premises in Quebec Street and successfully ran the business for many years.

Jack Ardley was born in 1890 and attended the British School in the village. He and the future Mrs. Groves were the first boy and girl to be granted a scholarship to the Durham Johnstone School. Furthering his education Mr. Ardley went to St. Luke's College, Exeter.

Before the First World War he took up a teaching post at Sacriston and from 1914 – 1918 served in the Royal Artillery. Returning home he went back to Sacriston and later taught at Earls House, then a young offenders home.

Jack had met Lily Gibson who was a dedicated nurse at the local Isolation Hospital. The couple married and Mr. Ardley began teaching at Langley Park.

Always an enthusiastic cricketer in the 1920s-1930s he was well known as captain, batsman and wicket keeper with Langley Park Cricket Club. Considered by many to be of county standard he was never selected to play. During the 1939 – 1945 War Mr. Ardley was Head of the Local A.R.P. Wardens.

Rising to Deputy Headmaster at Langley Park County School he retired in the summer of 1955. In his retirement gardening was his favourite hobby.

Mr. and Mrs. Ardley had two children. John who married Miss Sally Robinson at Preston under Scar in May 1944. During war service in the R.A.M.C. he was one of the first British servicemen to enter the notorious Belsan Concentration Camp. Later he became Medical Officer of Health at Blackburn. He died in 2001. Daughter Laura and her husband Frank Heppell still live in Langley Park. Mr. and Mrs. Heppell have a daughter Glynis who now resides in Harrogate.

Jack Ardley died in 1962. His wife died in 1948.

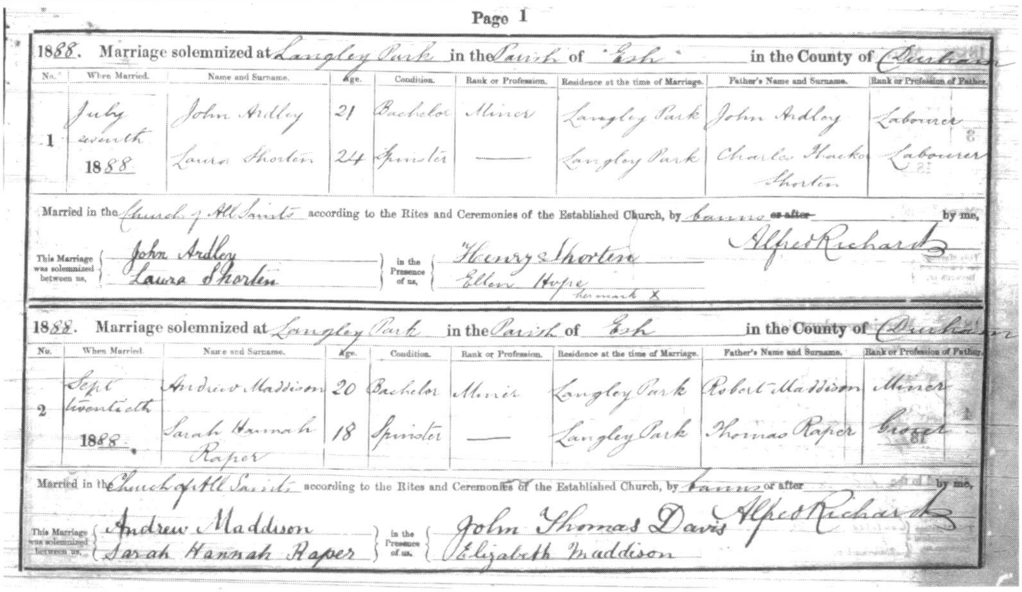

Marriage Certificate for first wedding at All Saints Church, Langley Park   July 1888. Below the 'happy couple' in later life. Right: Mr Ardley standing right, his father centre and son Jack left.

SYBIL MITCHELL
School teacher.
Sister of Jack Ardley

JACK ARDLEY
Teacher at Langley Park County School and well known cricketer

J. B. MITCHELL (Brian) son of Sybil (right) during service in the R.A.F. in the late fifties.

FAMILY ALBUM

175

LANGLEY PARK PEOPLE

Left: The Garrod family outside their home in Quebec Street and following a look at the lives of some of the people who were resident in the village.

FREDERICK BURDON

Charles Frederick Burdon, often known as 'Tibby', died at the beginning of 1961 at the age of 77. Born in 1884 in Quebec Street in a house adjoining his father's tailoring shop he himself became a master tailor and carried on the family business. But it as a musician that he was probably best remembered in Langley Park. Self taught he built himself a manual organ in the sitting room of his house. At sixteen he was playing the organ at Esh Parish Church before taking over at Langley Park. This was in the days when the organ was blown manually. Later All Saints got a new organ. Mr. Burdon was organist in Esh Parish for 31½ years. In 1911 on the opening of the Hippodrome in the village he began playing the piano for silent films continuing until the arrival of the talkies. He also played the piano at the Kings Cinema, Annfield Plain for 6 ½ years. For many years he gave piano lessons visiting pupils in their homes and he was also well known in the Durham area as a pianist in a number of public houses. Married he had two daughters and five sons.

MATTHEW KING

Mr. King died at the home of his niece in Logan Street in February 1959. He was 79. He began working underground at Langley Park Colliery and his working life spanned 52 years. He began on the screens and was then employed in the Hutton Seam. For the majority of his working life he was a boilermaker. Mr. King retired in March 1946. He was an ex Chairman of the Durham County Enginemen, Boilermakers and Firemen's Association having been a member for 26 years. For thirty years he was church warden/treasurer of All Saints Church and a member of the Ruri Decanal Conference for many years. He was known in the village as an authority on Durham history and was a long serving member of Langley Park Cricket Club who honoured him in 1958 by making him a life member.

W. E. COOPER

Mr. Cooper began work at the age of 12 and worked for 50 years at Langley Park Colliery. During both world wars he was secretary of S.A.A.F.A. At All Saints Church he was a founder member of the Parochial Church Council, a post he held for 41 years and he was also involved in organising many of the social activities run by the church. Mr. Cooper was a well known contributor to the Durham County Advertiser - in those days a newspaper which could be purchased every week on Friday and contained items concerning village activities throughout the area.

RICHARD A. SWINBANK

Mr. Swinback was a bachelor who lived for some time in a caravan in the Hill Top area of the village. He was just over 4' tall and was living in a vehicle that was 8' long, 6 5" wide and 5' 6" high. It had cardboard panels on a metal framework, an oil stove for cooking, no sanitary accommodation and had only a single bench seat. Water had to be carried from the village. The caravan had been bought with money left to him by his father. By the early days of 1956 the accommodation had become uninhabitable. Mr. Swinbank was offered a place at a hostel in Barnard Castle but he was insistant he wanted to live near Langley Park.

MARTHA HEPPELL

Mrs. Heppell was a Wrekenton born lady who lived in Front Street, Langley Park and who died in February 1936 aged 94. She had lived in the village for nearly sixty years and in the same house for over forty years. She remembered Langley Park when villagers had to walk half a mile for water and carry lanterns with them when it was dark. Her husband, William, died in 1915. He was a pioneer member of the Primitive Methodist Church in Quebec Street, a local preacher and a Sunday School teacher.

JOHN PEEL

Another Langley Park veteran was John Peel of Langley Street and he could also remember villagers having to go to the well at the top of Langley Park near the 'Silly Steps' for water. Just at the time he was old enough to carry out the task a water supply and taps were put into all the houses. In February 1939 he retired after 45 years at Langley Park Colliery. He came to the village aged two and during his working life was employed as an on setter until in 1910 he became an official. He was the original treasurer of the Langley Park Aged Miners Homes Committee and Treasurer of the Old People Christmas Treat from the start. He was a regular attender at Trinity Methodist Church.

JANE BUCHAN

Known to her family and friends as Jenny. Miss Buchan died suddenly on Christmas Day 1960. The death came as a shock to all who knew her. She had been to midnight service at All Saints Church and a few hours later had gone to the garage to collect her car to take her parents to her brother's house to spend the day. At the garage she collapsed and died shortly afterwards in Dryburn Hospital. Aged 30 she had trained as a schoolteacher at Lincoln College and had been on the staff of Langley Park Junior School as Deputy Head. An active member of All Saints Church she was particularly interested in working with young people and had also become a member of the local Women's Institute. She appeared regularly in productions staged by the Langley Park Players. Her good friend Marjorie Preston was organist for her funeral at All Saints.

HAROLD ARDLEY

Aged 88 and 87 in the late 1950s, Mr. and Mrs. Harold Ardley were the oldest married couple living in Langley Park at that time. Mr. Ardley was born in Coggleshalll, Essex circa 1869. He began his working life as a baker but by 1889 he had gone to work in the mines. He spent 49 years at Langley Park Colliery retiring at the age of 69.

As a huntsman he was well known and was associated with the South Durham Foot Harriers. A keen cricketer he played in the North West Durham and Durham Senior Leagues eventually becoming an umpire in the latter. In 1958 he was made a life member of Langley Park Cricket Club. Mr. Ardley was also a life member of the Langley Park Workmen's Club having been a member for sixty years.

Catherine, Mrs. Ardley, came from Newcastle to Langley Park circa 1880 and having married Harold the couple had three children. Sons John and Harold and daughter Alice – all married by the late 1950s. Mrs. Ardley was one of the founding members of the Mother's Union in Langley Park (circa 1914) and served for many years on the Parochial Church Council.

Catherine died early in 1962. Harold died a year earlier. They had been married for 65 years   Harold Ardley was brother to Jack Ardley Senior.

ANN WOOD

Born in Bilsdale, Cleveland she was the only child of parents who were farmers. In her younger life she recalled baking 20 stones of flour into bread to feed the farm workers. She lived in Langley Park for over 43 years having moved into Durham County in 1891.

She was a member of Quebec Street Methodist Church and at the age of 94 and the village's oldest resident she still enjoyed reading, knitting and sewing. She said she owed her long life to plenty of fresh air and good food.

Her husband died circa. 1911. She had six daughters and one son and up to 1949 had 36 grandchildren, 68 great grandchildren and 15 great great grand children.

Ann Wood died in July 1949 aged 97. The Rev. A. E. Emmerson conducted the funeral service at Quebec Street Methodist Church.

Mrs. Wood's grandson, Stephen Hoggart became sub-postmaster at Langley Park. Having lived in the village his entire life Mrs. Woods's great grandson, George Hoggart is in 2006 one of the villages oldest residents having reached 93 years of age.

Since 1949 the branches of the family tree started by Mr. and Mrs. Wood all those years ago has further extended to include great great great grandchildren and great great great great grand children!!!!

ELEANOR MULCASTER

In April 1958 having reached the age of 92, Mrs. Eleanor Mulcaster died at her home in Finings Avenue. At 87 she was nearly blind and had become a pupil of the Blind Institute using the Moon Tonal System. She lived in Langley Park for most of her life. In 1890 she married a schoolteacher and they both worked in the profession. In later life they took over a grocery business in the Durham area. Mrs. Mulcaster could remember schools being supported by local authorities when pupils had to pay four-pence a week in order to receive their education. Mr. and Mrs. Mulcaster had two children. Despite her handicap, two years before her death, she was still knitting, baking, playing bridge with her neighbours and was an active member of the Mothers Union at All Saints Church.

RICHARD SHORTEN

Richard Shorten, aged 91 and then the village's oldest man, died in February 1946. Born in Sprowston, near Norwich circa 1854 he could remember the Franco-Prussian War of 1870. Mr. Shorten's home was in Cross Street and he had lived in Langley Park for 62 years. As a boy his entire school experience was one half day. Aged six years he worked in Colman's Starch Factory and at eight went to sea with the Great Yarmouth fishing fleet spending many years at sea. In 1872 he came north to Gateshead arriving in Langley Park from Sunniside in 1884 to take up work at Langley Park Coke Works. His working life lasted more than sixty-six years. He finally retired at the age of 74. His last job was as a lamp-man at the Colliery. Mr. Shorten was one of the founders of All Saints Church and the first sexton and verger. His wife died in 1922. They had two sons and two daughters, thirteen grandchildren and fifteen great grand children. Brothers, in 1946, aged 79, 74 and 70 and a sister 88 survived him from what was a family of five.

WILLIAM DUNN HALL

Sixty years a miner, William Dunn Hall of Clifford Street was born in Burnhopfield. At the age of thirteen he was a trapper boy at the pit earning ten-pence a shift. He went on to be a driver, putter and hewer and in 1901 became, for twenty-seven years, a deputy. Later he was employed as a stonemason. A founder member of Langley Park Workmen's Club, he was treasurer, committee member and electrician. From 1937 he was Clerk to Esh Parish Council and served on Lanchester Rural District Council. Mr. Hall was also Captain of the Langley Park Ambulance Association team during the 1914-1918 war and was presented with a medallion. During the 1926 strike he took a leading role in making arrangements for the feeding of local school children. Mr. Hall was well known for his beautiful handwriting and wrote all the Parish Council notices by hand. Mr. Hall died in March 1946 aged 73.

DAWSON G. HARRON

In January 1946 Dawson G. Harron died aged 68. He served in the 1914 – 1918 war and was wounded in the right arm. At Langley Park Colliery he worked for 55 years the last 34 as an official. Mr. Harron and his wife had a family of nine children. At the time of his death his daughter was serving in the Land Army and four sons were in the armed forces. Another was a well-known cricketer with Leeds City, Joseph was an ex-professional footballer and there was another son John.

WESTGARTH ADAMSON

Westgarth Adamson, of Palm Street, retired at the end of September 1944. He had been a telephone attendant and previously, for fifteen years, a check weigh man at Langley Park Colliery. Born at Rookhope in Weardale he began work aged eleven at the lead crushing mills. At 27 he was living in New Brancepeth and circa. 1923 came to Langley Park. He completed 20 years service with Langley Park Miner's Lodge retiring as correspondence secretary in June 1944. George Eccleston was his successor. Mr. Adamson was a member of the Langley Park and Witton Gilbert Nursing Association Committee and had been one of those who helped to start the Langley Park Comforts Fund in the early days of the Second World War. On Esh Parish Council he served for 14 years and had been a Methodist local preacher for nearly forty years. It was in 1906 he joined the Crook Methodist Church and at the time of his retirement was on the Durham Circuit. As a member of the Trinity Methodist Church in Langley Park he was a Trustee and Vice-President of the Wesleyan Guild.

WILLIAM FOSTER

Known by local people as 'Lloyd George' because of his resemblance to the famous statesman of that name, William Foster died in July 1939 aged 93. He claimed he had had only three days illness in his life and his longevity was due to eating plenty of brown bread, good home fed fat bacon and a glass of milk. His mother had lived to the age of 95 and his father to 84. At the age of nine he commenced work at Coundon Colliery and over the years was employed at Leasingthorne, Auckland Park, Rainton, Wheatley Hill and Binchester. He returned to Langley Park at the age of 74. Married for 56 years he had been living in the Aged Miners Homes in Langley Park for ten years. A married son was living in Ireland and a daughter in Winlaton.

ROBERT HOWE

Robert Howe, who lived next door to Mr. Foster in the Aged Miners Homes, died in September 1942. He had reached the age of 92 and at the time had been the village's oldest inhabitant. He was born at sea on a journey his mother was making from India. His father was killed at the Battle of Lucknow during the Indian Mutiny. Aged nine years he began work at Backworth Colliery, Newcastle. He walked two miles and worked 12 or 13 hours a day. He left home at 5 a.m. and got home at 7 p.m. His earnings – ten-pence a day. At the age of seventeen he had moved to Elswick and prior to coming to Langley Park circa. 1901 he had been an official at Boldon Colliery for 20 years receiving a handsome clock on leaving. Mr. Howe was employed at Langley Park Colliery for a further 35 years. He retired, aged 72, in 1923. In retirement he enjoyed reading and a pipe of tobacco. For fifteen years he was President of Langley Park Workmen's Club and a Methodist preacher for a number of years. Married with a family of nine, Mrs. Howe had died in 1936 in her 80th year She came from Marley Hill near Blaydon.

A.W. ELLIOTT

Known in Langley Park for his service as a Special Constable, A. W. Elliott of Church Street died in July 1940. He had been a horse-keeper at Langley Park Colliery for 35 years. His son Sergeant Cecil Elliott was serving in the 7th Queen's Hussars. After five years in Egypt he had been home and found his father to be seriously ill in hospital but had left England again before the death occurred.

J. S. ELLIOTT

J. S. Elliott, who began working at Langley Park Colliery aged 13 and was 55 years a Horse-Keeper underground died in January 1959 aged 76.

ERNEST EDWIN ELLIOTT

Early in August 1950, Head Horse-Keeper Ernest Edwin Elliott retired after 53 years at Langley Park Colliery. His father came to the village in 1879 and Ernest was the last of five members of the family who were Horse-Keepers.

NED MILLER

Ned Miller was, in August 1957, Head Horse-Keeper at Langley Park Colliery and won the National Coal Board No. 5 Area prize for the best pit pony at Darlington Show. Mr. Miller was very proud of his large collection of rosettes he had been presented with over his years working with pit ponies.

A MODEL MAN

Langley Park resident Mr. E. E. Murray was well known as a model engineer. Mr Murray started his working life as an apprentice in his father's firm Messrs. John Murray and Sons, Blacksmiths, of Crook. Service in the Durham Light Infantry during the First World War followed and in 1921 he married. He began model engineering by building a toy pithead for his two sons in 1930. Adding to it from time to time his hobby got out of control and became too big for the house. He built a wagon 14' x 7' which soon became completely filled with a perfect working model of a colliery surface and underground with coke ovens. There were also coal shutters, tubs and trailer prams, putters, men with 'windy picks' and ponies. A realistic touch was given with electric rams pushing red coke from the coke ovens, aerial flight and well-equipped fitting shops manned by model men. There were coal and coke trucks, tanks and locomotives. Mr. Murray used to take his model and exhibit at seaside resorts during the summer months. In 1952 he parted with the model. It was sent to South Africa and was on exhibition in Johannesburg.

Mr. Murray retired from work in 1951 after being employed as a blacksmith at Malton Colliery for several years. Aged 73 Mr Murray, who lived in Thomas Street, died in hospital in late August 1957 after a long illness.

MR AND MRS JOHN AGAR

In late 1945 Mr. and Mrs. John Agar who were resident in The Aged Miners Homes celebrated their 53rd wedding anniversary. Mr. Agar was born at Ewe Hill near Chester-le-Street circa 1869. Coming to Langley Park in 1880 he began his working life at the age of eleven at the pit working ten hours each day and earning 10d a shift. He was a trapper boy, a putter, a coal hewer and a deputy and for some time and much later he also worked in a bank. Mr. Agar retired at the end of December 1935. He enjoyed football and cycling. In the football world he had been Secretary for Langley Park Rovers F.C. and played the game himself. During his active life he had played in teams against most of the sides in the Mid and North West Durham League. In 1891 club members had presented him with a Seal and an inscribed football bag in recognition of his service. His first venture into cycling was the 'high cycle' usually known as the penny-farthing and he competed in numerous cycle races in and around Durham. For sixteen years he was elected unopposed as Treasurer of the Langley Park Lodge of the Durham Miners Association. First appointed aged 24 he eventually resigned when he became a deputy. In 1912 he was re-elected Treasurer and remained in office until 1944. Around this time he and his wife moved into The Aged Miners Homes. During his lifetime he had also served on Annfield Plain Co-operative Society Committee and on the Committee of the Langley Park Workmen's Club. Mr. and Mrs. Agar were married at St. John's Church, Meadowfield. She was born in the village of Tudhoe Colliery in 1871 and had lived all her married life in Langley Park The couple had five sons and four daughters and up to February 1945 could count 31 grand and great grand children. In 1945 one son was a Regimental Sergeant Major in the Royal Artillery serving in the Middle East and a number of grandsons were also in the forces. Mrs. Agar (Sarah) died aged 78 in March 1949.

MOLLY AGAR

Molly Agar lived a quiet but active life in Oak Street made remarkable because she was deaf. However her handicap developed her skills as a lip reader and she became well known for her outstanding ability. Taking part in competitions in many parts of the country she regularly appeared alongside most of the top exponents of the art and won national acclaim and awards. Mrs. Agar was also well known as the maker of ginger snaps and gingerbread men that became a feature of after meeting refreshments at many social gatherings.

DAVID JOHN OUGH

Mr. Ough of Dean Street, Langley Park died in July 1924 aged 76. A stone-mason by trade he came to Langley Park circa. 1874 and was employed by Consett Iron Company. He was one of the workmen who helped to build the first colliery houses in the village. He worked for the Consett firm for 45 years and was then caretaker at the local Institute and Library. He and his wife had celebrated their Golden Wedding in 1921. They had eight daughters.

NORMAN RICHARDSON

Norman Richardson's parents lived in Bridge Street, Langley Park and as a child Norman was becoming well known for appearances at local social events. He soon had his own orchestra and undertook engagements all over the North East being particularly well known at the Regal and Princess's Ballroom in Durham. During the Second World War he served in the R.A.F.V.R. in Canada and became a flying instructor. In 1947 he established a travel, shipping and forwarding agency in a small shop in Claypath, Durham City and two years later he was appointed a member of the World Institute of Travel Agents becoming one of the youngest members. When Langley Park Gymkhana was established in the late 1940s he proved to be a popular commentator. Eventually he was announcer for Houghall Show and was invited to provide a similar service at the Aldershot Tattoo. Gradually his travel business grew in popularity and he extended his interests into other areas. Elected to Durham City Council he eventually served as Lord Mayor of Durham and became an Alderman of the City.

ELLA McNAY

In the summer of 1964 Miss Ella McNay retired from the post of Headmistress of Langley Park Infants' School. She had been at the school for 15 years. Previously she had taught at Houghton-le-Spring Infants' School for 27 years, making a total of 42 years in the profession. She had begun her career as an actress and played with a professional repertory company at the Palace Theatre, Durham. However, she eventually took her parents advice to join a more stable profession and attended St. Hilds College, Durham. During the 1939-1945 war she ran a concert party and became pianist for a local English Folk Drama Society. She also trained choirs and was interested in puppetry. She was Entertainment's Secretary for Framwellgate Moor Womens' Institute.

JOHN DODGSON

Mr. and Mrs. John Dodgson of South View, Langley Park celebrated their Golden Wedding in late August 1934. Born at Washington Mr. Dodgson began work in brickyards at West Stanley at the age of 10. He was then at the 'Kettledrum' Pit, Burns Colliery, West Stanley. In 1878 he moved to Langley Park with his family and worked at the local colliery doing various jobs before retiring in December 1930. During this time he spent four years at South Shields. Mr. Dodgson was associated with Trinity Methodist Church for over 50 years He married on 30 August 1884 at Durham Register Office. Mrs. Dodgson was born in Craghead They had two sons (the eldest was killed during the First World War) and one daughter. There were two grandchildren.

HENRY SUTTERSFIELD

Henry Suttersfield who was living in a house in Esh Terrace died in March 1934 aged 75.... Born in Boston, Lincolnshire he came to Esh Winning in younger days and was to live in Langley Park for over 30 years. He worked as a keeker at Langley Park until he retired in 1925. For some time he was caretaker for Langley Park Council Schools. He was a loyal member and a deacon of the Baptist Church in the village.

WILLIAM HALL

William Hall who resided at May House in Langley Park retired as Schools Attendance Officer for the district in March 1930. The son-in-law of the late Dr. Wilson M. P., he worked at Framwellgate Moor Colliery before coming to Langley Park Colliery as a winding engineer. Circa. 1905 he was appointed Schools Attendance Officer for Durham County Council Education Committee.. At the time of his retirement he was a Superintendent and Trustee of the Primitive Methodist Church in the village and was still teaching there.

DAN GREGORY

Dan Gregory was born in Walsall. He began singing at St. Asaph Cathedral, North Wales. Four years later he was at Christchurch College, Oxford where he served under Dr. H. G. Ley who became precenter at Eton College. At Kings College, Cambridge he came under Dr. A. H. Mann. Having been appointed to Durham Cathedral Choir in 1914 he eventually became solo bass. He was conductor for Durham Choral Society and had a long association with All Saints Church in Langley Park being choirmaster for over thirty years.

DAVID RICHARDSON

David was born in Pine Street, Langley Park and spent the whole of his life in the village. The son of the late Elsie and Frank Richardson and sister of Barbara, he worked at Mackay's Carpet Factory until that firm ceased to trade. He was then briefly with Derwentside District Council. An active member of the local cricket club as a player and secretary and a keen football supporter he also had a keen interest in Langley Park Workmen's' Club being a well liked concert chairman. Sadly Mr. Richardson died suddenly in February 2006 at the age of 56. His popularity as a member of the community was apparent at his funeral when family and villagers filled All Saints Church to overflowing.

Mr. Richardson's life began in the middle period of these memories and this brief tribute to him and recollections of a few Langley Park people brings 'Looking At Langley Park' to an end.

Apologies are offered to all those people and organisations, together with events, that, for various reasons have been omitted. During the 20th Century Langley Park grew from a few streets of houses to the village it is today. Residents have come and gone, businesses and clubs have thrived. Many of the well-known shops have disappeared. Some organisations continue to exist being kept alive by 'old stagers' who still have the old community spirit. There is no colliery or coke works today.

What will the chronicler record of life in another 50 – 100 years time when Langley Park will no doubt be a very different place?